COMM
TRADER'S
ALMANAC
2009

Jeffrey A. Hirsch and John L. Person

WILEY

John Wiley & Sons, Inc.

Published by John Wiley & Sons, Inc., Hoboken, New Jersey
Published simultaneously in Canada

Editor	Jeffrey A. Hirsch, stocktradersalmanac.com
Contributing Editor	John L. Person, nationalfutures.com
Director of Research	J. Taylor Brown
Statistics Director	Christopher Mistal
Graphic Design	Darlene Dion Design
Data & Research	GenesisFT.com
Additional Data	Pinnacledata.com

For general information about our other products and services, please contact our Customer Care Department within the United States at 800-762-2974, outside the United States at 317-572-3993 or fax 317-572-4002.

Wiley also publishes its books in a variety of electronic formats. Some content that appears in print may not be available in electronic books.

For more information about Wiley products, visit our Web site at www.wiley.com. Also visit www.almanacinvestor.com for information about the *Commodity Trader's Almanac* and other market data.

ISBN 13 978-0-470-23061-9
ISBN 10 0-470-23061-4

10 9 8 7 6 5 4 3 2 1

Printed in China

FOREWORD

The Third Edition of the *Commodity Trader's Almanac* has been completely revamped and vastly improved. We have spent the past three years converting our annual bestseller, the *Stock Trader's Almanac,* into a product that translates into the commodities complex. We feel after much work and consideration that we have produced a product worthy of the Almanac banner.

The changes to this edition are numerous, but the single most important one is that this year we have brought on board a commodities expert nonpareil. Many of you are no doubt familiar with John Person. A 28-year veteran of the futures and options industry, John is an independent trader, broker, and analyst.

Moreover, he is an accomplished author who is widely quoted in the financial press and newswires and makes regular media appearances on CNBC. John also presents at a plethora of investment conferences worldwide and regularly hosts full-house trading seminars and workshops.

With John's expertise, we have hand-selected 54 specific seasonalities for 17 different commodities on both the long and short side. In addition to traditional commodities, we have added data for major foreign currencies, namely the euro, Swiss franc, Japanese yen and the British pound. Detailed historical trades and in-depth data are available in the databank section in the back of the book.

The *Almanac* is broken down by month; and for each month we have offered specific and actionable guidance on how to forge an investment strategy in an attempt to capitalize on specific historical strengths and weaknesses. The diary pages contain the beginning and end for both rallies and breaks. The book was designed for an investor to utilize both the diary pages and databank to generate investment ideas. It is not intended to be a black box investment strategy, but rather, a vital resource of historical reference and seasonal patterns.

The *Commodity Trader's Almanac* is based on the same tenet that has shaped the Hirsch Organization's research since the late 1960s: There is a cyclical pattern to free markets. Weather, holidays, and human behaviors — to name but a few influencing factors — hold sway over demand and supply, and therefore the price of a commodity.

We carefully crafted this publication to be a practical tool for investors of all levels. More importantly, this edition of the *Commodity Trader's Almanac* was designed to be used not only for trading futures contracts in the pits, but stocks and ETFs as well.

The historical patterns contained within this text will expand the knowledge base of traders and investors of all levels. Understanding these historical patterns will give the seasoned trader a leg up and the most novice investor a solid foundation as they cut their teeth in the world of commodities.

INTRODUCTION TO THE THIRD EDITION

The new *Commodity Traders Almanac 2009* is designed to give the reader a look at the past seasonal tendencies of the top 13 commodity markets and four of the top major currencies pairs against the U.S. dollar. To help traders understand not only the price behavior of the underlying futures but also the supply and demand cycles that create these pricing patterns. Inside the Almanac you will learn:

- How natural production and consumption cycles drive prices during specific times of the year.

- How the futures markets often factor in demand and supply concerns prior to the actual event.

- How similar, but different markets often react stronger or weaker to the natural consumption/production cycle.

- That prices are often driven by regularly recurring patterns (or cycles) surrounding the calendar year and how often these patterns have continued or reversed.

The Almanac also provides a monthly overview of pertinent statistics and highlights the seasonal tendencies of each particular futures market. In total, the Almanac is designed to help point traders and investors in the general direction of the normal natural supply/demand cycle of the market. The Almanac highlights specific strategies you may wish to employ, monthly overviews and historical statistics

The Almanac is intended to be used as a tool to assist market participants in making informed decisions. Within these pages the historical statistics and studies can serve as a framework and guide when entering a new position (long or short) or deciding to either move a stop loss or add to a position.

The trading strategies presented here have been selected from the highest winning percentage seasonal trades based on the major and minor annual tops and bottoms of these markets. Starting on page 120 in the Databank section are the historic results of the best seasonal trades in chronological order. The data used here are based on the continuously linked front contract months, which are the most liquid contracts and not back- or inflation-adjusted. These specific strategies illustrate the results from trading one contract each year data was available at the best historical entry and exit days. Included are the win/loss performance and total gain. A summary of all these "best trades" appears on pages 114 and 116, Commodity Seasonality: Top Percentage Plays, and reminders are listed throughout the Almanac on the weekly planner pages.

For each seasonal trade there is an entry day and an exit day. At the top of each table the entry day specified as a particular trading day of the month, not a calendar day, and the exit day is the last day of the specified holding period. For example, the January short euro trade begins on the third trading day and is held for 23 days. The third trading day of January 2009 is the sixth and 23 days later is February 9. So you would entry this trade on January 6 and exit February 9. Actual entry and exit dates are provided in the tables, along with the closing prices, profit/loss, profit at high, and loss at low.

The remainder of the Databank section is devoted to each commodity's particular nuances, cycles, patterns and historical data. Monthly Almanac pages summarize these seasonal trades and alerts you to other tendencies, dangers and opportunities.

This Almanac has evolved along with the changing times, market participants, products and ways to trade the commodity markets. In just a few short years and even months, more and more markets are no longer open outcry, or they are migrating toward all electronic access. In addition, it is our intention to point out to investors the most advanced ways to profit from history, as it pertains to the commodity markets. The futures industry is by no means considered the gamblers market it was when I first came in the industry some 30 years ago.

Due to the heightened awareness and ripple effect that commodities have on each of our daily lives as well as our investments, this Almanac also gives insights on how to take advantage of commodity markets in several formats. There are several ways to capture trading and investing opportunities in the commodity and futures markets. One is through the futures markets outright, then there are options on the futures markets. There are specific stocks that correlate or are tightly linked to specific commodity markets price moves. There are also options on these stocks. Now there are exchange-traded funds (ETFs) that directly track commodities, and there are options on these ETFs. And finally, there is one more way to invest in this asset class, and that is investing in shares in the exchanges themselves that have gone public that clear these products.

When selecting stocks that pertain to a specific commodity, there are simply too many choices and companies to illustrate within these pages. However, we have included individual stocks and ETFs that relate to these commodity markets throughout this Almanac that are closely correlated to the underlying commodity. My rule of thumb for picking stocks is to include companies that trade on average over 500,000 shares per day. In addition, here are more criteria that I use for picking stocks that relate to commodities.

STOCK FILTERING RULES

Balance Sheet or Cash Flows: When you examine a company's cash flow, if it is extremely positive, it will help give investors an idea of the company's working capital and can indicate its efficiency in not only its negotiating power but also its ability to diversify and utilize its resources and expand its marketing ability and capture more market share.

Price Earnings Ratio: It is also important to look at the company's P/E (price-to-earnings ratio) as it is compared to its competitors and the sector. Companies with longer histories and better relations with producers and suppliers or companies that have been in business longer and have deep-rooted positive public relations most likely may be trading at a premium to other less-well-known companies. Generally, if the sector and industry are performing well, then it most times justifies a higher P/E ratio. Keep in mind valuations have to justify the company's growth and earnings potential. A company's bottom line, or larger profit margins, helps hold and appreciate a stock's value and/or keeps dividend payments coming.

History and Management: Above all, look at the company's history and who's in charge and running the company. What is its business background? It helps to know who is running things, what their motives are, and if they are invested in the company as well. It is good to know the intentions of the people who run the company, because they could either run things well or run things into the ground. A company's leader and management team are responsible for the survival of the company and, in turn, for integrity of a shareholder's concern. Remember that when you invest in a company you are a participant—you share in the company's profits.

There are exceptions to this rule. For example, many of the U.S. futures and stock exchanges have been in business for many decades and in fact over 100 years. However, up until recently, they have not been publicly traded. Therefore, they do not have a "long history" of P/E ratios or leadership roles since exchange chair people have been voted in. These companies' share can be excellent proxies for the general trend of the commodities and other securities that trade on their exchanges.

The *Commodity Traders Almanac 2009* brings to you a new flavor and guidance on how to invest in this asset class, not only through the traditional commodity markets but also how to capitalize on the seasonal swings in these markets using various stocks, options and exchange-traded funds. This Almanac will help all investors by providing information on the seasonal tendencies of the various markets and then identify specific trading dates and holding days for specific market trends. Commodities have a dominant seasonality that tends to create a timely high and low in prices. However, some years these moves can be magnified or muted due to cyclical forces from periods of economic expansion and then periods of economic contractions or recessions. Therefore, it is important to remember to use this Almanac as a reference guide and to compare current events against history. We have included the data that allow the reader to distinguish which years had predominantly bigger price moves to compare where current prices and trends are against past historic data.

I wish you a healthy and prosperous 2009!

John L. Person

2009 COMMODITY MARKET OUTLOOK

The major price moves for 2008 in the commodity sector were magnified, as secular trends appeared to have affected the seasonal tendencies of this asset class. Several events helped manifest this secular trend. One of the main culprits that helped create a spike in commodity prices was the decline in the value of the U.S. dollar. No matter how many times Washington kept announcing the "best interest of the U.S. is to have a strong dollar," the policy statement generally led to another wave lower for the American greenback. It got to the point where people were referring to it as the American peso.

Since most commodities such as crude oil and gold are priced internationally in U.S. dollars, when the dollar's value declines, it creates a rise in these products value in terms of foreigner's purchasing power. The decline in the dollar created several surprising news stories. One such story was that a supermodel announced she would only accept payment in euros. The cause of the dollar's decline was in part due to the budget deficits from the war in Iraq, the decline in interest rates as a result of banks and financial institutions subprime mortgage dealings, and improved economic outlook in Europe.

Moreover, countries that were rich in natural resources saw dramatic improvements in their countries' wealth as a result of higher commodity prices, particularly Canada and Australia. Other factors included increased global demand for fossil fuels. The passage of ethanol legislation here in the United States had a dramatic effect on grain prices and helped push over-all inflationary pressures on food and services sharply higher.

In addition, a rough planting season in 2008 as a result of excess rain forced many farmers to replant or abandon acres entirely. Corn and soybean prices soared to record price levels, and most companies that had anything to do with planting and production of agricultural seed food products, including fertilizer suppliers, marketing of crop nutrients and animal feed products, also reaped the benefit from these higher commodity prices as share prices of these companies shot sharply higher.

Stocks like Monsanto (MON), Potash Corp. Saskatchewan (POT), Terra Industries (TRA), CF Industries (CF) and the Mosaic Company (MOS) had more than doubled since the beginning of 2007, when the commodity boom started gaining momentum. Besides fertilizer and seeding companies, agricultural equipment-related companies such as Deere (DE) enjoyed a stellar rally, as did transportation companies related to transportation of commodities.

Another event was the coming of age of underdeveloped and emerging countries' energy demands and the wealth effect of the overall increase in the gross domestic product (GDP) for these countries. Due to legislature changes in corporate tax codes early in the new millennium, many U.S.-based corporations began to outsource jobs overseas. As more jobs were created, the wealth effect increased, and that led to the ability for more consumption of goods and services. This, in turn, was partly what helped increase the global demand for fossil fuel that caused or helped ignite a tremendous price surge in crude oil. That caused higher costs for transportation and led to higher inflationary expectations. Furthermore, this is what led to support precious metals as gold traded over $1033 per ounce in 2008 for the very first time.

I believe the global markets will continue to demonstrate excess volatility as we deal with continued supply and demand issues in the energy complex as well as the agricultural markets that supply our food sources. I also believe that as living standards increase in developing countries, it is the energy, food, and agricultural sector that may see further sustained momentum. As a result of increased demand for food products, farmers' incomes are on the rise and they now have more money to invest in their farm operations. Therefore, they should improve their yield per acre output. That will help support fertilizer suppliers. The Federal Reserve will also be faced with combating inflationary pressures and at the same time making sure there is plenty of liquidity to help support financial institutions as they sort through the aftermath of the subprime fallout. In 2009, I am expecting a round of monetary tightening, which could help support the dollar, putting pressure on Treasury bond and commodity prices and a return of historical seasonal patterns. Overall, I expect the markets to remain volatile and present vast opportunities for the well-informed trader.

— John L. Person, June 27, 2008

THE 2009 COMMODITY TRADER'S ALMANAC

CONTENTS

2009 STRATEGY CALENDAR

	MONDAY	TUESDAY	WEDNESDAY	THURSDAY	FRIDAY	SATURDAY	SUNDAY
JANUARY	29	30	31	1 JANUARY New Year's Day	2	3	4
	5	6	7	8	9	10	11
	12	13	14	15	16	17	18
	19 Martin Luther King Day	20	21	22	23	24	25
	26	27	28	29	30	31	1 FEBRUARY
FEBRUARY	2	3	4	5	6	7	8
	9	10	11	12	13	14 ♥	15
	16 Presidents' Day	17	18	19	20	21	22
	23	24	25 Ash Wednesday	26	27	28	1 MARCH
MARCH	2	3	4	5	6	7	8 Daylight Saving Time Begins
	9	10	11	12	13	14	15
	16	17 St. Patrick's Day ♣	18	19	20	21	22
	23	24	25	26	27	28	29
	30	31	1 APRIL	2	3	4	5
APRIL	6	7	8	9 Passover	10 Good Friday	11	12 Easter
	13	14	15 Tax Deadline	16	17	18	19
	20	21	22	23	24	25	26
	27	28	29	30	1 MAY	2	3
MAY	4	5	6	7	8	9	10 Mother's Day
	11	12	13	14	15	16	17
	18	19	20	21	22	23	24
	25 Memorial Day	26	27	28	29	30	31
JUNE	1 JUNE	2	3	4	5	6	7
	8	9	10	11	12	13	14
	15	16	17	18	19	20	21 Father's Day
	22	23	24	25	26	27	28

Market closed on shaded weekdays; closes early when half-shaded.

2009 STRATEGY CALENDAR

MONDAY	TUESDAY	WEDNESDAY	THURSDAY	FRIDAY	SATURDAY	SUNDAY	
29	30	1 JULY	2	3	4 Independence Day	5	JULY
6	7	8	9	10	11	12	JULY
13	14	15	16	17	18	19	JULY
20	21	22	23	24	25	26	JULY
27	28	29	30	31	1 AUGUST	2	JULY
3	4	5	6	7	8	9	AUGUST
10	11	12	13	14	15	16	AUGUST
17	18	19	20	21	22	23	AUGUST
24	25	26	27	28	29	30	AUGUST
31	1 SEPTEMBER	2	3	4	5	6	SEPTEMBER
7 Labor Day	8	9	10	11	12	13	SEPTEMBER
14	15	16	17	18	19 Rosh Hashanah	20	SEPTEMBER
21	22	23	24	25	26	27	SEPTEMBER
28 Yom Kippur	29	30	1 OCTOBER	2	3	4	OCTOBER
5	6	7	8	9	10	11	OCTOBER
12 Columbus Day	13	14	15	16	17	18	OCTOBER
19	20	21	22	23	24	25	OCTOBER
26	27	28	29	30	31	1 NOVEMBER Daylight Saving Time Ends	OCTOBER
2	3 Election Day	4	5	6	7	8	NOVEMBER
9	10	11 Veterans' Day	12	13	14	15	NOVEMBER
16	17	18	19	20	21	22	NOVEMBER
23	24	25	26 Thanksgiving	27	28	29	NOVEMBER
30	1 DECEMBER	2	3	4	5	6	DECEMBER
7	8	9	10	11	12 Chanukah	13	DECEMBER
14	15	16	17	18	19	20	DECEMBER
21	22	23	24	25 Christmas	26	27	DECEMBER
28	29	30	31	1 JANUARY New Year's Day	2	3	DECEMBER

JANUARY ALMANAC

ENERGY: January tends to see continued weakness in crude oil (page 145) and in natural gas (page 147) before the typical bottom is posted in February. Traders should prepare for the strongest buy month for crude oil and natural gas (page 123). Crude oil suffers from yearend inventory liquidation due to tax liabilities. Refineries in large producing states are subjected to paying taxes on unsold inventories of crude and refined products such as gasoline and heating oil. End users tend to postpone purchases of additional inventory until after the New Year. Demand tends to be stable and prices generally stay depressed until February, as inventories have been built up into yearend by consumers and end users until supplies start to decline from demand for heating oil consumption in winter and gasoline into early spring. Natural gas prices tend to be weakest in January, as storage of inventories by utility companies through end-of-year has not been readily consumed by January. Typical severe cold weather snaps in February begin to draw increased demand for additional inventories from the Louisiana Henry Hub gas line. This pipeline serves much of the Northeast, Midwest, and Gulf Coast regions.

METALS: Gold has a strong history of making a seasonal peak from mid-January into early February. Shorting gold from mid-January to mid-March has been a winning strategy 23 out of 34 years (page 121). Silver also has a tendency to peak in late February and follows gold price weakness into March (page 123 & 155). Coming off its seasonal December bottom, copper tends to show mild strength in January (page 149).

GRAINS: Soybeans tend to post a low in late January or early February (page 122 & 161). Wheat prices are in the midst of seasonal weakness in January (page 142 & 164). However, corn prices tend to buck that trend as we enter a new marketing year (page 140 & 158).

SOFTS: Cocoa shows signs of strength in January and continues higher until March (page 124 & 167). Coffee tends to show a mixed performance in the month of January giving back some of Decembers gains (page 170). Sugar tends to show a mixed performance in January as beet and continued sugar cane harvest in the South East United States and India puts pressure on prices (page 173).

MEATS: Live cattle price strength continues through January (page 176) and lean hog prices tend to remain under pressure from making any significant moves up until March (page 179).

CURRENCIES: The euro has a short life span since beginning in 1999; however, since inception, it has a stellar trade by going short on the third trading day and holding for 23 days. It has generated 9 gains and only registered 1 loss (page 121). The Swiss franc and the British pound both show a strong seasonal tendency to continue lower from late December. The yen also demonstrates weakness from December into February.

DECEMBER/JANUARY 2009

MONDAY
29

If you don't keep [your employees] happy, they're not going to keep the [customers] happy.
— David Longest (Red Lobster VP, *NY Times* 4/23/89)

TUESDAY
30

In nature there are no rewards or punishments; there are consequences.
— Horace Annesley Vachell (English writer, *The Face of Clay*, 1861–1955)

WEDNESDAY
31

Nothing gives one person so much advantage over another as to remain always cool and unruffled under all circumstances.
—Thomas Jefferson (3rd U.S. president, 1743–7/4/1826

New Year's Day (Market Closed)

THURSDAY
1

Pretend that every single person you meet has a sign around his or her neck that says, "Make me feel important."
Not only will you succeed in sales, you will succeed in life. — Mary Kay Ash (Mary Kay Cosmetics)

End Long Swiss Franc (Nov. 26, 2008)

FRIDAY
2

Of 120 companies from 1987 to 1992 that relied primarily on cost cutting to improve the bottom line, 68 percent failed to achieve profitable growth during the next five years. — Mercer Management Consulting (*Smart Money Magazine*, August 2001)

SATURDAY
3

SUNDAY
4

EURO PEAKS AGAINST U.S. DOLLAR

The euro currency was first introduced to the world markets in 1999 and was finally launched with bank notes and physical coins in 2002. As of May 2008, the following countries use the euro as their official currency: Andorra, Austria, Belgium, Cyprus, Finland, France, Germany, Greece, Ireland, Italy, Luxembourg, Malta, Monaco, Montenegro, Netherlands, Portugal, San Marino, Slovenia, Spain, and Vatican City.

The European Central Bank dictates monetary policy and puts more emphasis on inflation concerns rather than on economic contraction. We have seen in the past where the ECB would rather maintain steady interest rates than stoke the flames of inflationary pressures. As a result, the ECB is less likely to adjust interest rates.

Seasonally speaking, we do see in the 10-year history of the euro a tendency for prices to head lower against the U.S. dollar on or about the third trading day in January through the first week of February. The typical holding period is 23 trading days ending on or about February 8th.

This particular event has a 90% success rate, with the 10-year cumulative gain adding up to over $25,650 based on a total of 9 winning years with 1 losing year, which was $3,975 back in 2003. The greatest gain was $5,850 in 1999, and the second highest gain was $5,763 in 2005. Theory suggests this has worked in the past due to the fact that multinational conglomerate corporations based here in the U.S. repatriate funds after the New Year, and this has a tendency to depress prices in the first quarter.

There are several ways to take advantage of this market—in particular, through an ETF that tracks the euro directly. By examining the chart below you will see the euro currency futures contract with the line chart based on the closing prices of the CurrencyShares euro (FXE). Notice how it mirrors the underlying futures market as well as looks at the seasonal price moves.

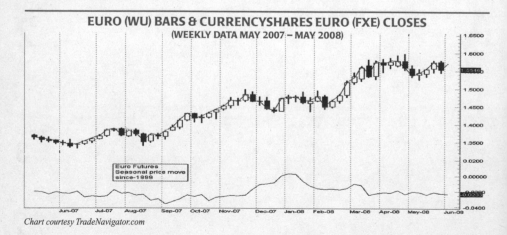

Chart courtesy TradeNavigator.com

JANUARY

The only thing that saves us from the bureaucracy is its inefficiency.
— Eugene McCarthy (U.S. Congressman & Senator Minnesota 1949–1971, 3-time presidential candidate, 1916–2005)

Start Short Euro — 90.0% Accuracy Since 1999 — End Feb. 9 — Page 121

TUESDAY

6

Knowing others is intelligence; knowing yourself is true wisdom. Mastering others is strength; mastering yourself is true power.
— Lau Tzu (Shaolin monk, founder of Taoism, circa 6th–4th century B.C.)

WEDNESDAY

7

If I had my life to live over again, I would elect to be a trader of goods rather than a student of science.
I think barter is a noble thing. — Albert Einstein (German/American physicist, 1921 Nobel Prize, 1934, 1879 1955)

THURSDAY

8

You are your own Promised Land, your own new frontier. — Julia Margaret Cameron (19th century English photographer)

FRIDAY

9

Almost any insider purchase is worth investigating for a possible lead to a superior speculation.
But very few insider sales justify concern. — William Chidester (*Scientific Investing*)

SATURDAY

10

SUNDAY

11

GOLD RALLY LOSES ITS LUSTER

Selling gold on the 14th trading day of January and holding for 38 days has resulted in a cumulative profit of $44,410 the past 34 years (page 121). In the last 34 years, this trade has been a winner 23 times, for a 67.6% success rate. However, in the last two years, 2008 and 2007, it has not fared so well.

One explanation as to why the seasonal aspects failed is there were cyclical forces such as booming inflationary pressures combined with lower interest rates, reducing the dollars value and this in turn led to higher values for stored commodities. In addition, due to the subprime housing situation and the failure of Bear Stearns, there was tremendous uncertainty in the banking and financial sector.

Due to the weaker U.S. dollar, inflationary pressures mounted and a surge in energy costs sent investors around the globe scrambling to buy gold as a hedge against these uncertain times. But things can and do revert back to historical norms and seasonal pressures can still have a negative effect on gold headed into 2009.

For example, if we do enter in a period of global economic contraction in late 2008 this could have a particular effect on gold. This is when demand is the weakest especially since this is after the holidays, and it is after the wedding season in India.

The best time to sell gold from a historical point of view is, apart from the last two years, during the second half of January on or about the 14th trading day holding for 38 trading days until on or about March 17, St. Patrick's Day. Equity traders may consider Agnico-Eagle Mines (AEM) close correlation to gold below.

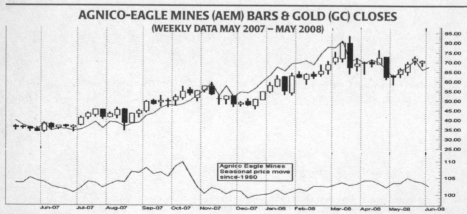

Chart courtesy TradeNavigator.com

JANUARY

MONDAY
12

There is no tool to change human nature ... people are prone to recurring bouts of optimism and pessimism that manifest themselves from time to time in the buildup or cessation of speculative excesses.
– Alan Greenspan (Fed Chairman 1987–2006, July 18, 2001 monetary policy report to the Congress)

TUESDAY
13

There is no great mystery to satisfying your customers. Build them a quality product and treat them with respect. It's that simple.
– Lee Iacocca (American industrialist, former Chrysler CEO, b. 1924)

WEDNESDAY
14

In all recorded history, there has not been one economist who has had to worry about where the next meal would come from.
– Peter Drucker (Austria-born pioneer management theorist, 1909–2005)

THURSDAY
15

Regret for the things we did can be tempered by time; it is regret for the things we did not do that is inconsolable.
– Sydney J. Harris (American journalist and author, 1917–1986)

FRIDAY
16

History is replete with episodes in which the real patriots were the ones who defied their governments.
– Jim Rogers (Financier, *Adventure Capitalist*, b. 1942)

SATURDAY
17

SUNDAY
18

COT REPORT—COMMODITY TRADERS' "INSIDE SCOOP"

One technique to gauge the market is to use the Commodity Futures Trading Commission's (CFTC) Commitment of Traders (COT) report available at *www.cftc.gov*. It is a report that reveals who is doing what or whose hands the market is in. Many investors who have never traded futures think of it as "insider trading."

This report breaks down the three main categories of traders and shows their overall net positions. The first group is called the commercials, the next group is called non-commercials (the large speculators) and the third group is called non-reportable (the small speculators). As a rule, when you trade a large number of contracts, these positions need to be reported to the CFTC. The number of allowable positions that must be reported varies by different futures contracts.

The data are taken from the close of business on Tuesday and then released on the following Friday at 2:30 PM CST for futures only. They are also released twice a month or every other Monday for futures, combined with the figures for options.

The commercials are considered to be hedgers. They could be producers or users of a given product. Due to the fact that they do or will own the underlying product, they are trying to hedge their risk in the cash market from adverse price moves. They do this in the futures market and they generally receive a discount from the margin requirements set for speculators. When a commercial entity fills out its account application, it usually discloses the fact that it is hedging. The exchanges recognize that hedgers are on the other side of the market from a cash standpoint and can usually, financially speaking, support their futures position. Therefore, they set lower margin rates for those accounts. Commercials are considered to be the "smart money" or the strong hands, because they are in the business of that commodity. They are considered to have the "inside scoop."

The large speculators category is considered to be the professional traders. It may also be an individual trader who holds a substantial position in the market. The theory is, if you are a large trader, you are committing a large amount of capital to a risky investment and have confidence in that position. You are either a very good trader that started small and built your capital up, or you are a professional trader with a good track record. Either way, professional traders with large reportable positions on are still speculating in the market with the motive for profit. They are well financed and typically have significant amounts of money to defend their positions.

The last group is the small speculators. Their positions are small enough not to need to be reported to the CFTC, but by subtracting the sum of the positions for the commercials and large traders from the total open interest, you can determine the small traders' position. These are the contracts held by the general trading public. Since it is estimated that 80% or more of small traders who enter the markets lose, this is the category that one generally does not want to follow. It is noted that the little guys win once in a while. A lot of individual investors have a good knack for calling market direction, but have a hard time with timing when it comes to entering or exiting the market. They are usually undercapitalized in the market and cannot defend their positions during periods of volatility.

What you want to watch for is the net positions for each category, and if you see a lopsided market position and prices are at an extreme high or an extreme low, this could signal a major turnaround in price direction.

JANUARY

Martin Luther King Jr. Day (Market Closed)

MONDAY
19

the end, we will remember not the words of our enemies, but the silence of our friends.
- Martin Luther King Jr. (Civil rights leader, 1964 Nobel Peace Prize, 1929–1968)

TUESDAY
20

he price of a stock varies inversely with the thickness of its research file.
- Martin Sosnoff (Atalanta Sosnoff Capital, *Silent Investor, Silent Loser*)

WEDNESDAY
21

ow a minority, Reaching majority, Seizing authority, Hates a minority. — Leonard H. Robbins

Start Short Gold — 67.6% Accuracy Since 1975 — End Mar. 18 — Page 121

THURSDAY
22

ack of money is the root of all evil. — George Bernard Shaw (Irish dramatist, 1856–1950)

FRIDAY
23

u don't learn to hold your own in the world by standing on guard, but by attacking and getting well hammered yourself.
- George Bernard Shaw (Irish dramatist, 1856–1950)

SATURDAY
24

SUNDAY
25

FEBRUARY ALMANAC

ENERGY: Crude oil makes a strong seasonal bottom registering a whopping 84.0% win ratio with 21 gains in 25 years (page 123). Natural gas also generates a stellar trade from its mid-winter bottom that blasts above crude's statistics with an 88.9% success rate, gaining 16 out of the last 18 years (page 22).

METALS: Gold is still in the seasonal downturn, and February is time to be short or flat the market (page 16). Silver tends to make tremendous price declines falling with gold's seasonal declines. In the past 37 years, silver has declined 26 years for a 70.3% success rate (page 26). Copper prices tend to move in the opposite direction of gold and silver; however, the best trade from December suggests exiting longs on strength during February on or about the 24th of the month (page 144).

GRAINS: Soybeans register a recovery rally from January's break that lasts into the May peak. Soybeans have seen price advances from mid-February to late May 32 out of the 41 years for a 78.0% win probability (page 24). Corn has a tendency to move higher in step with soybeans (page 158). Wheat marches to a different beat than soybeans and corn and generally sees price declines during February (page 164).

SOFTS: Cocoa prices tend to pause in February before advancing and peaking out in March (page 30). Coffee prices see average gains in February lasting though mid-May (page 48). Sugar prices tend to peak in mid month triggering a 72.2% win statistic with 26 years out of 36 performing well, including the last four years straight (page 122).

MEATS: Live cattle has a tendency to see further price gains following January's strength. However, March is a tough month for beef prices: Buyers beware, as the bottom generally does not come in until June (page 176). Lean hog prices tend to move lower in February and into March, which is the time where one wants to be long headed toward Memorial Day weekend (page 179).

CURRENCIES: The euro tends to be flat during February, but we do see the market correct from Januarys decline. As such, our best trade short position is covered on or about the 8th of the month. The Swiss franc also sees price corrections, and this is time to cover short positions from the December best trade on or about February 27 (page 144). The British pound tends to remain in a downtrend until mid-March. Look for continued weakness in February (page 144 & 182). The yen posts a secondary low in February, creating a solid long trade from early February through early May with a win ratio of 71.9%. In the last 32 years this trade has worked 22 times, including four straight (page 121).

JANUARY/FEBRUARY

Women are expected to do twice as much as men in half the time and for no credit. Fortunately, this isn't difficult.
— Charlotte Whitton (Former Ottawa Mayor, feminist, 1896–1975)

A.I. (artificial intelligence) is the science of how to get machines to do the things they do in the movies.
— Professor Astro Teller (Carnegie Mellon University)

Who so would be a man, must be a non-conformist...Nothing is at last sacred but the integrity of your own mind.
— Ralph Waldo Emerson (American author, poet and philosopher, *Self-Reliance*, 1803–1882)

Drawing on my fine command of language, I said nothing. — Robert Benchley (American writer, actor and humorist, 1889–1945)

I'm not better than the next trader, just quicker at admitting my mistakes and moving on to the next opportunity.
— George Soros (Financier, philanthropist, political activist, author and philosopher, b. 1930)

NATURAL GAS SURGES

Our long natural gas trade from late February to late April boasts an 88.9% success rate, gaining 16 out of the last 18 years. The cumulative profit is $55,340, with only two years (1994 and 2003) not profitable during this period (page 123).

One of the factors for this seasonal price gain is consumption driven by demand for heating homes and businesses in the northern cold weather areas in the United States. In particular when December and January are colder than normal we see depletions in inventories through February, and this has a tendency to cause price spikes lasting through mid-April.

This best trade scenario has a holding period of approximately 41 trading days lasting until on or about April 22. It is at this time when inventories start to replenish and demand tapers off until mid-July when demand for generating electricity is highest in order to run air conditioners during heat spells.

The chart below is natural gas (NG), with the United States Natural Gas (UNG) ETF overlaid displaying the strong correlation in price moves. In addition, the bottom portion shows the average seasonal price tendency since 1990, illustrating the bottom that occurs in February.

Chart courtesy TradeNavigator.com

The best place to start investigating natural gas stocks is in their premier sector index, the Amex Natural Gas Index (XNG). The XNG's 15 component companies are focused on natural gas exploration and production and pipeline transportation and transmission. XNG also tracks natural gas closely.

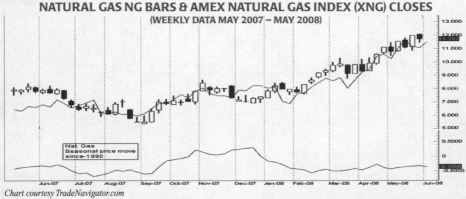

Chart courtesy TradeNavigator.com

FEBRUARY

MONDAY
2

When you get into a tight place and everything goes against you, till it seems as though you could not hang on a minute longer, never give up then, for that is just the place and time that the tide will turn. — Harriet Beecher Stowe (American writer and abolitionist)

TUESDAY
3

Don't compete. Create. Find out what everyone else is doing and then don't do it. — Joel Weldon

WEDNESDAY
4

Those who are of the opinion that money will do everything may very well be suspected to do everything for money. — Sir George Savile (British statesman and author, 1633–1695)

THURSDAY
5

Companies already dominant in a field rarely produce the breakthroughs that transform it. — George Gilder

End Long Live Cattle (June 19, 2008)

FRIDAY
6

Central Bankers are brought up pulling the legs off ants.
— Paul A. Volcker (Fed Chairman 1979–1987, Quoted by William Grieder, *Secrets of the Temple*)

SATURDAY
7

SUNDAY
8

STRENGTH IN SOYBEANS

Soybeans have seen price advances from mid-February to the end of May, 32 out of the last 41 years, for a 78.0% success rate. The history of this recovery rally on page 122 illustrates the continuing validity of this trade, with seven straight wins in a row.

Generally, we have heavier livestock demand, as animals consume more food during cold winter months. It is well after harvest and inventories have started to decline from harvest time. Then after the New Year, export business begins to pick up again.

It is usually after the January crop production report that traders get a better indication of what supply estimates are after the harvest and what demand prospects are based on domestic and export needs. Transportation during harsh winter months can hinder deliveries and this can cause price spikes. In addition, supplies from the Southern Hemisphere regions such as Brazil and Argentina are at their lowest levels.

Another event that can and has weighed in on our export business, particularly in our agriculture business, especially the grain markets, is the value fluctuation of the U.S. dollar. Exports tend to rise from a weakening dollar. Since the U.S. dollar has been on a massive decline since a peak in 2002, our exports for overseas demand have been very strong. This also has helped magnify this seasonality in the last few years.

Soy meal is used as an animal feed and is not a storable commodity. Therefore, demand for soybeans to crush into meal is strong during this period. Demand lasts well into May as we go through the planting process and potential delays from wet spring weather (as occurred in 2008). South American harvest gets underway and puts pressure on prices in late May, which is why our exit period is on or about May 30.

The following chart is the fertilizer company Mosaic (MOS), with the price of soybeans overlaid. The bottom section shows the seasonal tendency of Mosaic that has a strong correlation to the price moves in soybeans over the four years the company has been in existence. Traders looking to capture moves in soybeans besides trading futures or options on futures may want to explore taking positions out in companies such as Mosaic that tend to correlate to commodity seasonal price moves.

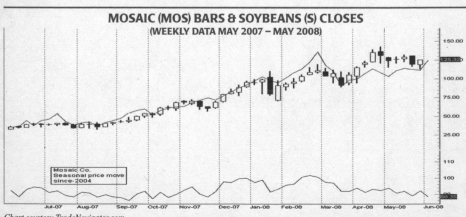

Chart courtesy TradeNavigator.com

FEBRUARY

Start Long Yen — 68.8% Accuracy Since 1977 — End May 8 — Page 121
End Short Yen (Oct. 16, 2008)
End Short Sugar (Nov. 25, 2008)
End Short Euro (Jan. 6)

MONDAY

9

It is the mark of many famous people that they cannot part with their brightest hour.
— Lillian Hellman, (Playwright, *The Children's Hour* and *Little Foxes*, 1905–1984)

TUESDAY

10

Never will a man penetrate deeper into error than when he is continuing on a road that has led him to great success.
— Friedrich von Hayek (*Counterrevolution of Science*)

WEDNESDAY

11

To find one man in a thousand who is your true friend from unselfish motives is to find one of the great wonders of the world.
— Leopold Mozart (Quoted by Maynard Solomon, Mozart)

Start Long Soybeans — 78.0% Accuracy Since 1968 — End May 29 — Page 122

THURSDAY

12

The first human being to live to 150 years of age is alive today, but will he get Social Security for 85 years of his longer life span, more than twice the number of years he worked? — John Mauldin (Millennium Wave Advisors, 2000wave.com, 2/2/07)

FRIDAY

13

Methodology is the last refuge of a sterile mind. — Marianne L. Simmel (Psychologist)

Valentine's Day ♥

SATURDAY

14

SUNDAY

15

SILVER TARNISHES IN FEBRUARY

Over the years, silver has peaked in February, and most notably so in 1980 when the Hunts Brothers plot to corner the silver market was foiled. Our seasonal study shows that selling on or about February 19 and holding until about April 24 has worked 26 times in the last 37 years, for a success rate of 70.3%.

But as you can see in the short silver trade on page 123, the usual February silver break has been trumped by an overarching commodity bull market three times in the last seven years. With talk of "stagflation" and "recession" permeating economic commentary in 2008 and as the stock market is in dire straits, we wonder if this seasonal trade will come to life in 2009.

Silver is considered the "poor man's" gold, and it does in fact tend to mirror the price move of gold. However, it does have a demand base for jewelry, and it is also used in the electronics industry for its high electrical conductivity and because it is extremely resistant to corrosion.

In decades past, it was used in the manufacturing of coins by the U.S. mint, but was discontinued in 1965. It is still used in some photo-processing applications, but demand in this area has declined with the rise of the digital age of computer imaging.

The chart below is of ASA Limited (ASA), a mining company that produces silver, with the actual price of silver overlaid on top. The bottom section is the average seasonal tendency of ASA showing how this stock closely mirrors silver's seasonal price moves as well. Traders of all asset classes can look for hidden trading gems by looking at "like" or highly correlating markets to the underlying commodity, such as ASA to silver.

Chart courtesy TradeNavigator.com

FEBRUARY

Presidents' Day (Market Closed)

MONDAY
16

---

*Any human anywhere will blossom in a hundred unexpected talents and capacities
simply by being given the opportunity to do so.* — Doris Lessing (British novelist, born in Persia 1919)

TUESDAY
17

Things may come to those who wait, but only the things left by those who hustle. — Abraham Lincoln (16th U.S. president, 1809–1865)

WEDNESDAY
18

---

*Time and money are two sides of a single coin. No person gives you his money until he has first given you his time.
WIN THE TIME OF THE PEOPLE, THEIR MONEY WILL FOLLOW.* — Roy II. Williams (*The Wizard of Ads*)

Start Short Sugar — 72.2% Accuracy Since 1971 — End Apr. 16 — Page 122
Start Short Silver — 70.3% Accuracy Since 1972 — End Apr. 24 — Page 123

THURSDAY
19

People become attached to their burdens sometimes more than the burdens are attached to them.
— George Bernard Shaw (Irish dramatist, 1856–1950)

FRIDAY
20

For a country, everything will be lost when the jobs of an economist and a banker become highly respected professions. — Montesquieu

SATURDAY
21

SUNDAY
22

MARCH ALMANAC

ENERGY: After January and February weakness, crude oil begins to strengthen in March at the outset of its best seven months March–September. The seasonal best trade from February is still long through mid-May (page 123). Natural gas prices also remain firm through March, as the seasonal best trade from February is still long as well headed into late April (page 22 & 123).

METALS: Gold posts bottoms during March, and this is the time to cover the seasonal best trade short position from January (page 16 & 121). Silver is still in a decline mode, as our seasonal best trade is holding a short position until late April (page 26 & 123). Copper prices can run higher in March and April, depending on the price gains from December through late February, which is our best trade time frame to be long (page 110 & 144). Look for a seasonal peak in April or May (page 54) to make trading decisions.

GRAINS: Soybeans during March are still in our best trade long scenario (page 24 & 122), but this month can produce consolidation or a pause in any strong price gain due to anticipation of the quarterly grain stocks report and the farmer planting intentions report, which shows how many acres farmers intend on devoting to corn, beans, wheat, and other crops. Wheat prices are still in a seasonal decline mode heading into the June harvest lows (page 104 & 142). Corn prices tend to defy gravity and continue higher into late April and early May (page 94 & 140).

SOFTS: Cocoa begins a seasonal decline instituting a short position in our seasonal best trade category (page 30 & 124). Coffee prices tend to see mild corrections after big up moves in February. This is the "frost scare" season in South America, coffee is susceptible to higher prices until the seasonal peak in May (page 48, 129 & 170). Sugar prices continue to decline (page 173).

MEATS: Live Cattle prices tend to post a seasonal high in March. This top seasonal trade that lasts until June conforms to a strong pattern of supply and demand forces. Producers liquidate inventories as packers and processors are preparing for BBQ season (page 32, 125, & 176). Lean hog prices tend to rise during March as demand for ham increases for Easter (page 179).

CURRENCIES: The euro currency, although only having a relatively short 10-year trading history, has revealed a tendency to decline during the second half of March in 8 out of 10 years (page 124). Perhaps this is due to multiconglomerate U.S. corporations repatriating dollars before the end of the first quarter (page 185). The Swiss franc also has a tendency to see price declines from mid-March through mid-May (page 187). The British pound has a distinct pattern of doing the opposite of the euro and Swiss franc; it has a strong tendency to move up against the U.S. dollar in mid-March (page 34 &125). The yen has a strong seasonal tendency to selloff in mid-March through early April (page 124).

FEBRUARY/MARCH

Start Long Crude Oil — 84.0% Accuracy Since 1984 — End May 13 — Page 123
End Long Copper (Dec. 12, 2008)

MONDAY
23

There is a perfect inverse correlation between inflation rates and price/earnings ratios...When inflation has been very high... P/E has been [low]. — Liz Ann Sonders (Chief Investment Strategist Charles Schwab, June 2006)

Start Long Natural Gas — 88.9% Accuracy Since 1991 — End Apr. 23 — Page 123

TUESDAY
24

In most admired companies, key priorities are teamwork, customer focus, fair treatment of employees, initiative, and innovation. In average companies the top priorities are minimizing risk, respecting the chain of command, supporting the boss, and making budget. — Bruce Pfau (*Fortune*)

Ash Wednesday

WEDNESDAY
25

Our philosophy here is identifying change, anticipating change. Change is what drives earnings growth, and if you identify the underlying change, you recognize the growth before the market, and the deceleration of that growth. — Peter Vermilye (Baring America Asset management, 1987)

End Short Swiss Franc (Dec. 26, 2008)

THURSDAY
26

The cause of the Dark Ages can be traced to the Y1K problem. — (A voice on the Internet)

FRIDAY
27

Friendship renders prosperity more brilliant, while it lightens adversity by sharing it and making its burden common. — Marcus Tullius Cicero (Great Roman Orator, Politician, 106–43 B.C.)

SATURDAY
28

SUNDAY
1

COCOA PEAKS BEFORE ST. PATRICK'S DAY

Cocoa begins a seasonal decline instituting a short position in our seasonal best trade category. Selling on or about March 14, right before St. Patrick's Day and holding until on or about April 16 for an average holding period of 23 trading days has been a winner 28 of the past 36 years, for a 77.8% success rate. The total cumulative gain is $18,070.

Even in the face of the 2008 great commodity bull-run, this seasonal tendency worked with a potential profit per contract of $2,600. Cocoa has two main crop seasons. The main crop from the Ivory Coast and Ghana in Africa accounts for 75% of the world production and runs from January through March. As inventories are placed on the market, this has a tendency to depress prices, especially as demand starts to fall for hot chocolate drinks and chocolate candy in the spring and summer time.

Investors may want to explore trading the short side of the futures markets through the Intercontinental Commodity Exchange (ICE). For stock traders, here is an interesting comparison. The chart below is Hershey Foods (HSY) with cocoa prices overlaid and the historic seasonal tendency of Hershey on the bottom. Notice the inverse relationship.

When cocoa prices rise, Hershey prices decline, and then as cocoa prices decline in March, we see a small advance in the stock price. Investors should be aware of the price swings of the underlying product that companies need to manufacture goods in order to produce a decent profit margin.

Besides the inverse relationship with cocoa prices, what is interesting about Hershey is that one of their competitors includes Cadbury PLC (CBY), which is a confectionery and nonalcoholic beverage company. Although the Cadbury chocolate products have been sold in the United States since 1988 under the Cadbury trademark name, the chocolate itself has been manufactured by Hershey.

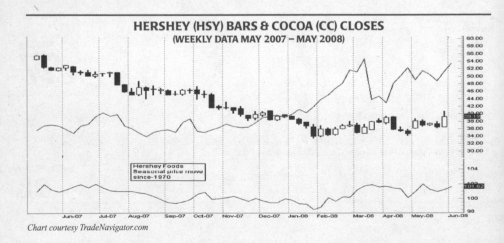

Chart courtesy TradeNavigator.com

MARCH

MONDAY
2

All you need is to look over the earnings forecasts publicly made a year ago to see how much care you need to give those being made now for next year. — Gerald M. Loeb (EF Hutton, *The Battle for Investment Survival*, predicted '29 Crash, 1900–1974)

TUESDAY
3

If you create an act, you create a habit. If you create a habit, you create a character.
If you create a character, you create a destiny. — André Maurois (Novelist, biographer, essayist, 1885–1967)

WEDNESDAY
4

When I talk to a company that tells me the last analyst showed up three years ago, I can hardly contain my enthusiasm.
— Peter Lynch (Fidelity Investments, *One Up On Wall Street*, b. 1944)

THURSDAY
5

Keep me away from the wisdom which does not cry, the philosophy which does not laugh and the greatness which does not bow before children. — Kahlil Gibran (Lebanese-born American mystic, poet and artist, 1883–1931)

FRIDAY
6

I do not rule Russia; ten thousand clerks do. — Nicholas I (1795–1855)

SATURDAY
7

Daylight Saving Time Begins

SUNDAY
8

BEEF PRICES HEAD SOUTH FOR SUMMER

Live cattle prices tend to post a seasonal high in March. Between the supplies of fattened beef coming out of feed lots from the cold winter months to competing meat products like poultry and pork, supply tends to outpace demand and we see a strong seasonal tendency for beef prices to decline starting on or about March 20 through the end of June.

In the past 38 years ending in 2007, this trade has worked 31 times, for a whopping cumulative profit of $41,590. There have only been seven years that this seasonality did not work. Since 1982, this phenomenon has worked each year except for in 2006 and 2004 (page 125).

Investors have other ways to trade the seasonality of the commodity markets by trading the outright futures contract. In the case of the meat complex, since there is not currently an ETF that is geared toward meat prices, investors can start examining which companies have not only a like or tandem price relationship, but also an inverse relationship with seasonal price moves in the underlying commodity markets, as is the case with live cattle and McDonald's.

The chart below is of McDonald's (MCD), one of the nation's, and most likely the world's, favorite fast-food hamburger establishments. As you can see, this stock has a seasonal tendency to move higher from late March into early June as beef prices decline. Then as beef prices tend to bottom in June we see the reverse occur in MCD stock prices.

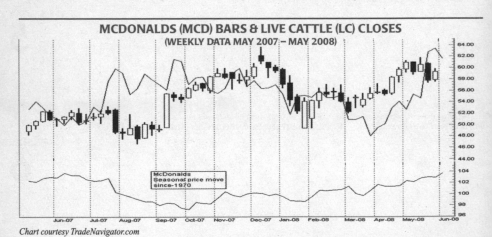

Chart courtesy TradeNavigator.com

MONDAY

9

It was never my thinking that made the big money for me. It was always my sitting. Got that? My sitting tight!
— Jesse Livermore (Early 20th century stock trader & speculator, *How to Trade in Stocks*, 1877–1940)

TUESDAY

10

When someone told me "We're going with you guys because no one ever got fired for buying Cisco (products)." That's what they used to say in IBM's golden age. — Mark Dickey (Former Cisco sales exec, then at SmartPipes, *Fortune* 5/15/00).

WEDNESDAY

11

Anytime there is change there is opportunity. So it is paramount that an organization get energized rather than paralyzed.
— Jack Welch (GE CEO, *Fortune*)

THURSDAY

12

Small volume is usually accompanied by a fall in price; large volume by a rise in price.
— Charles C. Ying ("Stock Market Prices and Volumes of Sales," *Econometrica*, July 1966)

Start Short Cocoa — 77.8% Accuracy Since 1973 — End Apr. 16 — Page 124
Start Short Yen — 71.9% Accuracy Since 1977 — End Apr. 2 — Page 124

FRIDAY

13

Governments last as long as the undertaxed can defend themselves against the overtaxed.
— Bernard Berenson (American art critic, 1865–1959)

SATURDAY

14

SUNDAY

15

MARCH BRITISH POUND INVASION

The British pound has a distinct pattern of doing the opposite of the euro and Swiss franc. It has a strong tendency to move up against the U.S. dollar from mid-March through early part of May. In fact, in the 34-year history, it has been positive 24 times, for a success rate of 70.6%.

Entering on or about March 21, holding a long position for 22 trading days and exiting on or about April 21, this trade has had a cumulative gain of $20,981. It has had a string of winners the last four years in a row, starting from 2004 (page 125).

Perhaps the fact that Britain's fiscal year begins in April helps to push the pound's value up against the U.S. dollar as money moves back overseas. Cross transactions between the pound versus the euro currency and the pound versus the yen may help influence the rise in the pound's value relative to the U.S. dollar.

The weekly chart below depicts the British pound with the exchange-traded fund on the British pound (FXB) overlaid to illustrate how the two instruments trade in tandem.

Traders have the ability to trade foreign currencies on a regulated marketplace such as the CME Group's futures and options exchanges that provides more electronic access than ETFs afford. Investors who require less leverage will find the FXB an adequate trading vehicle. Either way, the seasonal tendency is quite strong for the pound to move up in this time frame.

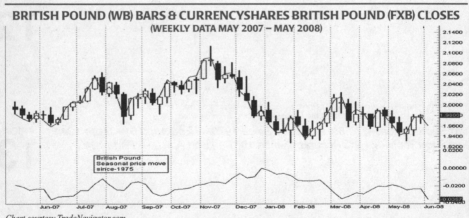

Chart courtesy TradeNavigator.com

Start Short Euro — 80.0% Accuracy Since 1999 — End Mar. 30 — Page 124

MONDAY
16

If there is something you really want to do, make your plan and do it. Otherwise, you'll just regret it forever.
— Richard Rocco (PostNet franchisee, *Entrepreneur* magazine 12/2006, b. 1946)

St. Patrick's Day ♣

TUESDAY
17

There have been three great inventions since the beginning of time: The fire, the wheel, and central banking.
— Will Rogers (American humorist and showman, 1879–1935)

End Short Gold (Jan. 22)

WEDNESDAY
18

Show me a good phone receptionist and I'll show you a good company. — Harvey Mackay (*Pushing the Envelope*, 1999)

Start Short Live Cattle — 81.6% Accuracy Since 1970 — End June 29 — Page 125
End Short British Pound (Dec. 26, 2008)

THURSDAY
19

Let us have the courage to stop borrowing to meet the continuing deficits. Stop the deficits.
— Franklin D. Roosevelt (32nd U.S. President, 1932, 1882–1945)

Start Long British Pound — 70.6% Accuracy Since 1975 — End Apr. 22 — Page 125

FRIDAY
20

Short-term volatility is greatest at turning points and diminishes as a trend becomes established.
— George Soros (Financier, philanthropist, political activist, author and philosopher, b. 1930)

SATURDAY
21

SUNDAY
22

PIVOT POINT ANALYSIS – COMPLEX EQUATIONS SIMPLIFY TRADING

Pivot Point Analysis is a famous technique that is used as a price forecasting method for determining Support and Resistance targets based on a mathematical formula. It is quite useful for trading almost any commodity, or stock or other security for that matter.

The variables are defined as: **P = Pivot Point, C = Close, H = High, and L = Low**.

The Pivot Point is the high, low and close summed and then divided by three.

$$P = (H + L + C) / 3$$

The first resistance level is the Pivot Point times two, then subtract the low.

$$(P \times 2) - L = \textbf{Resistance 1}$$

For the second resistance, take the Pivot Point and add the high, then subtract the low.

$$P + H - L = \textbf{Resistance 2}$$

For the first support, take the Pivot Point times two, then subtract the high.

$$(P \times 2) - H = \textbf{Support 1}$$

For the second support, take the Pivot Point, subtract the high, then add the low.

$$P - H + L = \textbf{Support 2}$$

As you can see it is a detailed formula, but fairly simple to apply. Consider the Pivot Point as the average of the previous sessions trading range combined with the closing price. The numbers of support and resistance that are calculated indicate the potential ranges for the next time frame based on the past weight of the markets strength or weakness derived from the calculations of the high, low, and distance from the close of those points. The previous session's trading range could be based on and calculated for an hour, a day, a week, or a month. Most trading software includes these numbers on a daily basis so that you do not have the tedious chore of doing it the old fashion way, by hand or using a calculator.

The daily numbers at the end of the day identify the next day's potential range or support and resistance. It gives a trader a head start on their analysis so they are prepared for the next day's work. In short, it helps you plan your trades. Similarly, the weekly numbers are done at the end of every week, and the same goes for the monthly numbers.

Since most technical analysis is derived from mathematical calculations, the common denominators that are used are the high, low, close, and the open. This is what is used for plotting a bar chart. Many technical analysis techniques, like moving averages, relative strength index, stochastics, and Fibonacci numbers, are all calculated using mathematics based on those points of interest. As technical analysts, we are trying to use past price behavior to help us indicate future price direction.

MARCH

Financial genius is a rising stock market. — John Kenneth Galbraith (Canadian/American economist and diplomat, 1908–2006)

The only things that evolve by themselves in an organization are disorder, friction and malperformance.
— Peter Drucker (Austria-born pioneer management theorist, 1909–2005)

Everyone wants to make the same three things: money, a name, and a difference.
What creates diversity in the human race is how we prioritize the three. — Roy H. Williams (*The Wizard of Ads*)

Foolish consistency is the hobgoblin of little minds.
— Ralph Waldo Emerson (American author, poet and philosopher, *Self-Reliance*, 1803–1882)

If all the economists in the world were laid end to end, they still wouldn't reach a conclusion.
— George Bernard Shaw (Irish dramatist, 1856–1950)

APRIL ALMANAC

ENERGY: Crude oil has a tendency to fall the first part of April and rally through mid-May. Buying this break has been a good decision in the last 26 years, as this trade has worked 76.9% of the time (page 40). This is still one of the best seven months to be long, which are from March through September. Natural gas prices tend to peak in mid- to late April. Our long best seasonal trade from February signals an exit on or about April 22 (page 123).

METALS: Gold has a tendency to continue the seasonal decline in April as tax-related selling pressures prices (page 42). Our best seasonal short trade for silver from February signals an exit on or about April 25 (page 26). Copper tends to form a seasonal high toward the end of April and the first part of May (page 149).

GRAINS: Soybeans in April still see upside, as planting concerns and demand for both meal and oil remain strong as U.S. inventories decline and new supplies are not yet ready since South America's harvest is just beginning (page 161). Wheat is still under pressure, as harvest adds fresh inventories that outweigh demand (page 164). Corn has a tendency to remain strong, especially as April can lead to planting delays in cool wet spring conditions. In addition, April tax season has passed and farmers tend to start focusing on production rather than marketing, allowing inventories to build up on farm locations (page 158).

SOFTS: Cocoa's best seasonal short trade from March signals an exit on or about April 16 (page 124). Coffee prices are seasonally strong, as this is still just short of the Columbian and Brazilian harvest. It is also the time when the threat of frost damaging the South American crop is high (page 170). Sugar tends to remain weak during this time frame due to inventory from sugar cane harvests in the U.S. Southeast and Brazil (page 173).

MEATS: Live cattle prices are in a seasonally weak period through mid-June, but we do see times where prices consolidate especially if the month prior showed significant price declines (page 176). Ranchers tend to pay more attention to breeding in the spring rather than bringing livestock to market. This may have some effect on price stabilization, which allows supplies to remain in balance with demand. Lean hog prices on the other hand continue to remain firm in April from a seasonal perspective (page 179). As corn prices increase feed costs, hog producers have shifted towards liquidating inventories and are preparing for breeding as well. Furthermore, competing pork producers from Canada have had more incentives marketing product with the increase in value of the Canadian dollar relative to the U.S. dollar. This has magnified the seasonal peak which comes in late May (page 128).

CURRENCIES: The euro best seasonal short trade from March signals an exit on or before April 1 (page 124). The Swiss franc continues its seasonally flat period from March until the first part of August (page 187). The British pound best seasonal long trade from March signals an exit on or about April 22 (page 125). The yen best seasonal trade short trade from March signals an exit on or about April 3 (page 124).

End Short Euro (Mar. 16)

MONDAY

30

A cynic is a man who knows the price of everything and the value of nothing. — Oscar Wilde (Irish-born writer and wit, 1845–1900)

TUESDAY

31

Since 1950, the S&P 500 has achieved total returns averaging just 3.50% annually during periods when the S&P 500 price/peak earnings ratio was above 15 and both 3-month T-bill yields and 10-year Treasury yields were above their levels of 6 months earlier. — John P. Hussman, Ph.D. (Hussman Funds, 5/22/06)

WEDNESDAY

1

When I have to depend upon hope in a trade, I get out of it.
— Jesse Livermore (Early 20th century stock trader & speculator, *How to Trade in Stocks*, 1877–1940)

End Short Yen (Mar. 13)

THURSDAY

2

The soul is dyed the color of its thoughts. Think only on those things that are in line with your principles and can bear the light of day. The content of your character is your choice. Day by day, what you do is who you become.
— Heraclitus (Greek philosopher, 535–475 BC)

FRIDAY

3

Economics is a very difficult subject. I've compared it to trying to learn how to repair a car when the engine is running.
— Ben Bernanke (Fed Chairman 2006-, June 2004, Region interview as Fed governor)

SATURDAY

4

SUNDAY

5

CRUDE OIL STRIKES A WINNER IN APRIL

Crude oil has a tendency to fall the first part of April and then rally through mid-May. It is that early April break that can give traders an edge by buying low in a seasonally strong period. In the 26-year history, this trade has worked 20 years, for an impressive 76.9% success rate. The massive price advance made in 2008 gave by far the single biggest seasonal profit of $16,800 (page 126).

The seasonal influence that causes crude oil to move higher in this time period is partly due to the fact that during this time there is still demand for heating oil and diesel fuel in northern states, but also refineries shut down operations in order to switch production facilities from producing heating oil to reformulated unleaded gasoline in anticipation of heavy demand for the upcoming summer driving season. This has refiners buying crude oil in order to ramp up the production for gasoline.

Traders seek high probability trades that limit risk and volatility. When the futures markets seem hazardous and unstable, there are other alternatives. One such opportunity is to trade the exchange-traded funds United States Oil Fund (USO) or Select SPDR Energy (XLE) or options on these ETFs.

One other aspect is to look for stocks that trade inversely to the underlying commodity market or stocks like Chesapeake Energy (CHK) that have a direct correlation to the underlying futures market and trade that product under the seasonal aspects. This company meets our criteria of good management, P/E outlook, and trades in excess of 700,000 shares per day.

CHK is an oil and natural gas exploration and production company. Notice the direct correlation between crude oil futures and the price value in the stock in the chart below. The bottom section shows the seasonal tendencies for the company dating back to 1993. This company stock has a strong resemblance to the seasonal price moves in crude oil (page 145).

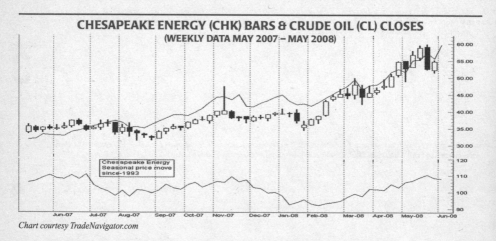

Chart courtesy TradeNavigator.com

APRIL

Love your enemies, for they tell you your faults. — Benjamin Franklin (U.S. founding father, diplomat, inventor, 1706–1790)

Make it idiot-proof and someone will make a better idiot. — Bumper sticker

Towering genius disdains a beaten path. It scorns to tread in the footsteps of any predecessor, however illustrious. It thirsts for distinction. — Abraham Lincoln (16th U.S. president, 1809–1865)

Passover
Start Long Crude Oil — 76.9% Accuracy Since 1983 — End May 15 — Page 126

One only gets to the top rung on the ladder by steadily climbing up one at a time, and suddenly all sorts of powers, all sorts of abilities, which you thought never belonged to you-suddenly become within your own possibility.... — Margaret Thatcher (British prime minister 1979–1990, b. 1925)

Good Friday

The worst trades are generally when people freeze and start to pray and hope rather than take some action. — Robert Mnuchin (Partner Goldman Sachs)

Easter

APRIL TAX TIME TAKES A BITE OUT OF GOLD

Gold has a tendency to continue the seasonal decline that begins in January, leaving April vulnerable to price declines. April tends to see tax related selling pressure on Gold prices along with other financial markets specifically the U.S. stock markets and more predominantly it happens in the tech sector as represented by the NASDAQ. It seems that some investors raise capital to pay the IRS by liquidating portions of assets such as gold and stocks (see *Stock Traders Almanac 2009* page 38).

Generally speaking, April is also a weak month from a demand perspective. The two forces of increased sales (supply) and no major demand cause the downside price pressure on gold during April. The monthly percent changes show a distinct price decline on gold (page 154).

The weekly chart below shows the price comparison of gold to a gold mining stock, Newmont Mining (NEM). NEM is a major producer of gold and other metals. This company manages properties in the United States, Australia, Peru, Indonesia, Ghana, Canada, Bolivia, New Zealand, and Mexico. The company was founded in 1916 and is based in Denver, Colorado. Not only are they diversified in various countries, but they also have a long history of being in business. This stock also meets our criteria, as it trades well over an average of 6 million shares per day.

As you can see, the April selloff is predominant not only in the price of gold but also in the shares of this company. The bottom chart shows the average seasonality since 1983 of the actual stock prices making declines in the month of April. Here again is another example of trading opportunities using seasonalities of commodities that have direct correlation to other markets and trade that product under the seasonal aspects. Newmont Mining is one such example that mirrors the price movement of gold.

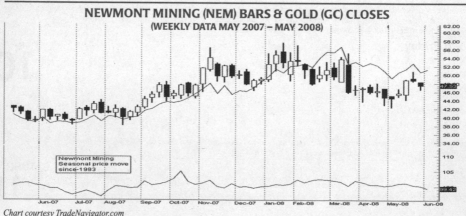

Chart courtesy TradeNavigator.com

APRIL

MONDAY

13

0K ought to be enough for anybody. — William H. Gates (Microsoft founder, 1981; Try running Microsoft Vista on less than a gig.)

TUESDAY

14

a man has no talents, he is unhappy enough; but if he has, envy pursues him in proportion to his ability.
Leopold Mozart (to his son Wolfgang Amadeus, 1768)

come Tax Deadline

WEDNESDAY

15

ople with a sense of fulfillment think the world is good, while the frustrated blame the world for their failure.
Eric Hoffer (*The True Believer*, 1951)

nd Short Cocoa (Mar. 13)
nd Short Sugar (Feb. 19)

THURSDAY

16

weak currency is the sign of a weak economy, and a weak economy leads to a weak nation.
H. Ross Perot (American businessman, *The Dollar Crisis*, two-time 3rd-party presidential candidate 1992 & 1996, b. 1930)

FRIDAY

17

arket risk tends to be poorly rewarded when market valuations are rich and interest rates are rising.
John P. Hussman, Ph.D. (Hussman Funds, 5/22/06)

SATURDAY

18

SUNDAY

19

BULLISH ON COMMODITIES—OWN THE EXCHANGES

If trading in the underlying commodity market becomes too volatile or if the margin requirements soar as contract values increase, traders can instead own the underlying U.S. exchanges. Here is a select group of publicly traded exchanges:

Chicago Mercantile Exchange Group (CME) operates two self-regulatory futures exchanges, the Chicago Mercantile Exchange and the recently acquired Chicago Board of Trade. The company now offers a complete spectrum of markets across various asset classes, including futures and options on interest rates stock index products, foreign currencies, agricultural commodities and alternative investments, such as weather and real estate. The company also owns a clearinghouse, CME Clearing. In addition, CME Group offers market data and information products, and is involved in real estate.

Its primary trade execution facilities consist of its CME Globex electronic trading platform and open outcry trading floors, as well as privately negotiated transactions that are cleared and settled through its clearinghouse. The company's customer base includes professional traders, financial institutions, institutional and individual investors, corporations, manufacturers, producers, and governments worldwide. It has strategic relationships with BM&F, China Foreign Exchange Trade System and National Interbank Funding Center, NYMEX, Reuters, and Singapore Derivatives Exchange, Ltd. CME Group was founded in 1898 and is headquartered in Chicago, Illinois.

InterContinental Exchange (ICE) is the other major player in the electronic commodity exchange industry. In 2008, it acquired the rights to trade the Russell 2000, a popular stock index contract weighted toward the small cap markets. ICE also acquired the New York Board of Trade Exchange, where coffee, cocoa, sugar and, yes, frozen concentrated orange juice (FCOJ) were traded. The NYBOT was established in 1870 so it does have history, but is now under new management.

ICE is an Internet-based global electronic marketplace for trading in futures, over-the-counter (OTC) commodities, and derivative financial products in the United States and internationally. Its products also include contracts based on crude and refined oil products, natural gas, electricity and emissions. The company is headquartered in Atlanta, Georgia. ICE futures was formerly the International Petroleum Exchange, which is another example of a company that has been around a long time, and it does have a good business model and market share of products that is traded.

NYMEX Holdings (NMX), otherwise known as its subsidiary, the New York Mercantile Exchange, operates as a physical commodities exchange, offering futures and options trading in energy, metals, and other contracts and clearing services. Through a hybrid model of open outcry floor trading and electronic trading through the CME Globex electronic platform, as well as clearing off-exchange instruments through NYMEX ClearPort Clearing, the company offers crude oil, petroleum products, natural gas, coal, electricity, gold, silver, copper, aluminum, platinum group metals, emissions, and soft commodities contracts for trading and clearing.

NYMEX Holdings has a joint venture with Tatweer Dubai LLC to develop the Middle East's first energy futures exchange; and a strategic alliance with Bourse de Montreal, Inc. to form a joint venture company that focuses on offering trading and clearing of exchange-traded and over-the-counter products in Canada. The CME has a noncompete clause on NYMEX products, which should technically force it to shut down the CBOT metals complex when the merger deal is finalized. The NYMEX was founded in 1872 as the Butter and Cheese Exchange of New York and changed its name to the Butter, Cheese, and Egg Exchange of the City of New York. Here is one more example of a company with a rich history.

NYSE Euronext (NYX). The New York Stock Exchange traces its origins to 1792, when 24 New York City stockbrokers and merchants signed the Buttonwood Agreement. This agreement set in motion the NYSE's unwavering commitment to investors and issuers. Through its subsidiaries, it offers various financial products and services. It provides securities listing, trading, and market data products and services, including some of the stocks just mentioned on the futures exchanges and ETFs, many of which trade based on the price fluctuations of certain commodity markets.

The historic combination of NYSE Group and Euronext in 2007 marked a milestone for global financial markets. It brought together major marketplaces across Europe and the United States whose histories stretch back more than four centuries. The combination was by far the largest of its kind and the first to create a truly global marketplace group. In addition, the company provides international services for regulated cash markets and derivative markets in Belgium, France, the United Kingdom, the Netherlands, and Portugal. As of December 31, 2007, it operated six cash equities and six derivatives exchanges. The company is headquartered in New York, New York.

APRIL

*Individualism, private property, the law of accumulation of wealth and the law of competition...
are the highest result of human experience, the soil in which, so far, has produced the best fruit.*
— Andrew Carnegie (Scottish-born U.S. industrialist, philanthropist, *The Gospel of Wealth*, 1835–1919)

*Some people say we can't compete with Intel. I say, like hell you can't... Dominant companies usually don't change
unless they're forced to do so.* — David Patterson (Chip designing force behind R.I.S.C. and R.A.I.D., WSJ 8/28/98)

End Long British Pound (Mar. 20)

History is a collection of agreed upon lies. — Voltaire (French philosopher, 1694–1778)

End Long Natural Gas (Feb. 24)

If you don't know who you are, the stock market is an expensive place to find out.
— George Goodman (*Institutional Investor, New York,* "Adam Smith," *The Money Game,* b. 1930)

End Short Silver (Feb. 19)

Nothing is more uncertain than the favor of the crowd. — Marcus Tullius Cicero (Great Roman Orator, Politician, 106–43 B.C.)

MAY ALMANAC

ENERGY: Liquidate crude oil longs from February and April on or about May 13–15 (pages 123 & 126). Natural gas generally consolidates during the month of May prior to forming a mid-June peak, followed by early summer weakness (page 147).

METALS: Gold continues to remain weak from a seasonal perspective headed into the early summer month trading doldrums. Silver sees a strong tendency to peak — look to sell silver on or about May 14 (page 50). Get short copper on or about May 12 (page 54).

GRAINS: Soybeans tend to peak out and start a seasonal decline in most normal weather years, as planting is well established and the crop growing season is well underway. This is the time to take advantage of any further seasonal strength to liquidate long positions from February on or about May 29 (page 122). Wheat prices continue to trend lower under normal crop years before the harvest lows are made in June (page 164). Corn tends to peak out in May. Look to short corn on or about May 13 (page 52).

SOFTS: Cocoa sees some price consolidation as it heads toward its seasonal low in June (page 167). Coffee has its best seasonal trade as it typically hits a seasonal high in May, look to sell short on or about May 22 (page 48). Sugar sees some price consolidation, as it also tends to hit a seasonal low in June (page 173).

MEATS: Live cattle generally trends lower in May headed into June when it typically establishes its average seasonal low (page 176). Lean hogs usually peak in May (page 179). Short lean hogs on or about May 21 and hold through August 17 (page 128).

CURRENCIES: The euro has no real meaningful trend direction or influences from one particular seasonal factor during the month of May. The Swiss franc also drifts sideways, with a tendency to post a seasonal bottom in May, but typically does not advance higher against the U.S. dollar until August. The British pound can be shorted on or about May 29 and held through June 10. This trade worked 27 of 34 years, for a cumulative gain of $31,631 (page 129). In fact, this trade has been on a recent hot streak, registering five straight wins in a row since 2004 up to and including 2008. The yen should rally, giving traders a chance to liquidate the seasonal long best trade from February on or about May 8 (page 121).

MONDAY

27

The worst mistake investors make is taking their profits too soon, and their losses too long.

TUESDAY

28

Bill [Gates] isn't afraid of taking long-term chances. He also understands that you have to try everything because the real secret to innovation is failing fast. — Gary Starkweather (Inventor of laser printer in 1969 at Xerox, *Fortune*, July 8, 2002)

WEDNESDAY

29

Selling a soybean contract short is worth two years at the Harvard Business School.
— Robert Stovall (Managing director, Wood Asset Management)

THURSDAY

30

No horse gets anywhere until he is harnessed. No steam or gas ever drives anything until it is confined.
No Niagara is ever turned into light and power until it is tunneled. No life ever grows great until it is focused,
dedicated, disciplined. — Harry Emerson Fosdick (Protestant minister, author, 1878–1969)

FRIDAY

1

You know a country is falling apart when even the government will not accept its own currency.
— Jim Rogers (Financier, *Adventure Capitalist*, b. 1942)

SATURDAY

2

SUNDAY

3

COFFEE BUZZ FADES IN SUMMER

Coffee typically posts a seasonal high in May. This creates coffee's most powerful seasonal play under normal weather conditions, which means a lack of frost in the Southern Hemisphere growing regions of Columbia and Brazil. Traders should look to sell short on or about May 22 and hold through August 9. This trade has worked 28 out of the last 34 years with $158,194 in cumulative profits. This trade has a long history of success, registering an 82.4% success rate.

However, this trade has not fared so well in the past two years, 2007 and 2008 (page 128). One explanation as to why this market defied the seasonal tendency to decline in this time period was partly due to a much smaller crop than expected in Brazil back in 2007 and lack of rain during the key flower pollination stage. Trade estimates were looking for 50 million KG bags of production, but according to forecasts, that estimate backed down to 45 million KG bags of production. So in essence, supply declined due to poor weather conditions as demand remained steady. Therefore, we saw a price increase result in two years of poor performance.

If we have a normal weather in 2009, this trade could turn out to be a significant return on investment by selling futures or implementing a bearish option position. As for other trading opportunities, the chart below shows the coffeehouse and distributor Starbucks (SBUX) with an overlaid price line of coffee. The bottom section is the average seasonal price move of Starbucks, reflecting the inverse of coffee's price action.

When coffee declines, historically we have seen a price increase in share prices of SBUX. The reverse is also true. When coffee prices increased, share prices of SBUX declined. If in 2009 coffee prices have been up strong on or about May 22, and if SBUX is near its yearly or monthly lows, then traders may want to look to buy shares of SBUX or consider call options.

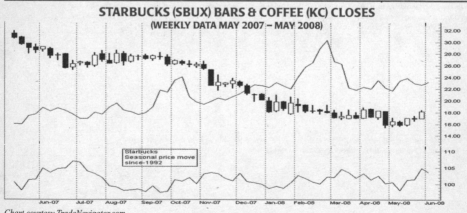

Chart courtesy TradeNavigator.com

MAY

MONDAY
4

Setting a goal is not the main thing. It is deciding how you will go about achieving it and staying with that plan. — Tom Landry (Head Coach Dallas Cowboys 1960–1988)

TUESDAY
5

In an uptrend, if a higher high is made but fails to carry through, and prices dip below the previous high, the trend is apt to reverse. The converse is true for downtrends. — Victor Sperandeo (*Trader Vic — Methods of a Wall Street Master*)

WEDNESDAY
6

An appeaser is one who feeds a crocodile — hoping it will eat him last. — Winston Churchill (British statesman, 1874–1965)

THURSDAY
7

A man isn't a man until he has to meet a payroll. — Ivan Shaffer (*The Stock Promotion Game*)

End Long Yen (Feb. 9)

FRIDAY
8

I have a love affair with America, because there are no built-in barriers to anyone in America. I come from a country where there were barriers upon barriers. — Michael Caine (Actor, Quoted in *Parade Magazine*, 2/16/03)

SATURDAY
9

Mother's Day

SUNDAY
10

SILVER SLIPS IN MAY

Silver has a strong tendency to peak or continue lower in May, bottoming in late June. Traders can look to sell silver on or about May 14 and hold until on or about June 25. In the past 36 years, this trade has seen declines 26 times for a success rate of 72.2%. This trade has a cumulative gain of $52,325. 2007 posted the greatest gain since 1972, chalking up a $24,400 gain (page 127).

The futures market has, without a doubt, been trading under extremely volatile conditions recently. This type of environment may not be suitable for all traders, especially those who cannot monitor positions closely. There are other products to trade, as the chart below shows an exchange-traded fund, the iShares Silver Trust (SLV). Notice the price action is identical on a closing basis with the underlying silver futures contract and SLV.

iShares Silver Trust (SLV), much like the gold counterpart SPDR Gold Shares (GLD), is unique in that the trust owns the underlying commodity that the ETF is attempting to track; each share represents 10 ounces of silver and the closing price of the ETF will represent, within reason, spot silver multiplied by 10. As of July 9, 2008, SLV owned 192,905,122.8 ounces of silver with 19.5 million of shares outstanding. Just like every other ETF, there is a premium to net asset value (NAV), which accounts for the difference. The banks have to make a buck too!

In fact, this ETF is optionable, and one can place electronic orders and receive confirmation of orders and fills. The bottom section shows the 27-year historic average seasonal price tendency of silver and the decline typically seen from the highs in February until the lows are posted in late June into early July. This May silver short trade captures the tail end of silver's weak seasonal period.

SILVER (SI) BARS & ISHARES SILVER TRUST (SLV) CLOSES
(WEEKLY DATA MAY 2007 – MAY 2008)

Chart courtesy TradeNavigator.com

MAY

End Long Corn (Oct. 28, 2008)

MONDAY
11

Buy a stock the way you would buy a house. Understand and like it such that you'd be content to own it in the absence of any market.
— Warren Buffett (CEO Berkshire Hathaway, investor & philanthropist, b. 1930)

Start Short Copper — 66.7% Accuracy Since 1973 — End May 29 — Page 126

TUESDAY
12

Change is the law of life. And those who look only to the past or present are certain to miss the future.
— John F. Kennedy (35th U.S. president, 1917–1963)

Start Short Corn — 72.5% Accuracy Since 1968 — End Jul. 20 — Page 127
End Long Crude Oil (Feb. 23)

WEDNESDAY
13

Live beyond your means; then you're forced to work hard, you have to succeed. — Edward G. Robinson (American actor)

Start Short Silver — 72.2% Accuracy Since 1972 — End Jun. 25 — Page 127

THURSDAY
14

In the realm of ideas, everything depends on enthusiasm; in the real world, all rests on perseverance.
— Johann Wolfgang von Goethe (German poet and polymath, 1749–1832)

End Long Crude Oil (Apr. 9)

FRIDAY
15

It's better to have your enemies inside the tent pissing out than outside pissing in.
— Lyndon B. Johnson (37th U.S. president, 1908–1973)

SATURDAY
16

SUNDAY
17

MOTHER NATURE MAKES CORN POP

Corn tends to peak in May under normal crop years as planting is complete and farmers are looking for cooperation from Mother Nature to produce increased production yields. Look to sell on or about May 13 and hold through July 20. This is when we typically get a "drought scare" or mid-summer rally. The 40-year history of this timing strategy shows a win in 29 of those years, for a success rate of 72.5% and a cumulative profit of $54,213 (page 127).

However, due to the change in legislation that boosted ethanol production and poor weather conditions that led to a slow planting season in 2008, this trade is not working well at press time. Trade estimates suggest we may have lost over 10% of the corn crop in 2008 due to flooding, and if that is the case, then we could see the tightest stocks-to-usage ratio in 35 years. The lowest percentage was 5% back in 1995–1996. June estimates for the crop year of 2008–2009 were about 6.7%, as condition are precarious. This could easily tighten if weather condition put further strain on the corn crop.

With the price increase in corn headed into summer, we would normally see the market settle back as farmers have a better idea of their crop size and start to hedge or forward contract sales out to lock in a profit. Depending on the levels of volatility, traders can look to sell futures or buy put options or once again look for alternative trading opportunities.

The chart below is Deere & Co. (DE) with corn prices overlaid. The bottom section shows the seasonal tendency of Deere stock prices since 1970. As you can see, there is a high correlation of the price of corn and the share price of DE. One can look to sell DE, buy puts, or write calls in the seasonally weak timeframe that starts in May and goes into July.

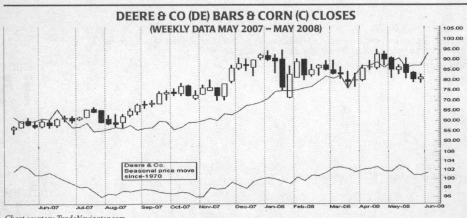

Chart courtesy TradeNavigator.com

MAY

End Short Wheat (Nov. 25, 2008)

MONDAY
18

Don't confuse brains with a bull market.
— Humphrey B. Neill (Investor, analyst, author, *Neill Letters of Contrary Opinion*, 1895–1977)

TUESDAY
19

While one person hesitates because he feels inferior, the other is busy making mistakes and becoming superior.
— Henry C. Link (Industrial psychologist, author, *Psychological Corporation*, 1889–1952)

WEDNESDAY
20

Unless you've interpreted changes before they've occurred, you'll be decimated trying to follow them.
— Robert J. Nurock (Editor of *The Astute Investor* newsletter)

Start Short Lean Hogs — 89.5% Accuracy Since 1970 — End Aug. 17 — Page 128

THURSDAY
21

We pay the debts of the last generation by issuing bonds payable by the next generation.
— Lawrence J. Peter (Educator and formulator of the "Peter Principle"

Start Short Coffee — 82.4% Accuracy Since 1974 — End Aug. 10 — Page 128

FRIDAY
22

The worst bankrupt in the world is the person who has lost his enthusiasm. — H.W. Arnold

SATURDAY
23

SUNDAY
24

COPPER TOPS IN MAY

Copper prices tend to peak out as construction season is underway. Supplies have built up, but demand tends to decline. Producers have a tendency to ship inventories when prices are the highest during periods of strong demand (page 149).

Builders order hand-to-mouth rather than stockpile copper tubing for plumbing installations when prices get too high. This could be one explanation for this short-term seasonal tendency.

Traders can look to sell copper on or about May 12, and then exit on or about May 29. This trade has racked up 24 wins out of the last 36 years. What is more impressive is the last two years. 2007 and 2008 have totaled $11,875 in profits. Besides selling a futures contract, one way to capitalize on this event is to look at BHP Billiton (BHP), which is a natural resource company that mines iron ore, aluminum, and, of course, copper, among other metals.

Notice the striking similarities of the seasonal tendencies that this company moves in relation to the price of copper. This is a company that meets our criteria as well since this company trades well over 1,000,000 share per day. The company was founded in 1860 so it does have a long history of staying in business. It is headquartered in Melbourne, Australia.

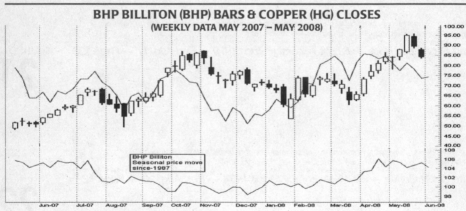

Chart courtesy TradeNavigator.com

MAY

Memorial Day (Market Closed)

MONDAY
25

Beware of inside information...all inside information.
— Jesse Livermore (Early 20th century stock trader & speculator, How to Trade in Stocks, 1877–1940)

TUESDAY
26

Iron rusts from disuse; stagnant water loses its purity and in cold weather becomes frozen;
even so does inaction sap the vigor of the mind. — Leonardo da Vinci (Italian Renaissance polymath, 1452–1519)

WEDNESDAY
27

Everyone blames the foreigners when the economy goes south. Always. It is human nature to blame others,
and it is the same all over the world. — Jim Rogers (Financier, *Adventure Capitalist*, b. 1942)

THURSDAY
28

While markets often make double bottoms, three pushes to a high is the most common topping pattern.
— John Bollinger (Bollinger Capital Management, Capital Growth Letter, Bollinger on Bollinger Bands)

Start Short British Pound — 79.4% Accuracy Since 1975 — End Jun. 10 — Page 129
End Long Soybeans (Feb. 12)
End Short Copper (May 12)

FRIDAY
29

Securities pricing is, in every sense a psychological phenomenon that arises from the interaction of human beings with fear.
Why not greed and fear as the equation is usually stated? Because greed is simply fear of not having enough.
— John Bollinger (Bollinger Capital Management, Capital Growth Letter, Bollinger on Bollinger Bands)

SATURDAY
30

SUNDAY
31

JUNE ALMANAC

ENERGY: Seasonally, this is still one of the best seven months, March to September, to be long crude oil. However, June tends to see price consolidations after major price moves in May (page 145). Natural gas prices tend to move lower in June until mid-July, when we typically see the market make its average seasonal low (page 68).

METALS: Most years Gold prices continue in a downtrend as it is in its seasonally weak price period until July-August (page 66). Cover short Silver position from May 14 on or about June 25 (page 50). Copper tends to have counter seasonal rallies in June (page 149).

GRAINS: Soybeans seasonal peak, sell on June 1, hold until October 6 (page 58). Wheat's best seasonal long trade is in June. Enter long position around June 8 and exit near November 4 (page 60). Corn is in the middle of seasonal decline especially in normal or above-average weather conditions. Some years we see countertrend rallies in early June that overlap the May short trade position (page 50). This rally offer traders a spot to add or enter new short positions by selling on or about June 16 and holding through the end of July. The last 40 years, this trade has worked 29 times, for a cumulative profit of $16,050 (page 131).

SOFTS: Enter new long cocoa position on or about June 2, exit on or about July 7. This trade worked 27 of 35 years for a 77.1% success rate; cumulative profits are $19,810 (page 130). Coffee continues its downtrend, as it is in the seasonally weak price period (page 48). Sugar also continues to trend down in June, as it is also in a seasonally weak price period through August (page 86).

MEATS: Close out short live cattle position from March around June 29 (page 32). This is seasonally the best time to buy beef. Fundamentals show that consumer demand generally declines in hot summer months, but so does supply. Statistically speaking, as our data reveal, traders should look to enter a long position on or about June 18 and hold through February 5 of the following year. This trade has worked 34 times in the last 38 years for a success rate of 89.5% and a total gain of $65,950 (page 62). Hogs continue their downtrend as they are in their seasonally weak price period.

CURRENCIES: The euro tends to trend lower into the end of the third quarter (page 185). Swiss francs generally move lower into August (page 76). Cover short British pound position from May 29 on or about June 10 (page 46). Prices tend to give traders another trade opportunity. In the past 33 years, reversing positions and going long on or about June 26 and holding into late July has produced 24 years of successful trades, for a success rate of 72.7%. The cumulative profit is $31,906 (page 132). The yen tends to trend lower into August (page 72).

JUNE

Start Short Soybeans — 70.0% Accuracy Since 1968 — End Oct. 6 — Page 129

MONDAY

1

If I had eight hours to chop down a tree, I'd spend six sharpening my axe. — Abraham Lincoln (16th U.S. president, 1809–1865)

Start Long Cocoa — 77.1% Accuracy Since 1973 — End Jul. 7 — Page 130

TUESDAY

2

The two most abundant elements in the universe are hydrogen and stupidity. — Harlan Ellison (Science fiction writer, b. 1934)

WEDNESDAY

3

The way a young man spends his evenings is a part of that thin area between success and failure.
— Robert R. Young (U.S. financier and railroad tycoon, 1897–1958)

THURSDAY

4

Most people can stay excited for two or three months. A few people can stay excited for two or three years.
But a winner will stay excited for 20 to 30 years — or as long as it takes to win. — A.L. Williams (Motivational speaker)

FRIDAY

5

Bankruptcy was designed to forgive stupidity, not reward criminality.
— William P. Barr (Verizon general counsel, calling for government liquidation of MCI-WorldCom in Chap. 7, 4/14/2003)

SATURDAY

6

SUNDAY

7

SHORT SOYBEANS FOR SUMMER

After planting season has finished through the bean belt of Illinois and up through Minnesota, soybeans tend to post a seasonal peak as we enter what is known as the blooming stage or pollination period. It is at this time where we have a good understanding of the crop size. Under ideal weather conditions, traders tend to sell the market as producers and grain elevators start hedging or forward contracting out their crops production. This marketing effort can last through harvest time.

The new genetically modified (GMO) seed, Roundup Ready, by Monsanto (MON) is more resistant than ever to insects and drought or heat stress. In addition, there has been more worldwide acceptance of this technology. U.S. farmers have increased usage and production over 85% of this variety and this may explain why, under normal weather growing years, prices tend to decline as there is a better estimate of the crop size.

Seasonally look to sell on June 1 and hold until October 6. In the last 40 years, the trade has worked 28 times, for a cumulative profit $54,213. The chart below is Monsanto (MON) with a line chart of the nearby soybean futures contract overlaid to help illustrate the corresponding price action of both.

Seasonally we see peaks in soybeans (page 161) and as the chart below shows the seasonality of the decline in price moves in Monsanto is closely correlated to the price declines in soybean prices through mid October.

Traders can look to sell futures short on any price rallies in June or look to buy put options as an alternative trading strategy. Stock traders may want to note that the best time to buy stock in this company is during the seasonally strong period or during harvest lows in October (page 92).

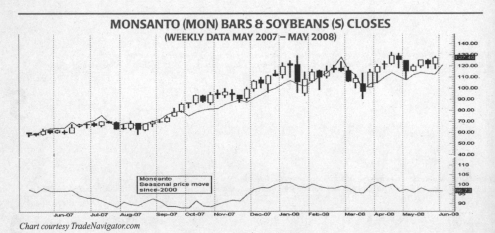

MONSANTO (MON) BARS & SOYBEANS (S) CLOSES
(WEEKLY DATA MAY 2007 – MAY 2008)

Chart courtesy TradeNavigator.com

JUNE

Start Long Wheat — 80.0% Accuracy Since 1968 — End Nov. 4 — Page 130

MONDAY

8

I am young, powerful and successful, and I produce at least $10,000 a month.
— (Mantra of Suze Orman, *The 9 Steps to Financial Freedom*, as a young Merrill Lynch broker)

TUESDAY

9

Anyone who has achieved excellence knows that it comes as a result of ceaseless concentration.
— Louise Brooks (Actress, 1906–1985)

End Short British Pound (May 29)

WEDNESDAY

10

The investor who concentrated on the 50 stocks in the S&P 500 that are followed by the fewest Wall Street analysts wound up with a rousing 24.6% gain in [2006 versus] 13.6% [for] the S&P 500.
— Rich Bernstein (Chief investment strategist, Merrill Lynch, *Barron's* 1/8/07)

THURSDAY

11

You win some, you lose some. And then there's that little-known third category.
— Albert Gore (U.S. vice president 1993–2000, former 2000 presidential candidate, quoted at the 2004 DNC)

FRIDAY

12

Oil has fostered massive corruption in almost every country that has been "blessed" with it, and the expectation that oil wealth will transform economies has lead to disastrous policy choices. — Ted Tyson (Chief investment officer, Mastholm Asset Management)

SATURDAY

13

SUNDAY

14

HARVEST BOOSTS WHEAT

The wheat market generally sees harvest lows in June, creating the best seasonal long trade. Enter long positions on or about June 8 and then exit on or about November 4. Out of the past 40 years, this trade has worked 32 times, for a 72.7% success rate; cumulative profits are $65,788 (page 130).

This commodity has a strong seasonal pattern (page 164) and in recent years we have seen unprecedented price gains. In fact, in February 2008 this market marked a record high of over $13.49 per bushel. CBOT wheat, now traded at the CME Group, is considered winter wheat as it is seeded in September-October time frame and during the winter it enters it's dormancy period.

In late winter through early spring it emerges and goes through what is called its heading stage. This is the phase that wheat is at most risk for frost or freeze damage. We do have times when these scares produce price spikes in late March or early April. Winter wheat begins harvesting in late spring through early summer.

Under normal weather years without late spring frost scares and ideal dry harvest conditions, we see sharp price breaks in late May until early June. It is this price decline that traders can take advantage of by entering long positions.

The chart below is of Kellogg (K), an end user or company that buys wheat to make cereals and snack cake items. The line chart overlaid is the price of Wheat and below is the seasonal price move of Kellogg. As you can see, wheat prices move mostly on an inverse relationship with this company.

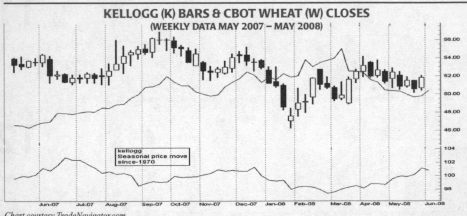

Chart courtesy TradeNavigator.com

JUNE

MONDAY
15

It wasn't raining when Noah built the ark. — Warren Buffett (CEO Berkshire Hathaway, investor & philanthropist, b. 1930)

Start Short Corn — 72.5% Accuracy Since 1968 — End Jul. 30 — Page 131

TUESDAY
16

What's going on... is the end of Silicon Valley as we know it. The next big thing ain't computers... It's biotechnology.
— Larry Ellison (Oracle CEO, quoted in *The Wall Street Journal*, April 8, 2003)

WEDNESDAY
17

The world has changed! You can't be an 800-pound gorilla; you need to be an economic gazelle.
You've got to be able to change directions quickly. — Mark Breier (*The 10-Second Internet Manager*)

Start Long Live Cattle — 89.5% Accuracy Since 1970 — End Feb. 5, 2010 — Page 131

THURSDAY
18

Institutions tend to dump stock in a single transaction and buy, if possible, in smaller lots, gradually accumulating a position.
Therefore, many more big blocks are traded on downticks than on upticks. — Justin Mamis

FRIDAY
19

One determined person can make a significant difference; a small group of determined people can change the course of history.
— Sonia Johnson (author, lecturer)

SATURDAY
20

Father's Day

SUNDAY
21

SUMMER BBQ SEASON GIVES BEEF A BOUNCE

This is seasonally the best time to buy live cattle. Fundamentally, beef consumption starts to decline in hot weather, but so does supply as feed lots are short of inventory. Cash grain prices tend to remain high as supply decreases before harvest season. This supply/demand imbalance creates a bid under the market and we have a tendency to see price increases in the summer months. Then before school season begins, federal government subsidies for school lunch programs kick in for beef purchases.

As winter and the holiday season approach, consumption increases. This helps keep a floor of support in cattle futures through mid-February (page 131). Enter long positions on or about June 18 then exit on or about February 5. Out of the past 38-year history, this trade has worked 34 times, for an 89.5% success rate. Cumulative profits add up to an impressive $65,950.

It is interesting to note that through the last 10 years, beef has certainly gone through many supply and demand shifts. For example, the price crash in December 2004 was based on a mad cow scare. Since then and through much of this new millennium, foreign buyers have shied away from U.S. beef due to hormone usage. All in all, demand has kept up and has remained stable, but there is a possibility that in 2009 and beyond, we could see a secular bull market that may magnify beef's seasonal price swings.

Due to the unprecedented high cost of feed grain (thanks to ethanol), ranchers have liquidated the breeding herd. If demand remains steady or if foreign buyers open the doors to buying more U.S. raised beef, then we could see sharply higher red meat prices in the next few years due to a decline in supplies.

The chart below is McDonald's (MCD) with the closing prices of the front contract live cattle futures overlaid and the seasonal price move of the stock on the bottom. It is interesting to note that while beef has a tendency to rise from June through August, MCD has a tendency to decline during this same time period on average since 1970.

Traders may want to look at long futures strategies on beef in June and stock traders certainly want to look for companies that would benefit or in this case see price weakness due to a commodity market move such as this inverse relationship between MCD and beef prices.

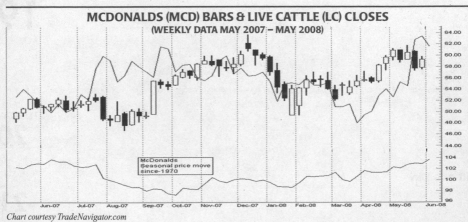

MCDONALDS (MCD) BARS & LIVE CATTLE (LC) CLOSES
(WEEKLY DATA MAY 2007 – MAY 2008)

Chart courtesy TradeNavigator.com

JUNE

worse a situation becomes the less it takes to turn it around, the bigger the upside.
George Soros (Financier, philanthropist, political activist, author and philosopher, b. 1930)

market can stay irrational longer than you can stay solvent. — John Maynard Keynes (British economist, 1883–1946)

ood new chairman of the Federal Reserve Bank is worth a $10 billion tax cut.
Paul H. Douglas (U.S. Senator Illinois 1949 1967, 1892 1976)

d Short Silver (May 14)

son has done more toward abolishing poverty than all the reformers and statesmen.
Henry Ford (Founder Ford Motors, father of moving assembly line, 1863–1947)

art Long British Pound — 72.7% Accuracy Since 1975 — End Jul. 21 — Page 132

biggest change we made was the move to a boundaryless company. We got rid of the corner offices, the bureaucracy,
the not-invented-here syndrome. Instead we got every mind in the game, got the best out of all our people.
ack Welch (retiring CEO of General Electric, *BusinessWeek*, September 10, 2001)

JULY ALMANAC

ENERGY: Crude oil continues to stay supportive during the month of July. Seasonally, this is one of the best months to get long natural gas. Buy natural gas on or about July 24 and hold until about October 21. In the past 18 years, this trade has worked 17 times for a success rate of 94.4%. The cumulative profit is a whopping $170,480 (page 68).

METALS: Seasonally, this is a strong price period for gold until October. Look to enter long positions on or about July 27 and hold until September. In the last 33 years, this trade has worked 26 times for a success rate of 78.8% (page 66). Silver can follow gold's strength in July, but seasonally speaking, September is a better month to go long (page 84). Copper prices tend to make counterseasonal uptrends in July, as summer construction season is underway (page 149).

GRAINS: Soybeans are seasonally in a weak period under normal weather markets until the harvest lows in October (page 161). Wheat remains in a strong uptrend after harvest lows are posted in June (page 164). Even though corn is in a seasonally weak time period, there are times when we see counterseasonal rallies due to weather scares such as drought or intense heat waves, which can reduce yields on the corn crop. Look at the past history of price moves in corn (page 159). This is the time to cover the short corn position from May on or about July 20 (page 52).

SOFTS: Liquidate long cocoa trades from June on or about July 7 (page 56). This is also the month to reverse the position toward the end of the month. Seasonally, we see downturns lasting into early November. Short cocoa on or about July 27 and hold until around November 3 (page 70). Coffee prices tend to remain under pressure until early August when we have a best seasonal trade (page 78). Sugar prices tend to be choppy during the month of July, as the market is trying to post a seasonal low. This is the peak harvest time in Brazil and India. Seasonal bottoms are typically posted in September (page 86).

MEATS: Seasonally, this is a strong price period for live cattle until February (page 176). Lean hogs are in a seasonally weak period until late October to early November (page 179).

CURRENCIES: Over its short 10-year history, the euro tends to consolidate into early September. July can produce rallies (page 185), but overall trends remain down against the dollar in this time frame. Exceptions have been 2006 through 2008, as the dollar has been in a torrid decline. Perhaps the 2008 elections and the new president can have a positive impact on the dollar. The Swiss franc seasonally enters a strong period (page 187). The Swiss franc correlates well with gold's price moves. Gold is strong in this period, so traders may want to watch this relationship between gold and the Swiss franc. August tends to produce the best seasonal trades (page 76). Cover the British pound long position from June (page 56) on or about July 21 (page 132). The yen continues to historically show weakness through the early part of August (page 190).

RESERVE YOUR *2010 ALMANAC* TODAY!

RESERVE YOUR *2010 COMMODITY TRADER'S ALMANAC* NOW BY MAIL OR CALL 800.356.5016!

☐ **Please reserve _____ copies of the *2010 Commodity Trader's Almanac.***

Just $31.96 each (regularly $39.95) plus shipping & handling!
Deeper discounts are available for orders of 5 copies or more—call us at 800-356-5016 for details.
Shipping: US: first item $5.00, each additional $3.00; International: first item $10.50, each additional $7.00.
Bulk discounts for 5 or more copies available. Call 800-356-5016.

$_____ payment enclosed

☐ Check made payable to **John Wiley & Sons, Inc.** *(US Funds only, drawn on a US bank)*

☐ Charge Credit Card (check one): ☐ Visa ☐ Mastercard ☐ AmEx

Name	E-mail address
Address	Account #
City	Expiration Date
State Zip	Signature

☐ **BECOME A SUBSCRIBER! I want to stay up-to-date! Please send me future editions of the *Commodity Trader's Almanac.*** You will automatically be shipped (along with the bill) future editions of the *Almanac* at the yearly pre-publication discount. It's so easy and convenient!

PROMO CODE: CTA10   ISBN 978-0-470-42217-5

SEND ME MORE OF THE *2009 COMMODITY TRADER'S ALMANAC!*

☐ **Please send me _____ copies of the *2009 Commodity Trader's Almanac.***
(ISBN 978-0-470-23061-9)

$39.95 for single copies plus shipping
Shipping: US: first item $5.00, each additional $3.00; International: first item $10.50, each additional $7.00.
Bulk discounts for 5 or more copies available. Call 800-356-5016.

$_____ payment enclosed

☐ Check made payable to **John Wiley & Sons, Inc.** *(US Funds only, drawn on a US bank)*

☐ Charge Credit Card (check one): ☐ Visa ☐ Mastercard ☐ AmEx

Name	E-mail address
Address	Account #
City	Expiration Date
State Zip	Signature

RESERVE YOUR *2010 COMMODITY TRADER'S ALMANAC* NOW AND SAVE 20%.

Mail the postage paid card below to reserve your copy.

NO POSTAGE
NECESSARY
IF MAILED
IN THE
UNITED STATES

BUSINESS REPLY MAIL
FIRST-CLASS MAIL PERMIT NO. 2277 HOBOKEN NJ

POSTAGE WILL BE PAID BY ADDRESSEE

A SPIVAK
JOHN WILEY & SONS INC
111 RIVER ST MS 5-01
HOBOKEN NJ 07030-9442

NO POSTAGE
NECESSARY
IF MAILED
IN THE
UNITED STATES

BUSINESS REPLY MAIL
FIRST-CLASS MAIL PERMIT NO. 2277 HOBOKEN NJ

POSTAGE WILL BE PAID BY ADDRESSEE

A SPIVAK
JOHN WILEY & SONS INC
111 RIVER ST MS 5-01
HOBOKEN NJ 07030-9442

End Short Live Cattle (Mar. 19)

MONDAY

29

The power to tax involves the power to destroy. — John Marshall (U.S. Supreme Court, 1819)

TUESDAY

30

I cannot give you a formula for success but I can give you a formula for failure: Try to please everybody.
— Herbert Swope (American journalist, 1882–1958)

WEDNESDAY

1

The "canonical" market bottom typically features below-average valuations, falling interest rates,
new lows in some major indices on diminished trading volume...and finally, a quick high-volume reversal in breadth....
— John P. Hussman, Ph.D. (Hussman Funds, 5/22/06)

THURSDAY

2

The incestuous relationship between government and big business thrives in the dark.
— Jack Anderson (Washington journalist and author, *Peace, War and Politics*, 1922–2005)

(Shortened Trading Day)

FRIDAY

3

That's the American way. If little kids don't aspire to make money like I did, what the hell good is this country?
— Lee Iacocca (American industrialist, former Chrysler CEO, b. 1924)

Independence Day

SATURDAY

4

SUNDAY

5

GOLD GLITTERS MID-SUMMER

Seasonally, this is a strong price period until October. Look to enter long positions on or about July 27 and hold until September 1. This trade has provided investors with some decent returns. In the last 33 years this trade has worked 26 times for a success rate of 78.8%. The last 9 years in a row provided an amazing win streak, for a cumulative profit of $9,670 per futures contract. Overall, in the 33-year trade history the cumulative profit was $26,410.

The chart below is a weekly chart of the price of gold with the exchange-traded fund known as the SPDR Gold Shares Trust (GLD) overlaid to show the direct price correlation between the two trading vehicles. The graph on the bottom section is the 33-year average seasonal tendency showing the market directional price trend.

SPDR Gold Shares (GLD), much like the silver counterpart iShares Silver Trust (SLV), is unique in that the trust owns the underlying commodity that the ETF is attempting to track; each share represents 1/10 ounces of gold and the closing price of the ETF will represent, within reason, spot gold divided by 10. As of July 9, 2008, GLD owned 21,187,192 ounces of gold with 214.9 million of shares outstanding. Just like every other ETF, there is a premium to net asset value (NAV), which accounts for the difference. The banks have to make a buck, too!

Traders looking for alternative ways to capture specific price moves in commodities now have, besides stocks, such as gold mining shares, exchange-traded funds that one can also implement option strategies. This vehicle is well within our stock picker's criteria, since it trades well in excess of 1,000,000 units per day.

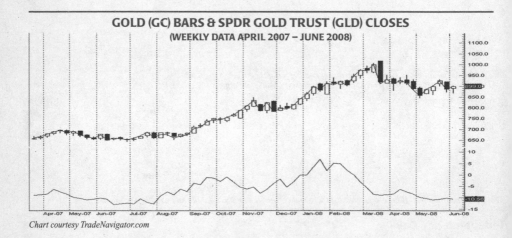

GOLD (GC) BARS & SPDR GOLD TRUST (GLD) CLOSES
(WEEKLY DATA APRIL 2007 – JUNE 2008)

Chart courtesy TradeNavigator.com

JULY

The political problem of mankind is to combine three things: economic efficiency, social justice, and individual liberty.
— John Maynard Keynes (British economist, 1883–1946)

End Long Cocoa (Jun. 2)

Real knowledge is to know the extent of one's ignorance. — Confucius (Chinese philosopher, 551–478 B.C.)

Wall Street has a uniquely hysterical way of thinking the world will end tomorrow but be fully recovered in the long run, then a few years later believing the immediate future is rosy but that the long term stinks. — Kenneth L. Fisher (*Wall Street Waltz*)

Stock prices tend to discount what has been unanimously reported by the mass media.
— Louis Ehrenkrantz (Ehrenkrantz, Lyons & Ross)

...those inquirers who desire an exact knowledge of the past as an aid to the interpretation of the future...
— Thucydides (Greek aristocrat and historian, *The Peloponnesian War*, 460–400 BC)

SUMMER AIR CONDITIONING
HEATS UP NATURAL GAS

Seasonally, July is the best month to get long natural gas ahead of its best five months, August through December. Buy natural gas futures on or about July 24 and hold until about October 21. In the past 18 years, this trade has worked 17 times, for a success rate of 94.4%. The cumulative profit is a whopping $170,480.

This unique commodity has a dual demand season based on hot and cold weather temperatures. In the U.S., natural gas, coal and refined petroleum products have been used as substitutes in electric power generation. Electric power generators have switched back and forth between natural gas, coal and or residual fuel oils, preferring to use whichever energy source was less expensive.

Natural gas is a cleaner-burning fuel source, and in recent years as crude oil has risen sharply, the less expensive product has been natural gas. But this has pushed prices higher in recent years. In addition, the effect of higher Crude Oil has caused demand to spike for natural gas, thus magnifying seasonal price moves.

The seasonal spikes in demand are obvious in the chart below as summer electricity demands for air conditioning lift prices in mid-July. As we exit the summer season, weather can still play a role in September as hurricanes can and have threatened production in the Gulf of Mexico, as occurred with Hurricane Katrina.

Besides options on futures, traders can take advantage of these seasonal price moves through ETFs. One in particular is the U.S. Natural Gas Fund (UNG), which trades well over 700,000 units a day, correlates very closely with natural gas futures as shown in the chart below.

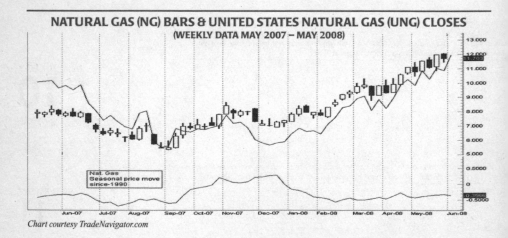

NATURAL GAS (NG) BARS & UNITED STATES NATURAL GAS (UNG) CLOSES
(WEEKLY DATA MAY 2007 – MAY 2008)

Chart courtesy TradeNavigator.com

JULY

MONDAY
13

There is nothing like a ticker tape except a woman—nothing that promises, hour after hour, day after day, such sudden developments; nothing that disappoints so often or occasionally fulfils with such unbelievable, passionate magnificence.
— Walter K. Gutman (Financial analyst, described as the "Proust of Wall Street" by *New Yorker, You Only Have to Get Rich Once,* 1961, *The Gutman Letter,* 1903–1986)

TUESDAY
14

Life is like riding a bicycle. You don't fall off unless you stop peddling.
— Claude D. Pepper (U.S. senator, Florida 1936–1951, 1900–1989)

WEDNESDAY
15

A gold mine is a hole in the ground with a liar on top.
— Mark Twain (1835–1910, pen name of Samuel Longhorne Clemens, American novelist and satirist)

THURSDAY
16

With enough inside information and a million dollars, you can go broke in a year.
— Warren Buffett (CEO Berkshire Hathaway, investor & philanthropist, b. 1930)

FRIDAY
17

[Look for companies] where the executives have a good ownership position — not only options, but outright ownership — so that they will ride up and down with the shareholder. — George Roche (Chairman, T. Rowe Price, *Barron's* 12/18/06)

SATURDAY
18

SUNDAY
19

TWIN COCOA CROPS CREATE MULTIPLE SUMMERTIME TRADES

Cocoa is split between two harvested crops. The so-called mid-crop falls between May and can last until August. The main crop is between October and March. This accounts for the fact that we see from a seasonal perspective downturns lasting into early November.

But as harvest is underway in the mid-crop, the market is vulnerable to volatility created by harvest and or shipping delays caused by weather conditions. Looking at this situation from a historical perspective, we have found that in the last 35 years selling cocoa on or about July 27 and holding until around November 3 has worked 25 times in the last 35 years. This trade has produced a cumulative profit of $16,850 per futures contract (page 133).

The weekly chart below shows the tremendous price move that occurred in 2007 to 2008. The graph in the bottom section shows the 35-year average seasonal price tendency. It is between June up until basically November that the market goes through a period of increased volatility during the mid-crop harvest.

The marketing year from approximately late November through mid-March not only from 2007-2008, but also from a historical perspective we see steady uptrending market conditions. Active futures traders with a good understanding of the seasonal forces are now armed with some pretty solid historical data to make educated trading decisions during the volatile summer months.

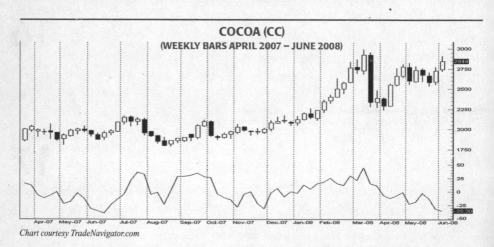

COCOA (CC)
(WEEKLY BARS APRIL 2007 – JUNE 2008)

Chart courtesy TradeNavigator.com

JULY

End Short Corn (May 13)

MONDAY
20

Ideas are easy; it's execution that's hard. — Jeff Bezos (Amazon.com)

End Long British Pound (Jun. 26)

TUESDAY
21

By the law of nature the father continues master of his child no longer than the child stands in need of his assistance; after that term they become equal, and then the son entirely independent of the father, owes him no obedience, but only respect. — Jean-Jacques Rousseau (Swiss philosopher, *The Social Contract*, 1712–1778)

WEDNESDAY
22

I've never been poor, only broke. Being poor is a frame of mind. Being broke is only a temporary situation. — Mike Todd (Movie producer, 1903–1958)

THURSDAY
23

Your organization will never get better unless you are willing to admit that there is something wrong with it. — General Norman Schwartzkof (Ret. Commander of Allied Forces in 1990–1991 Gulf War)

Start Long Natural Gas — 94.4% Accuracy Since 1990 — End Oct. 21 — Page 132

FRIDAY
24

The less a man knows about the past and the present the more insecure must be his judgment of the future. — Sigmund Freud (Austrian neurologist, psychiatrist, "father of psychoanalysis," 1856–1939)

SATURDAY
25

SUNDAY
26

AUGUST ALMANAC

ENERGY: Crude oil continues to stay supportive during the month of July. Seasonally, this is one of the best of five months to be long natural gas, from August through December. Best seasonal trade is long natural gas from about July 24 (page 68).

METALS: Seasonally, this is still in a strong price period for gold until October. Traders should be long from our seasonal best trade from July 27 (page 66). Silver follows gold's strength but, seasonally speaking, September is a better month to go long (page 84). Copper prices tend to continue the seasonal downturn in August as the dog days of summer causes a decline in demand as construction season slows to a crawl (page 149).

GRAINS: Soybeans are seasonally in a weak period under normal weather markets until the harvest lows in October (page 161). Wheat remains in a strong uptrend after harvest lows are posted in June (page 164). Even though corn is in a seasonally weak time period, there are times when we see counterseasonal rallies due to weather scares such as drought or intense heat waves, which can reduce yields on the corn crop. As a result, the short corn trade from June 16 should be covered on or about July 30 (page 131).

SOFTS: Cocoa encounters a countertrend seasonal trade. This is a potential conflict with positions established in July (page 70) as cocoa is, as we described, volatile during mid crop harvest. Active traders can look to take a secondary long trade on or about August 20 through September (page 74). Cover short coffee position from May on or about August 10 (page 48). Enter new long trade on or about August 18. This trade has only one loss since 1986 (page 78). Sugar prices tend to be choppy during the month of August as the market tries to post a seasonal low. This is the end of harvest time in Brazil and India. Seasonal bottoms are typically posted in September (page 86).

MEATS: Live cattle is in its seasonally strong price period until February (page 176). Cover short lean hogs position from May on or about August 17 (page 128).

CURRENCIES: The euro has a tendency to continue to decline against the U.S. dollar headed into Labor Day weekend. However, the first part of September marks a seasonal buying opportunity (page 82). Go long the Swiss Franc for its seasonal best trade on or about August 10 and hold until about October 1 (page 76). Short the British pound on or about August 3 and hold through until September 11 (page 80). Yen has a strong seasonal tendency to post bottoms against the U.S. dollar in late August-early September as it marks the half way point between Japan's fiscal year which runs April-March. In fact, seasonal bottoms are typically posted on or before September 1 (page 82).

JULY/AUGUST

Start Long Gold — 78.8% Accuracy Since 1975 — End Sep. 1 — Page 132
Start Short Cocoa — 71.4% Accuracy Since 1973 — End Nov. 3 — Page 133

MONDAY

27

Bull markets are born on pessimism, grow on skepticism, mature on optimism, and die on euphoria.
— Sir John Templeton (Founder Templeton Funds, philanthropist, 1994)

TUESDAY

28

Become more humble as the market goes your way.
— Bernard Baruch (Financier, speculator, statesman, presidential adviser, 1870–1965)

WEDNESDAY

29

If a man can see both sides of a problem, you know that none of his money is tied up in it. — Verda Ross

End Short Corn (Jun. 16)

THURSDAY

30

If you torture the data long enough, it will confess to anything. — Darrell Huff (*How to Lie with Statistics*, 1954)

FRIDAY

31

We go to the movies to be entertained, not see rape, ransacking, pillage and looting. We can get all that in the stock market.
— Kennedy Gammage (*The Richland Report*)

SATURDAY

1

SUNDAY

2

COCOA DELIVERS COUNTERSEASONAL TRADE

Active traders can look to take a secondary long trade on or about August 20 and exit approximately on September 24 (page 135). In the past 35 years, this trade has worked 25 times providing a success rate of 71.4% with a cumulative gain of $19,800.

On page 70, we described cocoa as having two crop harvests that can wreak havoc on the market, raising the level of volatility. It is during times of a heighten level of price moves that active traders can profit, if you are on the right side of the market.

Cocoa prices can also be influenced by political tensions, since most of this product is grown within 15 degrees latitude of the equator, a large portion of this commodity is grown in Africa, mainly the Ivory Coast, Ghana, and parts of Nigeria. There have been economic scandals such as the embezzlement of Ivory Coast cocoa funds back in October of 2007. Civil war in parts of these regions has also caused harvest and delivery delays, creating price spikes.

The chart below shows the average seasonal price swings for the past 35 years, depicting both the wild historic price swings as well as the price swings that occurred last year. The market did move within its seasonal norms.

If that is the case in 2009, then this particular trading opportunity may offer longer-term trader ammunition to expect a potential drawdown against the seasonal short position, and active traders can prepare for a fairly reliable short-term counterseasonal trading opportunity.

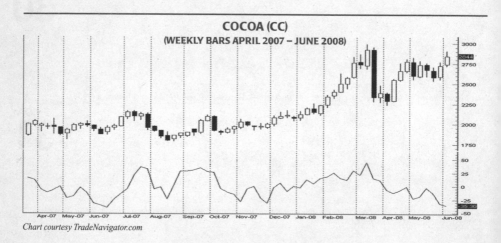

COCOA (CC)
(WEEKLY BARS APRIL 2007 – JUNE 2008)

Chart courtesy TradeNavigator.com

AUGUST

art Short British Pound — 69.7% Accuracy Since 1975 — End Sep. 11 — Page 133

MONDAY

3

know values is to know the meaning of the market. — Charles Dow (Co-founder Dow Jones & Co, 1851–1902)

TUESDAY

4

ly buy stocks when the market declines 10% from that date a year ago, which happens once or twice a decade.
Eugene D. Brody (Oppenheimer Capital)

WEDNESDAY

5

*a lot of fun finding a country nobody knows about. The only thing better is finding a country everybody's bullish on
d shorting it.* — Jim Rogers (Financier, *Investment Biker*, b. 1942)

THURSDAY

6

*ose companies that the market expects will have the best futures, as measured by the price/earnings ratios they are accorded,
ve consistently done worst subsequently.* — David Dreman (Dreman Value Management, author, *Forbes* columnist, b. 1936)

FRIDAY

7

the history of the financial markets, arrogance has destroyed far more capital than stupidity.
Jason Trennert (Managing Partner, Strategas Research Partners, March 27, 2006)

SATURDAY

8

SUNDAY

9

SWISS FRANC FOLLOWS GOLD HIGHER

The Swiss franc correlates well with gold's price moves. Gold is strong in this time period, so traders may want to watch this relationship between gold and the Swiss franc. August tends to produce the best seasonal trades.

The "Swissie," which is trader talk for the currency, has been a safe haven currency in the past, especially during times of financial and geopolitical instability. Due to this country's neutral stance and ability to close its borders, it has been well protected, as history shows.

However, under normal market conditions or a trading environment, the "Swissie" does tend to have seasonal forces against the U.S. dollar. One tendency for a relatively predictable move is in August.

Traders want to go long on this seasonal best trade on or about August 10 and hold until on or about October 16. In the last 33-year history of this trade it has worked 28 years for a success rate of 84.8%. The cumulative gain has been an impressive $68,713 (page 134).

The chart below shows the Swiss franc with the price of the exchange-traded fund the CurrencyShares Swiss Franc (FXF) overlaid showing how closely the two trading instruments are correlated. The graph at the bottom shows the 33-year average seasonal price move. As you can see, August through October tends to lead prices higher versus the U.S. dollar.

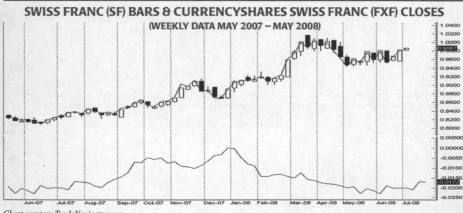

Chart courtesy TradeNavigator.com

AUGUST

Start Long Swiss Franc — 84.8% Accuracy Since 1975 — End Oct. 16 — Page 134
End Short Coffee (May 22)

MONDAY

10

News on stocks is not important. How the stock reacts to it is important. — Michael L. Burke (*Investors Intelligence*)

TUESDAY

11

It isn't as important to buy as cheap as possible as it is to buy at the right time.
— Jesse Livermore (Early 20th century stock trader & speculator, *How to Trade in Stocks*, 1877–1940)

WEDNESDAY

12

Those who cast the votes decide nothing. Those who count the votes decide everything.
— Joseph Stalin (Ruler USSR 1929–1953, 1879–1953)

THURSDAY

13

*The common denominator: Something that matters! Something that counts! Something that defines!
Something that is imbued with soul. And with life!* — Tom Peters (referring to projects, *Reinventing Work*, 1999)

FRIDAY

14

All the features and achievements of modern civilization are, directly or indirectly, the products of the capitalist process.
— Joseph A. Schumpeter (Austrian-American economist, *Theory of Economic Development*, 1883–1950)

SATURDAY

15

SUNDAY

16

AUGUST GIVES COFFEE A LIFT

Coffee has increased in popularity on an international scale in the last few decades. Most consumption has been from the United States, parts of Europe, and Canada. Many Europeans have switched from tea to coffee. With the introduction in late 2005 of Starbucks coffee in Europe more and more people are consuming "Vente Lattés."

Here in the United States, it is estimated that there are over 100,000,000 coffee consumers spending approximately $9.2 billion in the retail sector and $8.7 billion in the food service sector every year. That works out to about $164.71 per consumer each year spent on coffee.

As such, demand is improving, especially for higher grade and quality coffee. With increasing global consumption habits, if there are threats of supply disruptions or production declines for higher grade coffee the futures market can be prone to extreme price moves.

Coffee typically tends to start a seasonal bottoming process before distributors begin buying ahead of anticipated demand in the upcoming cold winter months. This is the time to cover the best seasonal trade short position from May on or about August 10.

It is also a time to look for a short term trade opportunity. Traders should look to enter a new long position on or about August 18 and hold this position for approximately 13 trading days until about September 4. This trade usually falls right after Labor Day weekend.

This trade has worked 27 times in the last 34 years for a cumulative gain of $58,988. In fact, since 1986 only one year, 2007, has produced a loss (page 135). The chart below shows the way the market traded in 2007, as well as the 35-year average seasonal trading pattern.

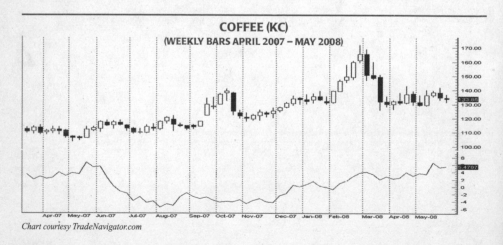

Chart courtesy TradeNavigator.com

AUGUST

End Short Lean Hogs (May 21)

MONDAY
17

Averaging down in a bear market is tantamount to taking a seat on the down escalator at Macy's.
— Richard Russell (*Dow Theory Letters*, 1984)

Start Long Coffee — 79.4% Accuracy Since 1974 — End Sep. 4 — Page 134

TUESDAY
18

I am sorry to say that there is too much point to the wisecrack that life is extinct on other planets because their scientists were more advanced than ours. — John F. Kennedy (35th U.S. president, 1917–1963)

WEDNESDAY
19

In the twenty-two presidential elections from 1900 through 1984, Americans chose the most optimistic-sounding candidate eighteen times. Martin E. Seligman, Ph.D (Professor of Psychology, University of Pennsylvania, *Learned Optimism*, 1990)

Start Long Cocoa — 71.4% Accuracy Since 1973 — End Sep. 24 — Page 135

THURSDAY
20

The stock market is that creation of man which humbles him the most. — Anonymous

FRIDAY
21

Chance favors the informed mind. — Louis Pasteur (French chemist, founder of microbiology, 1822–1895)

SATURDAY
22

SUNDAY
23

BRITISH POUND FALLS AGAINST THE DOLLAR

Here is a particularly interesting short-term trade, one that seems to have the opposite reaction with the trade direction in the yen, Swiss franc and euro currencies during this time period. The British pound has a strong seasonal tendency to decline against these other currencies as they are moving higher in this time frame.

Great Britain is a multi-trillion-dollar economy and its largest city, London, is considered the world's top financial trading center. Many market factors can influence the floating value of the pound versus other currencies, but when we look at a comparison versus the U.S. dollar, we see several trading opportunities throughout the year.

Seasonally speaking, the pound tends to trade lower in value against the U.S. dollar from about August 3 until about September 11. In the last 33 years, this trade has worked 23 times, for a success rate of 69.7% and a cumulative gain of $23,394 (page 133).

After September, we typically see rallies in October throughout the end of the calendar year. After that the market starts to fade against the dollar again before posting a bottom shortly before Britain's fiscal year begins in April. The chart below shows the Pound with the exchange-traded fund the CurrencyShares British Pound (FXB) overlaid to illustrate the close correlation to price movement these two trading vehicles have.

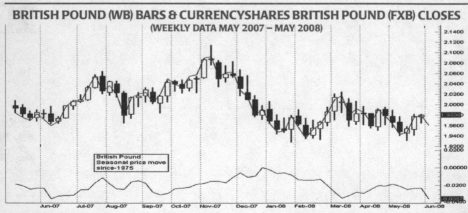

Chart courtesy TradeNavigator.com

AUGUST

MONDAY
24

Some people are so boring they make you waste an entire day in five minutes. — Jules Renard (French author, 1864–1910)

TUESDAY
25

All free governments are managed by the combined wisdom and folly of the people.
— James A. Garfield (20th U.S. president, 1831–1881)

WEDNESDAY
26

Give me a stock clerk with a goal and I will give you a man who will make history.
Give me a man without a goal, and I will give you a stock clerk. — James Cash Penney (J.C. Penney founder)

THURSDAY
27

Behold, my son, with what little wisdom the world is ruled.
— Count Axel Gustafsson Oxenstierna (1648 letter to his son at conclusion of *Thirty Years War*, 1583–1654)

FRIDAY
28

The mind is not a vessel to be filled but a fire to be kindled.
— Plutarch (Greek biographer and philosopher, *Parallel Lives*, 46–120)

SATURDAY
29

SUNDAY
30

SEPTEMBER ALMANAC

ENERGY: Crude oil tops out in September with the peak driving and hurricane seasons behind us. Refineries begin to focus on the production of heating oil and less on gasoline, thereby reducing capacity of crude oil inventories. Selling on or before September 11 and holding until on or about December 9 has produced 20 winning trades in the last 25 years. (page 88). Natural gas is in the midst of its best five-month span from August through December (page 68).

METALS: Liquidate the long gold position from July 27 on or about September 1 (page 66). Go long silver on or about September 1 and hold until on or about September 24. In the last 36 years, this relatively short trade has worked 27 times, for a success rate of 75% (page 84). Copper prices tend to stabilize in September but still lean toward a seasonal downturn until mid-December (Page 149).

GRAINS: Soybeans are in a weak period under normal weather markets until the harvest lows come by late October (page 161). Wheat continues to remain in an uptrend but prices have a tendency to stall or correct mid-month (page 164). Corn continues a seasonal decline in normal weather conditions apart from any early frost scare. Generally, the corn crop is made by now and prices tend to decline until the seasonal harvest lows are posted in late October or early November (page 158).

SOFTS: Exit the long cocoa trade from August 20 on or about September 24 (page 74). In addition, we have a trading opportunity that overlaps this trade and the July short (page 70), which is to sell short on or about September 15 and hold until on or about November 30. In the last 36-year history, this trade has worked 28 times for a success rate of 77.8% (page 137). We also exit the long coffee trade from August 16 on or about September 4 (page 78). Sugar bottoms are typically posted in the late August to early September. An excellent seasonal long opportunity occurs on or about September 1, holding until about November 30 (page 86).

MEATS: Live cattle prices tend to press higher through yearend as demand tends to rise in the fall. Fostering the bullish bias is that people generally eat more meat in cooler temperatures. Also bullish for cattle prices, with children back in school, government-sponsored lunch programs reinforce the demand outlook (page 176). Lean hog prices continue their seasonal decline, typically lasting through to November (page 179).

CURRENCIES: The euro tends to rally after Labor Day from approximately September 8 until about September 30. In the nine-year history this trade has worked eight times for a success rate of 88.9%, good for a cumulative profit of $17,475 (page 136). The Swiss franc is still in an uptrend until on or about October 16 (page 76). Cover the British pound short position from August 3 on or about September 11 (page 80). Look to reverse that position and go long around September 17, holding until about November 3. This trade has registered a cumulative profit of $39,875 and has worked 24 of the last 33 years, for a success rate of 72.7% (page 137). The yen has a strong seasonal tendency to post bottoms against the U.S. dollar in late August through early September. Buying the yen on or about September 1 and holding through September 22 has produced 24 gains in the last 32 years, for a success rate of 75.0%, for a cumulative profits of $33,273. We have seen three consecutive wins since 2005 (page 136).

AUGUST/SEPTEMBER

MONDAY
31

The finest thought runs the risk of being irrevocably forgotten if we do not write it down.
— Arthur Schopenhauer (German philosopher, 1788–1860)

Start Long Silver — 75.0% Accuracy Since 1972 — End Sep. 24 — Page 135
Start Long Sugar — 75.0% Accuracy Since 1972 — End Nov. 30 — Page 136
Start Long Yen — 75.0% Accuracy Since 1976 — End Sep. 22 — Page 136
End Long Gold (Jul. 27)

TUESDAY
1

To succeed in the markets, it is essential to make your own decisions. Numerous traders cited listening to others as their worst blunder.
— Jack D. Schwager (Investment manager, author, *Stock Market Wizards: Interviews with America's Top Stock Traders*, b. 1948)

WEDNESDAY
2

Learn from the mistakes of others; you can't live long enough to make them all yourself.
— Eleanor Roosevelt (First lady, 1884–1962)

THURSDAY
3

Success is going from failure to failure without loss of enthusiasm. — Winston Churchill (British statesman, 1874–1965)

End Long Coffee (Aug. 18)

FRIDAY
4

Get inside information from the president and you will probably lose half your money.
If you get it from the chairman of the board, you will lose all your money. — Jim Rogers (Financier, b. 1942)

SATURDAY
5

SUNDAY
6

SILVER SPIKES IN SEPTEMBER

Silver has a tendency to move up in September as jewelers and manufacturers accumulate inventories in preparation for increased demand for jewelry during the yearend holiday season. In addition, the harvest season in India is underway, where tradition has been that farmers sell grain and buy precious metals, including silver, in preparation for their wedding season.

This trade goes long silver on or about September 1 until about September 24. In the last 36 years, this trade has worked 27 times for a success rate of 75.0%. The cumulative profits are a stellar $73,075 (page 135).

The weekly chart below is Newmont Mining (NEM) stock prices overlaid on the price of silver. This company's main business is in mining precious metals such as gold and silver. The company was founded in 1916 and is headquartered in Denver, Colorado. This stock does meet our stock picker's criteria, as the company has been in business for a long time and trades well in excess of 1,000,000 shares per day.

As you can see, the stock price does move in close correlation with the price of silver, and the graph on the bottom shows the strong seasonal tendency for silver prices to move higher through the month of September.

Traders have several ways to take advantage of this seasonal tendency, with an outright long position in silver futures, options on the futures, the exchange-traded fund iShares Silver Trust (SLV), and stocks or options on stocks like Newmont Mining that correlate well with the underlying commodity price moves.

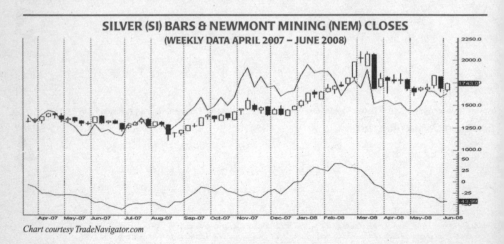

SILVER (SI) BARS & NEWMONT MINING (NEM) CLOSES
(WEEKLY DATA APRIL 2007 – JUNE 2008)

Chart courtesy TradeNavigator.com

SEPTEMBER

Labor Day (Market Closed)

MONDAY

7

I don't think education has a lot to do with the number of years you're incarcerated in a brick building being talked down to.
— Tom Peters (American writer, *In Search of Excellence, Fortune* 11/13/2000)

Start Long Euro — 88.9% Accuracy Since 1999 — End Sep. 30 — Page 136

TUESDAY

8

America, this brash and noble container of dreams, this muse to artists and inventors and entrepreneurs, this beacon of optimism, this dynamo of energy, this trumpet blare of liberty.
— Peter Jennings (Canadian-born anchor ABC World News Tonight, July 2003 after gaining U.S. citizenship in May, 1938–2005)

WEDNESDAY

9

Writing a book is an adventure. To begin with it is a toy, an amusement; then it is a mistress, and then a master, and then a tyrant.
— Winston Churchill (British statesman, 1874–1965)

THURSDAY

10

He who wants to persuade should put his trust not in the right argument, but in the right word. The power of sound has always been greater than the power of sense. — Joseph Conrad (Polish/British novelist, 1857–1924)

Start Short Crude Oil — 80.0% Accuracy Since 1983 — End Dec. 9 — Page 137
End Short British Pound (Aug. 3)

FRIDAY

11

"In Memory"

If there's anything duller than being on a board in Corporate America, I haven't found it.
— H. Ross Perot (American businessman, *NY Times*, 10/28/92, two-time presidential candidate 1992 & 1996, b. 1930)

SATURDAY

12

SUNDAY

13

SWEET SEPTEMBER SUGAR TRADE

Seasonal bottoms are typically posted in the late August to early September time period. A seasonal best long trade occurs from around September 1 through the end of November. This trade has worked 27 times in the last 36 years, for a cumulative gain of $31,338 (page 136).

If you examine the seasonal chart pattern of sugar (page 173) you will see the tendency for prices to rise starting in September through December. One reason is here in the United States both the sugar cane crop and the sugar beet crop are undergoing their harvests, often generating the "harvest lows" in September.

Now that there is a potential new demand base for sugar due to the push for increasing ethanol and alternative fuel source supplies, we may start to see more accelerated price moves in 2009 and beyond.

The chart below is of Archer Daniels Midland (ADM), often referred to as "the supermarket of the world." It has a global presence in the production of grain and oilseed production and distribution of other agricultural finished products such as corn products, including, but not limited to, starch sweeteners, feed, and meal. Plus, it processes soybean and other vegetable oils. It also produces syrups, including glucose, dextrose, sweeteners, and alcohol.

Its services division is in the business of working with independent farmers and charge for storing, cleaning, and transporting agricultural commodities. Archer Daniels Midland Company certainly meets our stock picker's criteria, as it has a long history of being in business; it was founded in 1898 and is headquartered in Decatur, Illinois. The stock trades well in excess of 1,000,000 shares per day.

This company makes money during harvest time, and as the chart below shows, it moves in direct correlation with the price of sugar and the historical average seasonal price move as shown in the bottom of the chart reflects sugar's seasonal price move. Traders have an alternative investment choice to buying sugar futures or options by looking at stocks like ADM that have a strong price correlation.

ARCHER DANIELS MIDLAND COMPANY (ADM) BARS & SUGAR (SB) CLOSES
(WEEKLY DATA MAY 2007 – MAY 2008)

Chart courtesy TradeNavigator.com

SEPTEMBER

MONDAY
14

Those who cannot remember the past are condemned to repeat it. — George Santayana (American philosopher, poet, 1863–1952)

Start Short Cocoa — 77.8% Accuracy Since 1972 — End Oct. 30 — Page 137

TUESDAY
15

The commodity futures game is a money game — not a game involving the supply-demand of the actual commodity as commonly depicted. — R. Earl Hadady (*Bullish Consensus, Contrary Opinion*)

WEDNESDAY
16

Every great advance in natural knowledge has involved the absolute rejection of authority. — Thomas H. Huxley (British scientist and humanist, defender of Darwinism, 1825–1895)

Start Long British Pound — 72.7% Accuracy Since 1975 — End Nov. 3 — Page 137

THURSDAY
17

Resentment is like taking poison and waiting for the other person to die. — Malachy McCourt (*A Monk Swimming: A Memoir*)

FRIDAY
18

History must repeat itself because we pay such little attention to it the first time. — Blackie Sherrod (Sportswriter, b. 1919)

Rosh Hashanah

SATURDAY
19

SUNDAY
20

CRUDE OIL TAKES A BREATHER

In most years, crude oil prices make significant price gains in the summer. Demand for unleaded gasoline increases as the summer driving season, created from vacationers and the annual trek of college students returning to school, peaks in August. The market also prices in a premium for supply disruptions due to threats of hurricanes in the Gulf of Mexico. However, toward the end of September, we see a seasonal tendency of prices to peak out as driving and hurricane season is behind us.

Selling on or before September 11 and holding until on or about December 9 has produced 20 winning trades in the last 25-year history. This gives us an 80.0% success rate with a cumulative gain of $32,480 (page 137).

If you study the seasonal chart pattern on crude oil (page 145) you will see the distinct pattern for declines in prices. Below is a chart on Frontline Limited (FRO), a company that primarily transports crude oil.

What better way to follow the price of a commodity that needs to be transported? This company's stock price does reflect that when demand goes up, prices rise for both crude oil and the stock due to the need for increased shipments of supply. In this scenario, the company should profit. However, as demand for crude oil declines, there is less need for shipping, and the company's revenues will decline.

This ebb and flow of supply and demand tendencies are prevalent, as the chart shows, with the price of crude oil overlaid and the seasonal historic price of the company at the bottom. It highly correlates to the seasonal price swings in crude oil.

This company also meets our stock picker's criteria as it has a long history of being in business. It was founded in 1948, and the stock trades well in excess of 1,000,000 shares per day.

Traders have many alternatives to capture seasonal price moves in the crude oil market. One can buy futures or its options, or trade stocks or stock options on companies that have a solid history of correlating with the seasonal price moves such as crude oil and FRO.

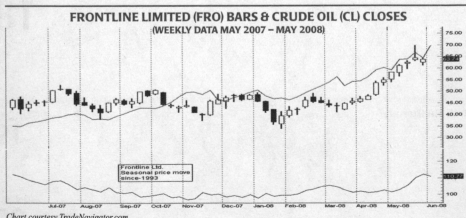

Chart courtesy TradeNavigator.com

MONDAY
21

Some men see things as they are and say "why?" I dream things that never were and say "why not?"
— George Bernard Shaw (Irish dramatist, 1856–1950)

End Long Yen (Sep. 1)

TUESDAY
22

The average man is always waiting for something to happen to him instead of setting to work to make things happen. For one person who dreams of making 50,000 pounds, a hundred people dream of being left 50,000 pounds.
— A. A. Milne (British author, *Winnie-the-Pooh*, 1882–1956)

WEDNESDAY
23

I don't know where speculation got such a bad name, since I know of no forward leap which was not fathered by speculation.
— John Steinbeck

End Long Cocoa (Aug. 20)
End Long Silver (Sep. 1)

THURSDAY
24

What investors really get paid for is holding dogs. Small stocks tend to have higher average returns than big stocks, and value stocks tend to have higher average returns than growth stocks. — Kenneth R. French (Economist, Dartmouth, NBER, b. 1954)

FRIDAY
25

Every man with a new idea is a crank until the idea succeeds.
— Mark Twain (American novelist and satirist, pen name of Samuel Longhorne Clemens, 1835–1910)

SATURDAY
26

SUNDAY
27

OCTOBER ALMANAC

ENERGY: Crude oil continues its seasonally weak period. We remain short from September 11 holding until about December 9 (page 88). Liquidate the natural gas long position from July on or about October 21 (page 68).

METALS: Enter a short gold position on or about October 2 and hold through until about November 6. In the last 33 years, this trade has worked 24 times, for a success rate of 72.7%, good for a cumulative gain of $11,910. However, the last two years this trade has not fared so well (page 138). Silver follows gold's lead, and traders can enter a short position on or about October 6, holding until on or about October 29. In the last 36 years, this trade has worked 25 times, for a success rate of 69.4%, posting a cumulative gain of $10,350. Much like gold, the massive commodity bull market of the last several years has also tarnished this trade, and the last three years have turned out to be disasters (page 138). Copper continues its seasonal downtrend as new construction begins to wind down for the winter months (page 149).

GRAINS: Cover the short soybean position from June on or about October 6 (page 58). Reverse your position and go long soybeans on or about October 22 holding until about November 9 (page 92). Wheat prices generally consolidate as harvest and new crop corn and soybean products dominate the trade (page 164). The seasonally best trade in corn is to go long on or about October 28 and hold until about May 11 (page 94).

SOFTS: Cocoa is wrapping its weak period. Close September short position October 30 (page 82). Coffee prices tend to stabilize as cold weather increases consumption, but not enough to offset inventories. Thus, there is no significant price move during this month (page 170). Sugar generally maintains its seasonal uptrend. Maintain the long position from September 1 until the end of November (page 86).

MEATS: Live cattle prices remain in a seasonal uptrend, as farmers and ranchers are focusing on grain harvest business. Demand for beef continues to rise as the temperature falls (page 176). Lean hogs prices remain in a seasonal downtrend. Producers are feeding newly harvested corn to fatten hogs. Weights are generally up, leading to a seasonal glut in pork through November (page 179).

CURRENCIES: During its 10-year history, the euro has been weak in October. A major factor to this bearishness is that U.S. corporations convert or transfer funds back to the United States after the new quarter for payroll and or pension fund distributions. 2008 is a presidential election year and we could see more of a magnified move in support of the dollar. However, we are in the beginning of a seasonally strong period until January (page 185). Liquidate the long Swiss franc from August on or about October 17 (page 76). The British pound is in a period of rising prices; maintain the long trade position from September 17 until on or about November 3 (page 82). The yen's seasonal weakness prevails versus the dollar. Traders can look to short the yen on or about October 16, holding that position until on or about February 9 (page 96).

SEPTEMBER/OCTOBER

Yom Kippur

There is only one corner of the universe you can be certain of improving, and that's yourself.
— Aldous Huxley (English author, *Brave New World*, 1894–1963)

Never tell people how to do things. Tell them what to do and they will surprise you with their ingenuity.
— General George S. Patton, Jr. (U.S. Army field commander WWII, 1885–1945)

End Long Euro (Sep. 8)

If the winds of fortune are temporarily blowing against you, remember that you can harness them and make them carry you toward your definite purpose, through the use of your imagination. — Napoleon Hill (Author, *Think and Grow Rich*, 1883–1970)

If I owe a million dollars I am lost. But if I owe $50 billion the bankers are lost. — Celso Ming (Brazilian journalist)

Start Short Gold — 72.2% Accuracy Since 1975 — End Nov. 6 — Page 138

The fear of capitalism has compelled socialism to widen freedom, and the fear of socialism has compelled capitalism to increase equality. — Will and Ariel Durant

SOYBEAN'S HARVEST LOWS OFFER POTENTIAL-FREE MEAL

This is generally not the time to sell short in the hole if traders are looking to sell any further weakness in early October. This is the time to cover short bean positions. In fact, this is the time of year where soybeans post their harvest lows.

Soybeans are a cash commodity because end users with feed operations that use soy meal to feed livestock and poultry must purchase hand-to-mouth, as soy meal does not have a long shelf life. Fresh new product is rushed to cattle feed lots, hog, and poultry operations, and exports of soybeans are being marketed. This wave of demand starts to create a floor of support in prices (page 161).

To take advantage of this seasonal trend, traders can go long soybeans on or about October 22 and hold until around November 9. In the last 40 years, this trade has worked 36 times, for an impressive 90.0% success rate. The cumulative profit totals $35,775. Looking back, since 1976 it has only registered two losses, in 1990 and in 2004 (page 139).

The chart below shows the price of soybeans overlaid on the stock of Monsanto (MON). This is the company that makes Roundup Ready soybean seed and who also has a joint venture with Cargill, Incorporated to commercialize a proprietary grain processing technology under the name Extrax.

As you can see, this company correlates very well with the price direction of soybeans, and as the graph at the bottom shows, it also forms its average seasonal lows right around the first of October and carries a strong push into November.

This company meets our stock picker's criteria, as it has a long history of being in business; it was founded in 1865, and is based in Minneapolis, Minnesota. This stock trades well in excess of 1,000,000 shares per day.

Traders now have many trading alternatives to capture seasonal price moves in the commodity markets. One can go buy futures or options or trade stocks or stock options on companies that have a solid history of correlating with the seasonal price moves, such as soybeans and MON.

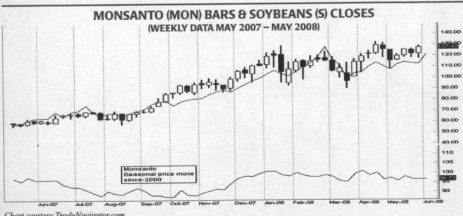

MONSANTO (MON) BARS & SOYBEANS (S) CLOSES
(WEEKLY DATA MAY 2007 – MAY 2008)

Monsanto
Seasonal price move
since-2000

Chart courtesy TradeNavigator.com

OCTOBER

e critical ingredient is getting off your butt and doing something. It's as simple as that. A lot of people have ideas,
there are few who decide to do something about them now. Not tomorrow. Not next week. But today.
e true entrepreneur is a doer, not a dreamer. — Nolan Bushnell (Founder Atari & Chuck E. Cheese's, b. 1943)

art Short Silver — 69.4% Accuracy Since 1972 — End Oct. 29 — Page 138
d Short Soybeans (June 1)

world hates change, but it is the only thing that has brought progress.
Charles Kettering (Inventor of electric ignition, founded Delco in 1909, 1876–1958)

*keting is our No. 1 priority... A marketing campaign isn't worth doing unless it serves three purposes.
ust grow the business, create news, and enhance our image.* — James Robinson III (American Express)

*spend $500 million a year just in training our people. We've developed some technology that lets us do simulations. Think of
ht Simulation. What we've found is that the retention rate from simulation is about 75%, opposed to 25% from classroom work.
oe Forehand (CEO, Accenture, Forbes, 7/7/03)*

ffect the quality of the day, that is the highest of the arts.
Henry David Thoreau (American writer, naturalist and philosopher, 1817–1862)

CORN HARVEST LOWS
FEED BULLS ALL WINTER AND SPRING

One of the best seasonal trades is to go long corn on or about October 28 and hold until about May 11. This trade has worked in 34 of the last 40 years, for a success rate of 85.0%. The cumulative profit is $44,838, and this trade has had a 10-year win streak that began in 1998 (page 140).

With the push for renewable energy and new changes in legislation, heightened ethanol demand has increased the production of corn. Now there is more competition for inventories of corn from animal feed, energy needs, and foreign business. These factors give support to prices as harvest gets underway.

When we combine years when weather does not cooperate and yields are less than estimated, then this seasonal tendency for price increases (page 158) could be magnified, further enhancing the pace and level of price moves.

It is important to look at alternative markets that trade in tandem with the underlying market. The chart below is Deere & Co. (DE). It is in the business of agricultural equipment manufacturing and servicing of farm equipment along with other business interests, including residential lawn and garden equipment and now wind-energy generation.

As you can see, the price of the stock highly correlates to the price of corn, and the average seasonal price moves of the stock also matches that of corn. Here is another example of a company that meets our stock picker's criteria, as it has a robust history of being in business. The company was founded in 1837 and is based in Moline, Illinois. This stock trades well in excess of 1,000,000 shares per day.

Traders now have many trading alternatives to capture seasonal price moves in the commodity markets. One can buy futures or options or trade stocks or stock options on companies that have a solid history of correlating with the seasonal price moves such as Corn and DE.

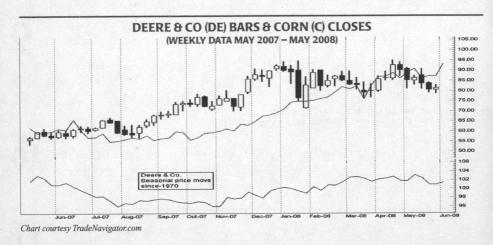

Chart courtesy TradeNavigator.com

OCTOBER

Columbus Day (Bond Market Closed)

MONDAY
12

All a parent can give a child is roots and wings. — Chinese proverb

TUESDAY
13

In this age of instant information, investors can experience both fear and greed at the exact same moment.
— Sam Stovall (Chief Investment Strategist Standard & Poor's, October 2003)

WEDNESDAY
14

I invest in people, not ideas; I want to see fire in the belly and intellect. — Arthur Rock (First venture capitalist)

THURSDAY
15

Don't delay! A good plan, violently executed now, is better than a perfect plan next week.
War is a very simple thing, [like stock trading] and the determining characteristics are self-confidence, speed, and audacity.
— General George S. Patton, Jr. (U.S. Army field commander WWII, 1885–1945)

Start Short Yen — 65.6% Accuracy Since 1977 — End Feb. 9, 2010 — Page 139
End Long Swiss Franc (Aug. 10)

FRIDAY
16

A "tired businessman" is one whose business is usually not a successful one.
— Joseph R. Grundy (U.S. senator, Pennsylvania 1929–1930, businessman, 1863–1961)

SATURDAY
17

SUNDAY
18

JAPANESE YEN DIVES AGAINST THE DOLLAR

The Japanese economy runs on a fiscal year running from April through March. The midpoint of the second half of their fiscal year is in October. Accounting and balance sheet adjustments are made at this point in time and are responsible for large currency transactions that have a seasonal influence on prices. Some years, of course, are more dramatic than others, but in normal economic times we see a seasonal weakness that prevails in the yen versus the dollar.

Traders need to be aware of several key elements at hand that can cause values to move violently. For one, intervention plays a role in the currencies. The Central Bank of Japan (BOJ) is known for intervention on behalf of managing the yen's value versus the U.S. dollar. One such example occurred in 1995, when the Bank of Japan felt threatened that its export business would suffer at the hand of an overvalued yen.

The BOJ intervened and sold yen and then, in turn, bought U.S. dollars. This type of situation would drastically impact a seasonal trade, so it is important to understand the relationship of the current markets value with past price action. Traders should be aware of these tendencies and the history of actions taken with respect to certain central bankers. If the yen does manage to overstep its value relative to the dollar, beware that the BOJ can and has stepped in to sell yen.

Based on our seasonal studies, traders can look to sell the yen on or about October 16 and hold until about February 9. The 32-year history of this trade has worked 21 years, for a success rate of 65.6% and a cumulative gain of $23,835 (page 139). Investors now have more opportunities to take advantage of this seasonal tendency, with an outright short position in yen futures, options on the futures, or, as the chart below shows, the exchange-traded fund, CurrencyShares Japanese Yen (FXY), and options on this investment vehicle. As you can see, the FXY is highly correlated with the underlying commodity price moves.

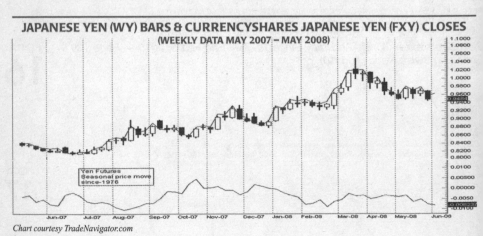

JAPANESE YEN (WY) BARS & CURRENCYSHARES JAPANESE YEN (FXY) CLOSES
(WEEKLY DATA MAY 2007 – MAY 2008)

Chart courtesy TradeNavigator.com

EXCLUSIVE ALMANAC INVESTOR PLATFORM TOOLS

Can you afford to ignore over 40 years of financial expertise? Few can and that's why we urge you to become a subscriber to Almanac Investor Platform. As a subscriber you'll have access to proprietary tools such as:

- **The Barometer Tool** devised by Yale Hirsch in 1972 allows you to test the January Barometer. The January Barometer indicator has a 90.9% accuracy ratio.
- **The MACD Calculator** (**M**oving **A**verage **C**onvergence/**D**ivergence) allows you to measure market sentiment for clues of trend reversals or continuation. You can track and confirm entry and exit points for the Best Months Switching Strategy.
- **The Year in Review Tool** allows you to observe daily, weekly and monthly trends.
- **Market & Stocks Tool** allows you to track your own portfolio and get updated information on nearly any stock, ETF, mutual fund.
- **Almanac Investor (AI) Watch List** allows you to create your own watch list.

These great tools and so much more are available to you at **stocktradersalmanac.com** Take advantage of these proprietary tools by subscribing *today!*

IT'S EASY TO SUBSCRIBE...

- **Online at stocktradersalmanac.com using promo code STA9**
- **Call us toll-free at 800-356-5016**
- **Fax us at 800-597-3299**
- **Mail the self-addressed card on the reverse side to our attention**

NO POSTAGE
NECESSARY
IF MAILED
IN THE
UNITED STATES

BUSINESS REPLY MAIL
FIRST-CLASS MAIL PERMIT NO. 2277 HOBOKEN NJ

POSTAGE WILL BE PAID BY ADDRESSEE

A SPIVAK
JOHN WILEY & SONS INC
111 RIVER ST MS 5-01
HOBOKEN NJ 07030-9442

OCTOBER

MONDAY
19

On [TV financial news programs], if the stock is near its high, 90% of the guests like it, if it is near its lows, 90% of the guests hate it. — Michael L. Burke (*Investors Intelligence*, May 2002)

TUESDAY
20

Try to surround yourself with people who can give you a little happiness, because you can only pass through this life once, Jack. You don't come back for an encore. — Elvis Presley (1935–1977)

End Long Natural Gas (Jul. 24)

WEDNESDAY
21

The future now belongs to societies that organize themselves for learning.
What we know and can do holds the key to economic progress. — Ray Marshall & Marc Tucker

Start Long Soybeans — 90.0% Accuracy Since 1968 — End Nov. 9 — Page 139

THURSDAY
22

It is not how right or how wrong you are that matters, but how much money you make when right and how much you do not lose when wrong. — George Soros (Financier, philanthropist, political activist, author and philosopher, b. 1930)

FRIDAY
23

I believe in the exceptional man—the entrepreneur who is always out of money, not the bureaucrat who generates cash flow and pays dividends. — Armand Erpf (Investment banker, partner Loeb Rhoades, 1897–1971)

SATURDAY
24

SUNDAY
25

NOVEMBER ALMANAC

ENERGY: Crude oil continues to be in a seasonally weak period. We are still short from September, holding that position until about December 9 (page 88). November is a mixed month for natural gas, depending on the temperatures in the Midwest. Beginning in October, if weather patterns are mild, then we see less demand; prices tend to consolidate (page 147).

METALS: Cover the short gold position from October on or about November 6 (page 90). Look to reverse that position and go long on or about November 18 until about December 3 (page 102). Look to go long silver on or about November 16, exiting on or about December 4. This trade has worked 26 times over the last 36 years, for a success rate of 72.2% and a cumulative profit of $40,725 (page 141). Copper's seasonal downtrend continues through December (page 149).

GRAINS: Liquidate the long soybeans positions from October on or about November 9 (page 92). Also liquidate the long wheat position from June on or about November 4 (page 60). Reverse your wheat position, as its seasonal peak is made in November. Sell wheat on or about November 24 and hold until on or about May 17 (page 104). Corn is just beginning its seasonal best long trade that was entered on or about October 28 and is held to about May 11 (page 94).

SOFTS: Cover the short cocoa position from July on or about November 3 (page 70). Enter a long Cocoa position on or about November 5 and hold until on or about December 24. This trade has worked 27 of 36 years, for a success rate of 75.0%, and has had a cumulative profit of $19,190 (page 141). Coffee prices continue to stabilize as cold weather increases consumption, but November rarely sees significant price moves (page 170). Sugar prices maintain a seasonal uptrend. Our best seasonal trade is long sugar from September 1 through the end of November (page 86). We have a slight overlapping seasonal trade. Reverse the long Sugar position on or about November 24 and hold to about February 8. This trade has worked 23 times over the last 36 years, for a success rate of 63.9% and a cumulative profit of $12,376 (page 143).

MEATS: Live cattle prices exhibit a push higher toward the middle of the month, but consumer demand declines as the turkey-centric Thanksgiving holiday diminishes beef sales. This can cause a short-term glut of inventory that can push prices lower through the first part of December (page 176). Buy lean hogs at the beginning of November and exit before Thanksgiving (page 100).

CURRENCIES: Over the last 10 years, the euro has rallied through yearend, but is not consistent enough to trade (page 185). The long Swiss franc position correlates with the seasonal strength in gold. Look to go long the Swiss franc on or about November 25 and hold until yearend (page 106). Liquidate the long British pound position from September on or about November 3 (page 137). The yen remains in a seasonal weak period versus the U.S. dollar. Maintain a short position from about October 16 until about February 9 (page 96).

OCTOBER/NOVEMBER

MONDAY
26

Around the world, red tape is being cut. Whether it's telecom in Europe, water in South America, or power in Illinois, governments are stepping back, and competition is thriving where regulated monopolies once dominated. — (Fortune, 12/20/99)

TUESDAY
27

He who knows nothing is confident of everything. — Anonymous

Start Long Corn — 85.0% Accuracy Since 1968 — End May 11, 2010 — Page 140

WEDNESDAY
28

Doubt is the father of invention. — Galileo Galilei (Italian physicist and astronomer, 1564–1642)

End Short Silver (Oct. 6)

THURSDAY
29

In my experience, selling a put is much safer than buying a stock. — Kyle Rosen (Boston Capital Mgmt., Barron's 8/23/04)

End Short Cocoa (Sep. 15)

FRIDAY
30

The worst crime against working people is a company that fails to make a profit. — Samuel Gompers

Halloween 🎃

SATURDAY
31

Daylight Saving Time Ends

SUNDAY
1

LEAN HOGS FATTEN UP BEFORE THANKSGIVING

Demand for pork increases as consumers switch meat products when beef prices are too high. In addition, Canadian imports have started to fall off, and now we begin a cycle of demand outpacing inventories.

Seasonally, we have a low posted in the hog market in November, so traders should look to buy lean hogs on or about November 3, and exit on or about November 20. In the last 39 years, this trade has provided 34 years of gains, for a success rate of 87.2%. The cumulative profit is $32,400, but most impressive is that this trade has had six straight wins in a row since 2002.

The chart below is of Smithfield Foods (SFD), with the lean hogs front month futures contract overlaid to illustrate the correlation in the price action. This company is in the business of processing pork and the production of hogs both in the United States and abroad.

As you can see, it has a strong seasonal tendency and these two securities do move in tandem. The seasonal chart of lean hogs (page 179) is very similar to the seasonal price move of this stock, as shown on the bottom of the chart.

SFD also meets our stock picker's criteria, as it has a solid history of being in business; it was founded in 1961, and is based in Smithfield, Virginia. This stock trades well in excess of 1,000,000 shares per day.

Traders can explore the trading alternatives in specific stocks to capture seasonal price moves in the commodity markets. One can buy futures or options or trade stocks or stock options on companies that have a solid history of correlating with the seasonal price moves, such as lean hogs and SFD.

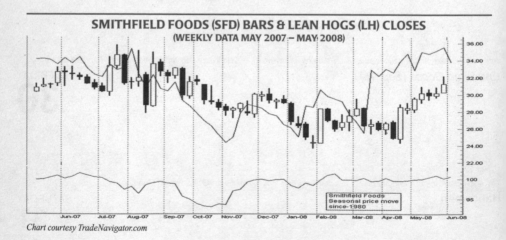

SMITHFIELD FOODS (SFD) BARS & LEAN HOGS (LH) CLOSES
(WEEKLY DATA MAY 2007 – MAY 2008)

Smithfield Foods
Seasonal price move
since-1980

Chart courtesy TradeNavigator.com

NOVEMBER

MONDAY

2

Prosperity is a great teacher; adversity a greater. — William Hazlitt (English essayist, 1778–1830)

Election Day
Start Long Lean Hogs — 87.2% Accuracy Since 1969 — End Nov. 20 — Page 140
End Short Cocoa (Jul. 27)
End Long British Pound (Sep. 17)

TUESDAY

3

Mankind is divided into three classes: Those that are immovable, those that are movable, and those that move.
— Arabian proverb (also attributed to Benjamin Franklin)

End Long Wheat (Jun. 8)

WEDNESDAY

4

Knowledge born from actual experience is the answer to why one profits; lack of it is the reason one loses.
— Gerald M. Loeb (EF Hutton, *The Battle for Investment Survival*, predicted '29 Crash, 1900–1974)

Start Long Cocoa — 75.0% Accuracy Since 1972 — End Dec. 24 — Page 141

THURSDAY

5

No one ever claimed that managed care was either managed or cared. — Anonymous

End Short Gold (Oct. 2)

FRIDAY

6

Politics ought to be the part-time profession of every citizen who would protect the rights and privileges of free people and who would preserve what is good and fruitful in our national heritage. — Dwight D. Eisenhower (34th U.S. president, 1890–1969)

SATURDAY

7

SUNDAY

8

GOLD BUGS GET A TREAT FOR THE HOLIDAYS

Gold prices tend to move up prior to the holidays. Seasonally speaking, it is best for traders to go long on or about November 18 and hold until about December 3. Over the last 33 years, this trade has worked 26 times for a success rate of 78.8%. The cumulative profit tallies up to $25,960. What is interesting is that this trade has had an eight-year win streak starting from 2000 (page 142).

The chart below shows the correlation with one other mining company, Freeport-McMoran Copper & Gold (FCX). It is in the business of exploration and development of gold. The FCX stock price line chart is overlaid on the front month gold futures contract. The graph on the bottom section is the 33-year average seasonal price move for gold.

As you can see, gold and FCX are highly correlated. What is important here is to see the seasonality of November's rally into December. Notice the price dip in November in gold and FCX. The chart on the seasonal history in gold shows a tendency for prices to then rally into the first week of December.

Last year, both gold and this stock traded in synch with the historic norm. Traders have the flexibility of trading seasonal price moves in commodities using alternative markets. Besides the futures and options markets, ETFs such as the SPDR Gold Shares (GLD), as we previously discussed, and specific stocks can be traded to capture seasonal price moves in the underlying futures markets such as gold and FCX.

This company meets our stock picker's criteria, as it has a solid history of being in business; it was founded in 1987 and is based in Phoenix, Arizona. This stock trades well in excess of 1,000,000 shares per day. This price relationship between gold and producers should continue unless a gold producer begins an aggressive hedging operation, which entails selling gold in the futures to lock in production profits. In this scenario, if gold prices continue to rise during the seasonal buy period and a gold producer sells futures contracts to lock in a profit, the company could reduce its maximum profit exposure, and that is when trading a stock versus a commodity would not be effective.

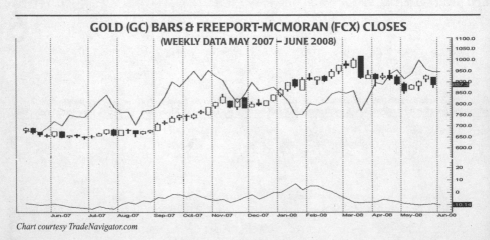

GOLD (GC) BARS & FREEPORT-MCMORAN (FCX) CLOSES
(WEEKLY DATA MAY 2007 – JUNE 2008)

Chart courtesy TradeNavigator.com

NOVEMBER

End Long Soybeans (Oct. 22)

MONDAY

9

If a battered stock refuses to sink any lower no matter how many negative articles appear in the papers, that stock is worth a close look. — James L. Fraser (*Contrary Investor*)

TUESDAY

10

It is impossible to please all the world and one's father. — Jean de La Fontaine (French poet, 1621–1695)

Veterans' Day

WEDNESDAY

11

Laws are like sausages. It's better not to see them being made.
— Otto von Bismarck (German-Prussian politician, 1st Chancellor of Germany, 1815–1898)

THURSDAY

12

Six words that spell business success: create concept, communicate concept, sustain momentum. — Yale Hirsch

FRIDAY

13

I never hired anybody who wasn't smarter than me. — Don Hewett (Producer, *60 Minutes*)

SATURDAY

14

SUNDAY

15

WHEAT TURNS TO CHAFF

Winter wheat (traded at the CME Group) is typically planted in the September through October time frame. Traders anticipate the crop size and this puts pressure on prices. In addition, the Southern Hemisphere crops are working through the export process, adding new supplies on the market. These events help explain how the seasonal peak is made in November (page 164).

Wheat is not a homogeneous crop, due to the many different classes that are grown (i.e., soft red winter (SRW), hard red spring wheat (HRS), and durum wheat). All have different protein contents and are used for different purposes, such as animal feed, seed, and food.

SRW is used for cracker-type products. It has a lower protein content. This is the wheat that is deliverable through the old CBOT or CME Group. HRS wheat is used in baking products and has a higher protein content, and durum is very high in protein and is used in pasta and spaghetti noodles. As winter wheat is planted in the fall, corn is harvested and wheat that may be used as feed can be replaced with less expensive corn, in most years.

Due to this event, traders can look to take advantage of this seasonality by selling on or about November 24 and hold until on or about May 17. This trade has worked 32 times in the last 40 years, for a success rate of 80.0%, and has a cumulative profit of $43,225 (page 142).

An additional avenue to consider would be a company that moves in step with the seasonal price swings in wheat. One such company is Excel Maritime Carriers, Ltd. (EXM). This company provides seaborne transportation services for dry bulk cargoes, such as wheat. This company also meets our stock picker's criteria, with a long history of being in business, as it was founded in 1988. It is headquartered in Hamilton, Bermuda. Plus, the stock trades over 700,000 shares per day.

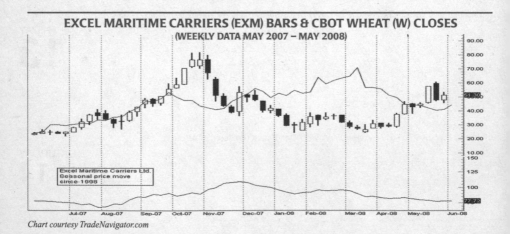

Chart courtesy TradeNavigator.com

NOVEMBER

Start Long Silver — 72.2% Accuracy Since 1972 — End Dec. 4 — Page 141

MONDAY
16

Develop interest in life as you see it; in people, things, literature, music — the world is so rich, simply throbbing with rich treasures, beautiful souls and interesting people. Forget yourself. — Henry Miller (American writer, *Tropic of Cancer, Tropic of Capricorn*, 1891–1980)

TUESDAY
17

Life is what happens while you're busy making other plans. — John Lennon (Beatle, 1940–1980)

Start Long Gold — 78.8% Accuracy Since 1975 — End Dec. 3 — Page 142

WEDNESDAY
18

I never buy at the bottom and I always sell too soon. — Baron Nathan Rothschild's success formula (London Financier, 1777–1836)

THURSDAY
19

Stocks are super-attractive when the Fed is loosening and interest rates are falling. In sum: Don't fight the Fed! — Martin Zweig (Fund manager, *Winning on Wall Street*)

End Long Lean Hogs (Nov. 3)

FRIDAY
20

From very early on, I understood that you can touch a piece of paper once... if you touch it twice, you're dead. Therefore, paper only touches my hand once. After that, it's either thrown away, acted on or given to somebody else. — Manuel Fernandez (Businessman, *Investor's Business Daily*)

SATURDAY
21

SUNDAY
22

SWISS FRANC TRADES LIKE GOLD

As we covered on page 76, the "Swissie" does track the price movement of gold. In the past, this currency had been a safe haven in times of geopolitical tensions. However, this relationship has tended to depart from the norm since the introduction of the Euro currency. But do not rule out that we will not see investors flock to the Swissie in times of trouble in the future.

There are periods of European upheavals, as occurred in 2004 when there was dissention among members of the European Union. In fact, there were riots in Paris, and some investors flocked to the Swiss franc as a short-term safe haven. This type of action did prop the value of the Swissie against all major currencies, including the U.S. dollar. It happened before, it could happen again. Be aware of what global events transpire; an event like what happened before could magnify a seasonal trade situation.

One of our seasonal studies suggests that traders can establish a long position that correlates with the seasonal trade in gold. Traders can look to go long the Swiss franc on or about November 25 and hold through yearend or so.

In the 33-year history, this trade has worked 25 times, for a success rate of 75.8%. The cumulative profit is $50,538 (page 143). The seasonal chart of gold (page 152) closely correlates to the Swiss franc. Therefore, traders may want to take note that trading both gold and the Swiss franc simultaneously would not be considered diversified trading strategies. If the trade works, since it does have a solid track record, then that would be great; however, traders are exposed to double the risk.

There are several ways to take advantage of this situation, such as the trade strategies for gold mentioned on page 102, with futures or a gold stock like Freeport-McMoran Copper & Gold (FCX), or this trade in the Swiss franc, or the exchange-traded fund Currency Shares Swiss Franc (FXF). The chart below shows the direct correlation of the Swiss franc futures and the ETF.

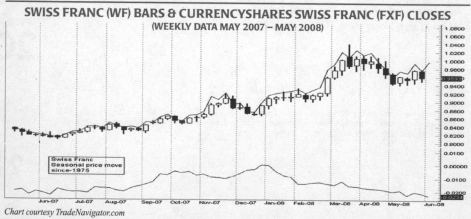

SWISS FRANC (WF) BARS & CURRENCYSHARES SWISS FRANC (FXF) CLOSES
(WEEKLY DATA MAY 2007 – MAY 2008)

Chart courtesy TradeNavigator.com

106

NOVEMBER

MONDAY
23

Capitalism without bankruptcy is like Christianity without hell. — Frank Borman (CEO Eastern Airlines, April 1986)

Start Short Wheat — 80.0% Accuracy Since 1968 — End May 17, 2010 — Page 142
Start Short Sugar — 62.9% Accuracy Since 1972 — End Feb. 8, 2010 — Page 143

TUESDAY
24

It has been said that politics is the second oldest profession. I have learned that it bears a striking resemblance to the first. — Ronald Reagan (40th U.S. president, 1911–2004)

Start Long Swiss Franc — 75.8% Accuracy Since 1975 — End Dec. 31 — Page 143

WEDNESDAY
25

The heights by great men reached and kept, were not attained by sudden flight, but they, while their companions slept, were toiling upward in the night. — Henry Wadsworth Longfellow

Thanksgiving (Market Closed)

THURSDAY
26

Always grab the reader by the throat in the first paragraph, sink your thumbs into his windpipe in the second, and hold him against the wall until the tag line. — Paul O'Neil (Marketer, *Writing Changes Everything*)

(Shortened Trading Day)

FRIDAY
27

You know you're right when the other side starts to shout. — I. A. O'Shaughnessy (American oilman, 1885–1973)

SATURDAY
28

SUNDAY
29

DECEMBER ALMANAC

ENERGY: Cover the short crude oil seasonal best trade from September on or about December 9 (page 88). Natural gas tends to see price declines, especially if inventories have not been worked off due to warmer than expected weather conditions (page 147).

METALS: Liquidate the long gold position from November on or about December 3 (page 102). Also liquidate the long silver position from November on or about December 4. Go long copper on or about December 14 and hold through on or about February 23 (page 110).

GRAINS: The end-of-year marketing for soybeans is winding down and farmers are reluctant to sell in front of end-of-year tax liabilities (page 161). December can see modest declines in the wheat market, which continues its seasonal downtrend (page 104). The corn market is in its seasonal period of strength, but much like soybeans, prices tend to consolidate due to yearend tax liabilities as farmers tend to defer sales until after the New Year (page 94).

SOFTS: Exit the long cocoa position from November on or about December 24 (page 98). Coffee prices tend to rise through yearend as cold northern winters help increase consumption (page 170). Make sure you have liquidated the long sugar position from September by the beginning of December and gone short (pages 86 & 98).

MEATS: Live cattle prices tend to stabilize. Most cash markets follow this trend as farmers try to minimize their tax liabilities by deferring sales until the New Year (page 176). Lean hogs prices tend to flat line or consolidate as producers work off inventories until prices begin to resume a seasonal uptrend in March (page 179).

CURRENCIES: The euro tends to rally through yearend. In the last 10 years, the average seasonal price tendency is for a push higher (page 185). There is a seasonal long position for the Swiss franc holding from November until yearend or thereabouts (page 106). We also have an overlapping trade situation where we reverse this position and go short on or about December 28 until on or about February 2. This trade has worked 25 times in the last 33 years for a success rate of 75.8% and a cumulative profit of $41,350 (page 144). Sell the British pound around December 28 and hold until about March 19 (page 112). The yen is in a seasonal weak period versus the U.S. dollar. The trade is to be short from about October 16 and hold until about February 9 (page 96).

NOVEMBER/DECEMBER

End Long Sugar (Sep. 1)

MONDAY
30

In business, the competition will bite you if you keep running; if you stand still, they will swallow you.
— William Knudsen (Former president of GM)

TUESDAY
1

Capitalism works because it encourages and rewards those who successfully take risks, adapt to change, and develop profitable opportunities. — Henry Blodget (former stock analyst, *NY Times* Op-Ed 12/20/06, *The Wall Street Self-Defense Manual*)

WEDNESDAY
2

Capitalism is the legitimate racket of the ruling class. — Al Capone (American gangster, 1899–1947)

End Long Gold (Nov. 18)

THURSDAY
3

…the most successful positions I've taken have been those about which I've been most nervous (and ignored that emotion anyway). Courage is not about being fearless; courage is about acting appropriately even when you are fearful.
— Daniel Turov (*Turov on Timing*)

End Long Silver (Nov. 16)

FRIDAY
4

Liberties voluntarily forfeited are not easily retrieved. All the more so for those that are removed surreptitiously.
— Ted Koppel (Newsman, managing editor Discovery Channel, *NY Times* 11/6/06, b. 1940)

SATURDAY
5

SUNDAY
6

COPPER STARTS TO
BUILD A BULLISH FOUNDATION

Copper prices tend to form seasonal bottoms during the month of December. Traders can look to go long on or about December 14 and hold until about February 23. This trade in the last 36-year history has worked 28 times, for a success rate of 77.8%.

Cumulative profit is a whopping $62,338. One third of that profit came from 2007, as the cyclical boom in the commodity market magnified that seasonal price move. However, this trade has produced other big gains per single contract, such as a $9,113 gain in 2003 and even back in 1973 it registered another substantial $9,100 gain. The biggest loss was for $6,000 back in 2006. These numbers show this trade can produce big wins and big losses.

Therefore, let's introduce a stock that mirrors the price moves of copper without the excess volatility. The chart below is BHP Billiton (BHP). This company mines copper, silver, lead, and gold in Australia, Chile, Peru, and the United States. These guys certainly meet our stock picker's criteria, as they have a solid history of being in business; they were founded in 1860. They are headquartered in Melbourne, Australia.

Notice the price correlation to copper. The bottom section of the graph illustrates BHP Billiton's average seasonal price moves, which also mirror that of copper (page 149).

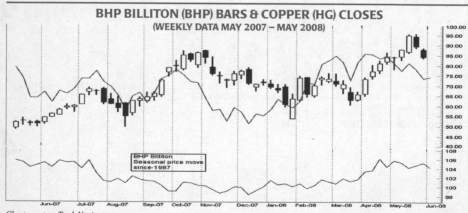

Chart courtesy TradeNavigator.com

DECEMBER

MONDAY
7

All great truths begin as blasphemies. — George Bernard Shaw (Irish dramatist, 1856–1950)

TUESDAY
8

I don't believe in intuition. When you get sudden flashes of perception, it is just the brain working faster than usual.
— Katherine Anne Porter (American author, 1890–1980)

End Short Crude Oil (Sep. 11)

WEDNESDAY
9

Don't worry about people stealing your ideas. If the ideas are any good, you'll have to ram them down people's throats.
— Howard Aiken (U.S. computer scientist, 1900–1973)

THURSDAY
10

In every generation there has to be some fool who will speak the truth as he sees it.
— Boris Pasternak (Russian writer and poet, 1958 Nobel Laureate in Literature, *Doctor Zhivago*, 1890–1960)

FRIDAY
11

Great spirits have always encountered violent opposition from mediocre minds.
— Albert Einstein (German/American physicist, 1921 Nobel Prize, 1879–1955)

Chanukah

SATURDAY
12

SUNDAY
13

BRITISH POUND INVASION FADES AWAY

We hear and see information daily on the values of currencies on CNBC, Bloomberg, Fox News and in print journals such as *The Wall Street Journal* or *Investors Business Daily*. Analysts and investors talk about the many effects currencies play in everyday finances one of which is the bottom line for multinational corporation's earnings. Another ramification of currency value fluctuations is on individuals needs as it applies to the cost of a vacation and how it may impact the business traveler abroad.

One currency, the British pound or "cable," as it is referred to, has a strong seasonal tendency to decline in December. The term cable refers to the British pound/U.S. dollar exchange rate. This was the term used due to the method it was reported by. Back in the mid-1800s, the rate was quoted via the transatlantic cable. The term is still used today as a slang word in traders talk. If you are an individual investor or just happening to visit London for the holidays, perhaps this statistical trading information will be of use. If you are traveling, I would suggest holding off buying pounds until late in December.

The British pound tends to show an average seasonal weakness from late December into March, partly as U.S. dollars tend to repatriate back in the United States and there is some book squaring pressure prior to England's new fiscal year which begins in April.

Traders can look to sell on or about December 28 and hold until on or about March 19. This trade has worked in the past 33-year history 26 times, for a success rate of 78.8%. The cumulative profit is sizable at $58,313.

If the Futures market exposes you to too much leverage or if the volatility is too dramatic, then traders could consider the exchange-traded fund, CurrencyShares British Pound (FXB), which also has options available just like the futures contracts.

The chart below shows the direct correlation between the British pound/U.S. Dollar futures and the FXB. The 33-year average seasonal price move is on the bottom section of the graph depicting the pound's tendency to peak in late December and decline through March.

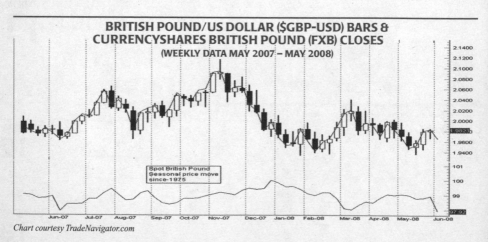

Chart courtesy TradeNavigator.com

DECEMBER

Start Long Copper — 77.8% Accuracy Since 1972 — End Feb. 23, 2010 — Page 144

MONDAY

14

Regardless of current economic conditions, it's always best to remember that the stock market is a barometer and not a thermometer.
— Yale Hirsch

TUESDAY

15

The test of success is not what you do when you are on top. Success is how high you bounce when you hit bottom.
— General George S. Patton, Jr. (U.S. Army field commander WWII, 1885–1945)

WEDNESDAY

16

In investing, the return you want should depend on whether you want to eat well or sleep well. — J. Kenfield Morley

THURSDAY

17

A market is the combined behavior of thousands of people responding to information, misinformation and whim.
— Kenneth Chang (*NY Times* journalist)

FRIDAY

18

If you want to raise a crop for one year, plant corn. If you want to raise a crop for decades, plant trees.
If you want to raise a crop for centuries, raise men. If you want to plant a crop for eternities, raise democracies.
— Carl A. Schenck (German forester, 1868–1955)

SATURDAY

19

SUNDAY

20

COMMODITY SEASONALITY: TOP PERCENTAGE PLAYS

Below and continued on page 116 are the seasonal trades that are the backbone of the *Commodity Trader's Almanac*. After parsing the data compiled from the continuously linked, nonadjusted front contract months, the best time to buy and the number of days to hold are determined for both the long and short. Inclusion of the trade is based primarily on the success rate.

The hold period begins the day after the purchase. Hold days correlate to the trading days, not calendar days. Weekends and days that the CME Trading Floor is closed as depicted in the Strategy Calendars on pages 10–11 and 118–119, and throughout the Almanac on the weekly planner pages are not counted in the hold period.

Whether you are buying or shorting the commodity, a correlating stock or ETF, the same logic applies; buy on or about the trading day listed and hold for the specified period. This is intended to be a guide for your trades, not gospel. If you are satisfied with your gain or have reached your threshold for losses, get out of the trade.

Results are based on trading one contract, commissions, fees and taxes are omitted from the history and the gain at high and loss at low are intraday. Moreover when a trade results in no gain, it is counted as a loss. The trades are also conveniently mapped to the weekly planner pages to alert you of activity throughout the year.

COMMODITY SEASONALITY: TOP PERCENTAGE PLAYS									
Commodity	Years	Trading Day	Hold Days	Success Rate	# Gains	# Losses	Total Gain	Best Gain	Worst Loss
January									
Euro Peaks (Short)	1999 - 2008	3	23	90.0%	9	1	$25,650	$6,138	$3,975
Gold Peaks (Short)	1975 - 2008	14	38	67.6	23	11	44,410	34,955	15,395
February									
Yen Bottoms (Long)	1977 - 2008	6	62	68.8	22	10	44,698	24,318	7,770
Soybeans Bottom (Long)	1968 - 2008	9	73	78.0	32	9	76,925	9,750	4,225
Sugar Peaks (Short)	1973 - 2008	13	39	72.2	26	10	32,278	9,800	2,968
Silver Peaks (Short)	1972 - 2008	13	45	70.3	26	11	103,375	98,000	18,175
Crude Oil Bottoms (Long)	1984 - 2008	15	56	84.0	21	4	67,190	25,830	7,220
Natural Gas Bottoms (Long)	1991 - 2008	16	41	88.9	16	2	55,340	13,650	20,200
March									
Cocoa Peaks (Short)	1973 - 2008	10	23	77.8	28	8	18,070	4,340	2,170
Yen Peaks (Short)	1977 - 2008	10	14	71.9	23	9	5,948	5,130	7,958
Euro Peaks (Short)	1999 - 2008	11	10	80.0	8	2	14,863	5,650	1,550
Live Cattle Peaks (Short)	1970 - 2007	14	70	81.6	31	7	41,590	5,220	3,880
British Pound Bottoms (Long)	1975 - 2008	15	22	70.6	24	10	20,981	7,531	5,594
April									
Crude Oil Bottoms (Long)	1983 - 2008	7	25	76.9	20	6	32,680	16,800	4,600
May									
Copper Peaks (Short)	1973 - 2008	8	13	66.7	24	12	20,550	8,875	3,875
Corn Peaks (Short)	1968 - 2007	9	46	72.5	29	11	15,288	7,100	5,588
Silver Peaks (Short)	1972 - 2007	10	29	72.2	26	10	52,325	24,400	14,250
Lean Hogs Peak (Short)	1970 - 2007	15	60	89.5	34	4	101,550	6,940	6,020
Coffee Peaks (Short)	1974 - 2007	16	54	82.4	28	6	158,194	40,875	17,531
British Pound Peaks (Short)	1975 - 2008	20	8	79.4	27	7	31,631	5,813	2,950

(Continued on page 116)

DECEMBER

If you don't profit from your investment mistakes, someone else will. — Yale Hirsch

A generation from now, Americans may marvel at the complacency that assumed the dollar's dominance would never end.
— Floyd Norris (Chief financial correspondent, *NY Times*, 2/2/07)

What people in the Middle East tell you in private is irrelevant. All that matters is what they will defend in public in their language.
— Thomas L. Friedman (*NY Times* Foreign Affairs columnist, "Meet the Press" 12/17/06)

(Shortened Trading Day)
End Long Cocoa (Nov. 5)

Amongst democratic nations, each generation is a new people.
— Alexis de Tocqueville (Author, *Democracy in America*, 1840, 1805–1859)

Christmas Day (Market Closed)

If you live each day as if it was your last, someday you'll most certainly be right.
— Favorite quote of Steve Jobs (CEO Apple & Pixar, Stanford University commencement address, 6/15/05)

COMMODITY SEASONALITY: TOP PERCENTAGE PLAYS

(Continued from page 114)

COMMODITY SEASONALITY: TOP PERCENTAGE PLAYS

Commodity	Years	Trading Day	Hold Days	Success Rate	# Gains	# Losses	Total Gain	Best Gain	Worst Loss
June									
Soybeans Peak (Short)	1968–2007	1	90	70.0	28	12	$54,213	$20,450	$17,850
Cocoa Bottoms (Long)	1973–2007	2	24	77.1%	27	8	19,810	3,520	4,560
CBOT Wheat Bottoms (Long)	1968–2007	6	105	80.0	32	8	69,788	13,800	6,900
Corn Peaks (Short)	1968–2007	12	31	72.5	29	11	16,050	4,425	5,700
Live Cattle Bottoms (Long)	1970–2007	14	160	89.5	34	4	65,950	5,600	5,460
British Pound Bottoms (Long)	1975–2007	20	16	72.7	24	9	31,906	8,438	6,656
July									
Natural Gas Bottoms (Long)	1990–2007	17	62	94.4	17	1	170,480	57,400	500
Gold Bottoms (Long)	1975–2007	18	26	78.8	26	7	26,410	6,450	1,970
Cocoa Peaks (Short)	1973–2007	18	70	71.4	25	10	16,850	10,590	9,980
August									
British Pound Peaks (Short)	1975–2007	1	28	69.7	23	10	23,394	7,913	4,688
Swiss Franc Bottoms (Long)	1975–2007	6	48	84.8	28	5	68,713	11,713	4,363
Coffee Bottoms (Long)	1974–2007	12	13	79.4	27	7	58,988	12,375	8,156
Cocoa Bottoms (Long)	1973–2007	14	24	71.4	25	10	19,800	3,800	1,710
September									
Silver Bottoms (Long)	1972–2007	1	16	75.0	27	9	73,075	35,000	8,850
Sugar Bottoms (Long)	1972–2007	1	62	75.0	27	9	31,338	12,544	4,368
Yen Bottoms (Long)	1976–2007	1	14	75.0	24	8	33,273	6,955	4,870
Euro Bottoms (Long)	1999–2007	5	16	88.9	8	1	17,475	7,363	4,125
Crude Oil Peaks (Short)	1983–2007	8	62	80.0	20	5	32,480	7,890	8,300
Cocoa Peaks (Short)	1972–2007	10	33	77.8	28	8	21,840	7,635	3,335
British Pound Bottoms (Long)	1975–2007	12	33	72.7	24	9	39,875	7,219	12,688
October									
Gold Peaks (Short)	1975–2007	2	25	72.7	24	9	11,910	9,600	8,380
Silver Peaks (Short)	1972–2007	4	17	69.4	25	11	10,350	8,600	8,450
Yen Peaks (Short)	1976–2007	12	78	65.6	21	11	23,835	11,205	9,633
Soybeans Bottom (Long)	1968–2007	16	12	90.0	36	4	35,775	4,050	1,075
Corn Bottoms (Long)	1968–2007	20	133	85.0	34	6	44,838	12,375	4,600
November									
Lean Hogs Bottoms (Long)	1969–2007	2	13	87.2	34	5	32,400	3,840	1,620
Cocoa Bottoms (Long)	1972–2007	4	34	75.0	27	9	19,190	5,900	5,250
Silver Bottoms (Long)	1972–2007	11	13	72.2	26	10	40,725	16,400	2,625
Gold Bottoms (Long)	1975–2007	13	10	78.8	26	7	25,960	4,800	1,720
CBOT Wheat Peaks (Short)	1968–2007	17	118	80.0	32	8	43,225	9,100	4,250
Sugar Peaks (Short)	1972–2007	17	50	63.9	23	13	12,376	21,504	9,016
Swiss Franc Bottoms (Long)	1975–2007	18	24	75.8	25	8	50,538	8,463	3,325
December									
Copper Bottoms (Long)	1972–2007	10	47	77.8	28	8	62,338	20,300	6,000
British Pound Peaks (Short)	1975–2007	19	56	78.8	26	7	58,313	9,300	9,000
Swiss Franc Peaks (Short)	1975–2007	19	41	75.8	25	8	41,350	8,925	6,963

DECEMBER/JANUARY 2010

Start Short British Pound — 78.8% Accuracy Since 1975 — End Mar. 19, 2010 — Page 144
Start Short Swiss Franc — 75.8% Accuracy Since 1975 — End Feb. 26, 2010 — Page 144

MONDAY
28

The most valuable executive is one who is training somebody to be a better man than he is.
— Robert G. Ingersoll (American lawyer and orator, "The Great Agnostic," 1833–1899)

TUESDAY
29

If buying equities seem the most hazardous and foolish thing you could possibly do,
then you are near the bottom that will end the bear market. — Joseph E. Granville

WEDNESDAY
30

Statements by high officials are practically always misleading when they are designed to bolster a falling market.
— Gerald M. Loeb (EF Hutton, *The Battle for Investment Survival*, predicted '29 Crash, 1900–1974)

End Long Swiss Franc (Nov. 25)

THURSDAY
31

If you bet on a horse, that's gambling. If you bet you can make three spades, that's entertainment.
If you bet cotton will go up three points, that's business. See the difference? — Blackie Sherrod (Sportswriter, b. 1919)

New Year's Day (Market Closed)

FRIDAY
1

Intense concentration hour after hour can bring out resources in people they didn't know they had.
— Edwin Land (Polaroid inventor & founder, 1909–1991)

SATURDAY
2

SUNDAY
3

2010 STRATEGY CALENDAR

	MONDAY	TUESDAY	WEDNESDAY	THURSDAY	FRIDAY	SATURDAY	SUNDAY
JANUARY	28	29	30	31	1 JANUARY New Year's Day	2	3
	4	5	6	7	8	9	10
	11	12	13	14	15	16	17
	18 Martin Luther King Day	19	20	21	22	23	24
	25	26	27	28	29	30	31
FEBRUARY	1 FEBRUARY	2	3	4	5	6	7
	8	9	10	11	12	13	14 ♥
	15 Presidents' Day	16	17 Ash Wednesday	18	19	20	21
	22	23	24	25	26	27	28
MARCH	1 MARCH	2	3	4	5	6	7
	8	9	10	11	12	13	14 Daylight Saving Time Begins
	15	16	17 ♣ St. Patrick's Day	18	19	20	21
	22	23	24	25	26	27	28
	29	30 Passover	31	1 APRIL	2 Good Friday	3	4
APRIL	5	6	7	8	9	10	11 Easter
	12	13	14	15 Tax Deadline	16	17	18
	19	20	21	22	23	24	25
	26	27	28	29	30	1 MAY	2
MAY	3	4	5	6	7	8	9 Mother's Day
	10	11	12	13	14	15	16
	17	18	19	20	21	22	23
	24	25	26	27	28	29	30
JUNE	31 Memorial Day	1 JUNE	2	3	4	5	6
	7	8	9	10	11	12	13
	14	15	16	17	18	19	20 Father's Day
	21	22	23	24	25	26	27

Market closed on shaded weekdays; closes early when half-shaded.

118

2010 STRATEGY CALENDAR

MONDAY	TUESDAY	WEDNESDAY	THURSDAY	FRIDAY	SATURDAY	SUNDAY	
28	29	30	1 JULY	2	3	4 Independence Day	JULY
5	6	7	8	9	10	11	
12	13	14	15	16	17	18	
19	20	21	22	23	24	25	
26	27	28	29	30	31	1 AUGUST	
2	3	4	5	6	7	8	AUGUST
9	10	11	12	13	14	15	
16	17	18	19	20	21	22	
23	24	25	26	27	28	29	
30	31	1 SEPTEMBER	2	3	4	5	SEPTEMBER
6 Labor Day	7	8	9 Rosh Hashanah	10	11	12	
13	14	15	16	17	18 Yom Kippur	19	
20	21	22	23	24	25	26	
27	28	29	30	1 OCTOBER	2	3	
4	5	6	7	8	9	10	OCTOBER
11 Columbus Day	12	13	14	15	16	17	
18	19	20	21	22	23	24	
25	26	27	28	29	30	31	
1 NOVEMBER	2 Election Day	3	4	5	6	7 Daylight Saving Time Ends	NOVEMBER
8	9	10	11 Veterans' Day	12	13	14	
15	16	17	18	19	20	21	
22	23	24	25 Thanksgiving	26	27	28	
29	30	1 DECEMBER	2 Chanukah	3	4	5	DECEMBER
6	7	8	9	10	11	12	
13	14	15	16	17	18	19	
20	21	22	23	24	25 Christmas	26	
27	28	29	30	31	1 JANUARY New Year's Day	2	

119

DIRECTORY OF TRADING PATTERNS & DATABANK

CONTENTS

YEAR	ENTRY DATE	ENTRY CLOSE	EXIT DATE	EXIT CLOSE	PROFIT/ LOSS	PROFIT AT HIGH	LOSS AT LOW
JANUARY SHORT EURO – TRADING DAY: 3 – HOLD: 23 DAYS							
1999	1/6	118.20	2/9	113.52	$5,850	$7,238	–$88
2000	1/5	104.24	2/8	99.33	6,138	9,075	–250
2001	1/4	94.75	2/7	93.32	1,788	3,888	–1,550
2002	1/4	89.33	2/7	86.49	3,550	4,725	–275
2003	1/6	104.56	2/7	107.74	–3,975	1,550	–5,400
2004	1/6	127.25	2/9	126.95	375	4,913	–1,513
2005	1/5	132.27	2/8	127.66	5,763	6,150	–1,075
2006	1/5	121.40	2/8	119.71	2,113	2,163	–2,513
2007	1/4	131.48	2/7	130.09	1,738	3,050	–150
2008	1/4	147.36	2/7	145.51	2,313	3,100	–2,425
				10-Year Gain $25,650		**Up 9**	**Down 1**
JANUARY SHORT GOLD – TRADING DAY: 14 – HOLD: 38 DAYS							
1975	1/21	179.8	3/18	179.0	$35	$485	–$965
1976	1/21	124.6	3/16	133.7	–955	75	–1,085
1977	1/20	133.7	3/16	150.0	–1,675	235	–1,875
1978	1/23	176.0	3/20	183.3	–775	215	–2,015
1979	1/19	232.8	3/15	244.0	–1,165	285	–2,645
1980	1/21	873.0	3/14	523.0	34,955	34,955	–45
1981	1/21	580.0	3/17	498.0	8,155	12,655	–145
1982	1/21	376.5	3/17	316.5	5,955	6,355	–1,975
1983	1/20	491.5	3/16	421.5	6,955	8,305	–2,895
1984	1/20	372.0	3/15	395.5	–2,395	905	–3,895
1985	1/21	307.8	3/15	291.0	1,635	2,475	–365
1986	1/21	359.0	3/17	349.2	935	2,685	–245
1987	1/21	408.2	3/17	407.5	25	1,635	–925
1988	1/21	476.3	3/16	448.5	2,735	5,075	–315
1989	1/20	405.4	3/10	393.0	1,195	2,295	–625
1990	1/19	410.8	3/15	399.2	1,115	1,365	–1,995
1991	1/21	379.0	3/15	364.7	1,385	2,155	–365
1992	1/21	357.8	3/16	345.8	1,155	1,155	–305
1993	1/21	329.7	3/17	329.3	–5	345	–535
1994	1/20	392.5	3/16	386.1	595	1,805	–215
1995	1/20	383.4	3/16	385.1	–215	845	–595
1996	1/22	402.5	3/15	396.5	555	975	–1,765
1997	1/21	354.9	3/17	353.0	145	1,575	–1,155
1998	1/22	295.0	3/18	289.2	535	535	–1,285
1999	1/22	287.5	3/18	284.4	265	505	–915
2000	1/24	287.7	3/17	286.7	55	425	–3,575
2001	1/22	266.5	3/16	261.1	495	1,005	–685
2002	1/22	283.1	3/18	291.0	–835	525	–2,485
2003	1/22	359.5	3/18	335.7	2,335	2,705	–2,545
2004	1/23	410.5	3/18	407.3	275	2,185	–795
2005	1/21	423.2	3/17	443.2	–2,045	1,125	2,525
2006	1/23	557.5	3/17	556.8	25	2,255	–2,245
2007	1/23	639.5	3/19	655.5	–1,645	385	–5,345
2008	1/22	864.0	3/17	1017.5	–15,395	–45	–15,395
				34-Year Gain $44,410		**Up 23**	**Down 11**
FEBRUARY LONG YEN – TRADING DAY: 6 – HOLD: 62 DAYS							
1977	2/8	34.84	5/9	36.00	$1,405	$2,555	–$108
1978	2/8	41.54	5/9	44.60	3,780	6,180	–133
1979	2/8	51.25	5/9	47.33	–4,945	18	–8,295
1980	2/8	41.65	5/8	42.98	1,618	2,093	–4,020
1981	2/9	49.46	5/8	46.70	–3,495	193	–3,995
1982	2/8	43.14	5/7	43.44	330	680	–2,983
1983	2/8	42.37	5/9	43.08	843	930	–1,070
1984	2/8	42.98	5/9	43.95	1,168	3,293	–383
1985	2/8	38.44	5/9	39.82	1,680	2,718	–670
1986	2/10	53.33	5/9	61.85	10,605	10,605	308
1987	2/9	65.21	5/8	71.96	8,393	9,480	–633
1988	2/8	77.70	5/6	80.44	3,380	4,705	–2,545
1989	2/8	77.60	5/9	74.63	–3,758	2,993	–3,883
1990	2/8	68.94	5/9	64.00	–6,220	705	–8,045
1991	2/8	78.11	5/9	71.93	–7,770	430	–9,683
1992	2/10	79.40	5/8	75.35	–5,108	5	–6,770
1993	2/8	80.40	5/7	90.66	12,780	13,893	–70
1994	2/8	92.10	5/9	97.60	6,830	9,280	–383
1995	2/8	101.46	5/9	120.95	24,318	29,380	–645
1996	2/8	94.25	5/7	95.75	1,830	3,030	–1,945
1997	2/10	81.95	5/9	82.40	518	1,830	–3,545
1998	2/9	80.61	5/8	75.81	–6,045	1,568	–7,608
1999	2/8	88.32	5/7	83.28	–6,345	155	–9,333
2000	2/8	92.29	5/8	92.78	568	8,793	–2,845
2001	2/8	86.60	5/9	82.53	–5,133	743	–8,770
2002	2/8	74.54	5/9	77.89	4,143	5,780	–533
2003	2/10	83.03	5/9	85.36	2,868	4,080	–1,083
2004	2/9	94.63	5/7	90.62	–5,058	2,768	–7,020
2005	2/8	94.85	5/9	94.93	55	2,955	–3,183
2006	2/8	84.76	5/9	90.15	6,693	7,093	–708
2007	2/8	82.80	5/8	84.00	1,455	5,480	–533
2008	2/8	93.33	5/8	96.02	3,318	13,030	–1,145
				32-Year Gain $44,698		**Up 22**	**Down 10**

YEAR	ENTRY DATE	ENTRY CLOSE	EXIT DATE	EXIT CLOSE	PROFIT/ LOSS	PROFIT AT HIGH	LOSS AT LOW
FEBRUARY LONG SOYBEANS – TRADING DAY: 9 – HOLD: 73 DAYS							
1968	2/14	275 1/4	5/31	266 1/4	–$450	$100	–$488
1969	2/13	266 1/2	6/2	267 1/2	50	263	–238
1970	2/12	258 3/4	5/28	272	663	675	–38
1971	2/11	309	5/27	309 1/2	25	250	–963
1972	2/11	318 3/4	5/26	353	1,713	2,363	–100
1973	2/13	548 1/2	5/30	656	5,375	5,825	–7,200
1974	2/14	640	5/31	555 1/2	–4,225	2,500	–6,000
1975	2/13	582	5/30	504	–3,900	1,675	–4,738
1976	2/12	480	5/27	582	5,100	5,100	–675
1977	2/11	742	5/31	937	9,750	16,100	–600
1978	2/13	560 1/4	5/30	735	8,738	9,363	N/A
1979	2/13	730	5/30	736 1/2	325	3,350	–450
1980	2/13	668 1/2	5/29	628	–2,025	200	–4,950
1981	2/12	746	5/29	763	850	4,650	–1,325
1982	2/11	633 1/2	5/27	654	1,025	2,525	–1,475
1983	2/11	595 1/2	5/27	614	925	3,875	–1,150
1984	2/13	703	5/29	883	9,000	9,800	–725
1985	2/13	577 1/2	5/30	558	–975	1,825	–1,050
1986	2/13	523	5/30	531 1/2	425	2,025	–388
1987	2/12	492 3/4	5/29	552	2,963	4,988	–663
1988	2/11	613 1/2	5/26	757	7,175	9,063	–275
1989	2/13	728	5/30	703	–1,250	3,325	–1,963
1990	2/13	564	5/30	606	2,100	5,375	–38
1991	2/13	572	5/30	572 1/2	25	2,063	–275
1992	2/13	566	6/2	626	3,000	3,550	N/A
1993	2/11	568 1/2	5/27	612 1/2	2,200	2,263	–188
1994	2/11	679 1/2	5/31	704	1,225	2,650	–1,575
1995	2/13	558	5/30	596	1,900	3,025	–250
1996	2/13	718 1/2	5/29	797	3,925	6,425	–250
1997	2/13	761	5/30	884	6,150	7,050	–50
1998	2/12	682	5/29	619	–3,150	100	–3,388
1999	2/11	500 3/4	5/27	457 1/2	–2,163	363	–2,425
2000	2/11	511	5/26	531	1,000	3,575	–750
2001	2/13	452 1/2	5/30	440	–625	875	–1,525
2002	2/13	436	5/30	495 3/4	2,988	3,213	–88
2003	2/13	564	5/30	631	3,350	4,700	–300
2004	2/12	832 1/2	5/27	858	1,275	11,575	–1,025
2005	2/11	517 1/2	5/27	673	7,775	8,700	–50
2006	2/13	580	5/30	585 1/2	275	2,000	–1,288
2007	2/13	746 1/2	5/30	794 1/2	2,400	3,325	–1,625
2008	2/13	1318	5/29	1358	2,000	13,425	–9,800
				41-Year Gain $76,925		**Up 32**	**Down 9**
FEBRUARY SHORT SUGAR – TRADING DAY: 13 – HOLD: 39 DAYS							
1973	2/22	9.00	4/18	8.77	$258	$907	–$616
1974	2/22	24.46	4/19	21.00	3,875	9,587	N/A
1975	2/24	32.75	4/21	26.05	7,504	11,245	–112
1976	2/23	13.70	4/19	14.38	–762	101	–2,083
1977	2/18	8.81	4/18	10.29	–1,658	571	–1,702
1978	2/23	8.90	4/20	7.77	1,266	1,971	–157
1979	2/21	9.07	4/18	8.26	907	1,075	–11
1980	2/22	25.45	4/18	24.45	1,120	8,960	–2,296
1981	2/20	25.60	4/16	16.85	9,800	9,800	–280
1982	2/19	13.70	4/16	10.00	4,144	4,144	–56
1983	2/18	7.12	4/18	7.08	45	1,086	–179
1984	2/21	6.92	4/16	6.20	806	930	–538
1985	2/21	4.17	4/18	3.56	683	717	–246
1986	2/21	6.11	4/18	8.76	–2,968	134	–3,886
1987	2/20	7.79	4/16	6.95	941	1,422	–806
1988	2/19	8.66	4/15	8.73	–78	1,277	–627
1989	2/21	11.77	4/18	12.23	–515	840	–1,434
1990	2/21	14.55	4/18	15.22	–750	414	–1,938
1991	2/21	8.40	4/18	8.24	179	370	–1,254
1992	2/21	8.47	4/16	9.47	–1,120	638	–1,602
1993	2/19	9.50	4/16	11.07	–1,758	134	–3,394
1994	2/18	11.48	4/18	11.32	179	1,098	–1,109
1995	2/21	14.65	4/18	11.48	3,550	3,550	–336
1996	2/21	11.68	4/17	11.05	706	806	–907
1997	2/21	11.00	4/18	10.88	134	358	–426
1998	2/20	10.15	4/17	8.83	1,478	1,602	–56
1999	2/19	6.42	4/16	4.79	1,826	1,826	–134
2000	2/18	5.20	4/14	6.18	–1,098	403	–1,109
2001	2/21	9.06	4/18	8.53	594	1,523	–403
2002	2/21	5.80	4/18	5.69	123	549	–638
2003	2/24	8.55	4/21	7.43	1,254	1,635	–45
2004	2/20	5.82	4/16	6.82	–1,120	11	–1,613
2005	2/18	9.30	4/18	8.25	1,176	1,310	–112
2006	2/21	17.75	4/18	17.53	246	1,747	–1,064
2007	2/21	10.50	4/18	9.70	896	1,030	–1,098
2008	2/21	13.73	4/17	13.36	414	2,778	–1,501
				36-Year Gain $32,278		**Up 26**	**Down 10**

YEAR	ENTRY DATE	ENTRY CLOSE	EXIT DATE	EXIT CLOSE	PROFIT/ LOSS	PROFIT AT HIGH	LOSS AT LOW
FEBRUARY SHORT SILVER – TRADING DAY: 13 – HOLD: 45 DAYS							
1972	2/17	157.5	4/24	161.0	–$175	$275	–$500
1973	2/21	231.0	4/26	216.0	750	1,075	–1,950
1974	2/21	576.0	4/26	553.0	1,150	7,275	–3,425
1975	2/21	464.5	4/28	438.0	1,325	3,050	–75
1976	2/19	411.0	4/23	447.5	–1,825	450	–2,750
1977	2/17	453.5	4/25	487.5	–1,700	75	–2,450
1978	2/21	505.0	4/26	501.0	200	675	–2,725
1979	2/20	782.0	4/25	764.0	900	3,350	–1,500
1980	2/20	3400.0	4/24	1440.0	98,000	101,400	–18,000
1981	2/19	1300.0	4/24	1155.0	7,250	11,000	–3,350
1982	2/18	832.0	4/23	730.0	5,100	6,600	–300
1983	2/17	1475.0	4/24	1232.0	12,150	22,950	–300
1984	2/17	907.0	4/24	936.0	–1,450	50	–6,250
1985	2/20	625.0	4/25	619.0	300	3,800	–3,250
1986	2/20	591.5	4/25	509.5	4,100	4,625	–825
1987	2/19	541.0	4/24	904.5	–18,175	100	–18,175
1988	2/18	648.0	4/22	640.0	400	2,000	–2,100
1989	2/17	584.0	4/25	582.0	100	500	–2,200
1990	2/20	535.0	4/25	498.0	1,850	2,250	–125
1991	2/20	369.5	4/25	387.5	–900	950	–2,725
1992	2/20	408.5	4/24	396.5	600	825	–700
1993	2/18	364.0	4/23	394.5	–1,525	650	–1,875
1994	2/17	529.5	4/25	508.0	1,075	1,275	–2,625
1995	2/17	471.5	4/25	565.0	–4,675	1,875	–6,375
1996	2/20	569.5	4/24	530.5	1,950	2,325	–175
1997	2/20	517.0	4/25	473.0	2,200	2,575	–1,325
1998	2/19	665.5	4/24	626.0	1,975	5,425	–925
1999	2/18	547.0	4/23	518.0	1,450	3,250	–850
2000	2/17	533.0	4/24	502.0	1,550	2,050	–125
2001	2/20	449.0	4/25	444.5	225	1,100	–450
2002	2/20	447.0	4/25	462.5	–775	650	–1,400
2003	2/20	461.0	4/25	463.5	–125	1,350	–575
2004	2/19	666.5	4/23	613.5	2,650	3,325	–8,225
2005	2/17	726.0	4/25	724.0	100	2,150	–2,100
2006	2/17	944.0	4/25	1240.0	–14,800	275	–25,700
2007	2/20	1397.0	4/25	1379.0	900	7,350	–3,700
2008	2/20	1738.0	4/24	1713.0	1,250	5,400	–17,825
				37-Year Gain $103,375		**Up 26**	**Down 11**
FEBRUARY LONG CRUDE OIL – TRADING DAY: 15 – HOLD: 56 DAYS							
1984	2/22	29.84	5/11	30.32	$480	$1,260	–$290
1985	2/22	26.80	5/14	27.12	320	2,400	–480
1986	2/24	14.20	5/14	15.15	950	1,700	–4,450
1987	2/23	17.40	5/13	19.11	1,710	1,880	–1,350
1988	2/22	16.50	5/11	17.68	1,180	2,340	–1,290
1989	2/22	17.65	5/12	18.75	1,100	3,950	–120
1990	2/22	21.81	5/14	19.08	–2,730	160	–4,460
1991	2/22	18.55	5/14	21.05	2,500	3,560	–1,100
1992	2/24	18.50	5/13	21.08	2,580	2,700	–370
1993	2/22	20.05	5/12	20.36	310	1,090	–310
1994	2/22	14.20	5/13	18.28	4,080	4,100	–300
1995	2/22	18.54	5/12	19.40	860	2,220	–710
1996	2/22	19.57	5/13	21.12	1,550	6,130	–790
1997	2/24	21.45	5/14	20.93	–520	900	–2,490
1998	2/23	15.68	5/13	15.20	–480	1,820	–2,880
1999	2/22	11.87	5/12	17.50	5,630	7,180	–10
2000	2/22	27.95	5/11	28.08	130	6,250	–4,250
2001	2/22	28.85	5/14	29.07	220	580	–3,360
2002	2/22	20.80	5/14	28.80	8,000	8,000	–400
2003	2/24	35.80	5/14	28.58	–7,220	4,190	–10,720
2004	2/23	34.27	5/12	40.21	5,940	5,940	–970
2005	2/22	49.24	5/12	50.41	1,170	9,040	–440
2006	2/22	62.50	5/12	73.10	10,600	12,850	–3,250
2007	2/21	58.89	5/11	61.89	3,000	9,200	–1,590
2008	2/21	100.01	5/12	125.84	25,830	26,260	–3,140
				25-Year Gain $67,190		**Up 21**	**Down 4**
FEBRUARY LONG NATURAL GAS – TRADING DAY: 16 – HOLD: 41 DAYS							
1991	2/25	1.342	4/24	1.385	$430	$930	N/A
1992	2/25	1.170	4/23	1.451	2,810	3,000	–240
1993	2/23	1.860	4/23	2.520	6,600	7,850	–1,100
1994	2/23	2.310	4/22	2.150	–1,600	100	–2,850
1995	2/23	1.450	4/24	1.710	2,600	3,500	–330
1996	2/23	2.330	4/23	2.340	100	4,200	–2,600
1997	2/25	1.830	4/24	2.075	2,450	4,100	–500
1998	2/24	2.225	4/23	2.435	2,100	5,000	–1,200
1999	2/23	1.705	4/22	2.215	5,100	5,100	–800
2000	2/23	2.510	4/20	3.060	5,500	6,650	–150
2001	2/23	5.180	4/24	5.200	200	5,600	–3,100
2002	2/25	2.400	4/24	3.535	11,350	13,000	–700
2003	2/25	7.700	4/24	5.680	–20,200	8,000	–28,150
2004	2/24	5.050	4/22	5.610	5,600	9,800	–200
2005	2/23	6.195	4/22	7.190	9,950	16,550	–550
2006	2/23	7.350	4/24	8.180	8,300	9,300	–9,000
2007	2/23	7.700	4/24	7.740	400	3,100	–8,800
2008	2/25	9.250	4/23	10.615	13,650	16,400	–4,650
				18-Year Gain $55,340		**Up 16**	**Down 2**

MARCH SHORT COCOA – TRADING DAY: 10 – HOLD: 23 DAYS

YEAR	ENTRY DATE	ENTRY CLOSE	EXIT DATE	EXIT CLOSE	PROFIT/ LOSS	PROFIT AT HIGH	LOSS AT LOW
1973	3/14	807	4/16	928	–$1,210	$30	–$1,310
1974	3/14	1521	4/17	1510	110	1,890	–4,330
1975	3/14	1400	4/17	1202	1,980	1,980	–90
1976	3/12	1433	4/14	1650	–2,170	260	–2,170
1977	3/14	3957	4/15	3523	4,340	5,850	–4,850
1978	3/14	3616	4/17	3516	1,000	3,400	–2,040
1979	3/14	3301	4/17	3053	2,480	2,480	N/A
1980	3/14	2932	4/17	2811	1,210	1,650	–2,430
1981	3/13	2045	4/15	2022	230	1,050	–730
1982	3/12	1937	4/15	1665	2,720	3,670	–180
1983	3/14	1795	4/15	1745	500	1,650	–520
1984	3/14	2516	4/16	2447	690	1,310	–620
1985	3/14	2195	4/17	2357	–1,620	370	–2,930
1986	3/14	2050	4/17	1930	1,200	2,330	–390
1987	3/13	1887	4/15	1986	–990	140	–1,070
1988	3/14	1582	4/15	1565	170	510	–370
1989	3/14	1405	4/17	1240	1,650	1,990	–950
1990	3/14	1102	4/17	1304	–2,020	910	–2,820
1991	3/14	1175	4/17	1129	460	1,050	–450
1992	3/13	1054	4/15	1010	440	1,170	–340
1993	3/12	865	4/15	951	–860	40	–1,180
1994	3/14	1199	4/15	1152	470	980	–530
1995	3/14	1368	4/17	1314	540	870	–70
1996	3/14	1210	4/17	1361	–1,510	50	–1,800
1997	3/14	1470	4/17	1450	200	1,000	–620
1998	3/13	1645	4/16	1566	790	820	–440
1999	3/12	1210	4/15	1144	660	1,370	–270
2000	3/14	885	4/14	852	330	1,020	–620
2001	3/14	1069	4/17	978	910	1,200	–190
2002	3/14	1552	4/17	1500	520	1,320	–260
2003	3/14	1940	4/16	1845	950	1,400	–1,300
2004	3/12	1398	4/15	1373	250	270	–1,640
2005	3/14	1794	4/15	1543	2,510	2,840	–560
2006	3/14	1446	4/17	1445	10	240	–770
2007	3/14	1785	4/17	1933	–1,480	320	–1,830
2008	3/14	2911	4/17	2650	2,610	6,940	–600
				36-Year Gain $18,070		**Up 28**	**Down 8**

MARCH SHORT YEN – TRADING DAY: 10 – HOLD: 14 DAY

YEAR	ENTRY DATE	ENTRY CLOSE	EXIT DATE	EXIT CLOSE	PROFIT/ LOSS	PROFIT AT HIGH	LOSS AT LOW
1977	3/14	35.47	4/1	36.15	–$895	$143	–$908
1978	3/14	43.50	4/4	46.25	–3,483	130	–3,820
1979	3/14	48.65	4/3	47.29	1,655	1,655	–983
1980	3/14	40.57	4/3	39.20	1,668	1,780	–270
1981	3/13	49.05	4/2	47.58	1,793	1,793	–408
1982	3/12	42.57	4/1	41.23	1,630	1,980	–170
1983	3/14	42.34	4/4	42.06	305	943	–933
1984	3/14	45.40	4/3	44.85	643	1,068	–358
1985	3/14	38.65	4/3	39.66	–1,308	43	–1,983
1986	3/14	56.95	4/4	55.86	1,318	1,680	–908
1987	3/13	65.68	4/2	68.36	–3,395	–45	–4,395
1988	3/14	79.44	4/4	81.18	–2,220	1,880	–2,258
1989	3/14	78.03	4/4	77.19	1,005	2,705	–383
1990	3/14	65.87	4/3	63.25	3,230	3,930	–170
1991	3/14	73.38	4/4	72.84	630	3,680	–120
1992	3/13	74.83	4/2	74.37	530	968	–1,208
1993	3/12	84.87	4/1	87.48	–3,308	568	–3,308
1994	3/14	94.98	4/1	97.28	–2,920	1,105	–4,133
1995	3/14	111.05	4/3	116.70	–7,108	618	–7,445
1996	3/14	96.22	4/3	94.50	2,105	2,905	–95
1997	3/14	81.86	4/4	81.45	468	593	–1,908
1998	3/13	78.92	4/2	75.55	4,168	4,230	–445
1999	3/12	84.60	4/1	84.49	93	1,055	–2,395
2000	3/14	96.93	4/3	96.60	368	3,493	–3,083
2001	3/14	84.39	4/3	80.25	5,130	5,918	–58
2002	3/14	78.12	4/4	76.21	2,343	3,843	–370
2003	3/14	84.67	4/4	83.94	868	3,043	–858
2004	3/12	90.08	4/1	96.41	–7,958	55	–8,133
2005	3/14	96.10	4/4	93.13	3,668	3,668	–1,108
2006	3/14	85.68	4/3	85.39	318	380	–2,508
2007	3/14	87.01	4/3	85.06	2,393	2,393	–308
2008	3/14	99.87	4/4	98.06	2,218	2,880	–4,945
				32-Year Gain $5,948		**Up 23**	**Down 9**

MARCH SHORT EURO – TRADING DAY: 11 – HOLD: 10 DAYS

YEAR	ENTRY DATE	ENTRY CLOSE	EXIT DATE	EXIT CLOSE	PROFIT/ LOSS	PROFIT AT HIGH	LOSS AT LOW
1999	3/15	109.93	3/29	107.52	$3,013	$3,013	–$1,275
2000	3/15	97.15	3/29	96.17	1,225	1,225	–1,425
2001	3/15	90.69	3/29	88.56	2,663	2,900	–288
2002	3/15	88.27	4/1	87.13	1,425	1,925	–138
2003	3/17	107.69	3/31	108.44	–938	3,738	–938
2004	3/15	122.52	3/29	120.99	1,913	2,438	–1,850
2005	3/15	134.14	3/30	129.62	5,650	6,663	–675
2006	3/15	120.97	3/29	120.63	425	1,000	–2,263
2007	3/15	132.64	3/29	133.88	–1,550	38	–2,088
2008	3/17	156.94	4/1	156.11	1,038	4,925	–1,763
				10-Year Gain $14,863		**Up 8**	**Down 2**

| | ENTRY | | EXIT | | PROFIT/ | PROFIT | LOSS |
YEAR	DATE	CLOSE	DATE	CLOSE	LOSS	AT HIGH	AT LOW
MARCH SHORT LIVE CATTLE – TRADING DAY: 14 – HOLD: 70 DAYS							
1970	3/19	32.000	6/30	31.800	$80	$1,040	N/A
1971	3/18	32.050	6/28	30.450	640	690	−860
1972	3/20	34.550	6/28	37.500	−1,180	420	−1,300
1973	3/20	47.000	6/28	47.150	−60	2,140	−420
1974	3/20	44.700	6/28	42.575	850	4,680	−1,240
1975	3/20	39.400	6/30	47.750	−3,340	130	−5,240
1976	3/18	36.600	6/28	43.300	−2,680	N/A	−5,160
1977	3/18	42.350	6/28	42.100	100	1,400	−1,700
1978	3/20	50.300	6/28	47.800	1,000	1,000	−4,380
1979	3/20	75.200	6/28	67.650	3,020	3,960	−1,820
1980	3/20	70.075	6/30	68.250	730	3,930	−70
1981	3/19	64.000	6/29	67.000	−1,200	330	−3,360
1982	3/18	67.300	6/28	64.500	1,120	2,060	−2,680
1983	3/18	66.650	6/28	63.200	1,380	2,230	−1,830
1984	3/20	70.750	6/28	64.250	2,600	3,580	−120
1985	3/20	62.050	6/28	58.450	1,440	1,950	−2,170
1986	3/20	58.050	6/30	56.750	520	3,280	−580
1987	3/19	66.000	6/29	63.300	1,080	1,640	−1,780
1988	3/18	73.600	6/28	64.600	3,600	4,710	−840
1989	3/20	78.150	6/28	70.400	3,100	4,480	−300
1990	3/20	77.950	6/28	73.200	1,900	2,220	−380
1991	3/20	80.850	6/28	72.075	3,510	3,850	−740
1992	3/19	77.400	6/29	71.700	2,280	2,870	−840
1993	3/18	82.600	6/28	74.700	3,160	3,720	−680
1994	3/18	76.400	6/29	63.350	5,220	5,900	−610
1995	3/20	69.450	6/28	62.500	2,780	4,320	−560
1996	3/20	64.900	6/28	64.675	90	4,360	−800
1997	3/20	68.900	6/30	64.475	1,770	2,360	−120
1998	3/19	65.350	6/29	64.750	240	900	−1,750
1999	3/18	66.800	6/28	62.900	1,560	2,470	−520
2000	3/20	72.400	6/28	66.700	2,280	2,410	−400
2001	3/20	77.500	6/28	75.350	860	3,070	−980
2002	3/20	71.425	6/28	63.350	3,230	4,840	−470
2003	3/20	74.875	6/30	69.750	2,050	3,170	−1,030
2004	3/18	76.900	6/29	86.600	−3,880	1,720	−6,320
2005	3/18	88.450	6/28	80.900	3,020	3,700	N/A
2006	3/20	78.250	6/28	86.950	−3,480	2,200	−3,880
2007	3/20	94.850	6/28	89.350	2,200	2,640	−960
				38-Year Gain $41,590		**Up 31**	**Down 7**
MARCH LONG BRITISH POUND – TRADING DAY: 15 – HOLD: 22 DAYS							
1975	3/21	235.20	4/23	230.00	−$3,250	N/A	−$3,875
1976	3/19	189.50	4/21	183.10	−4,000	844	−5,031
1977	3/21	168.85	4/21	171.15	1,438	1,438	−31
1978	3/21	189.75	4/21	181.55	−5,125	219	−5,344
1979	3/21	202.50	4/23	206.40	2,438	4,906	−250
1980	3/21	218.80	4/23	226.10	4,563	4,563	−3,750
1981	3/20	227.90	4/22	218.95	−5,594	281	−7,594
1982	3/19	180.60	4/21	177.65	−1,844	1,000	−3,500
1983	3/21	147.55	4/21	154.15	4,125	5,469	−1,719
1984	3/21	143.50	4/23	142.00	−938	1,719	−938
1985	3/21	114.70	4/23	126.75	7,531	9,094	N/A
1986	3/21	148.65	4/23	151.70	1,906	2,313	−3,500
1987	3/20	158.65	4/22	162.10	2,156	2,750	−438
1988	3/21	182.30	4/21	189.35	4,406	5,094	−281
1989	3/21	170.60	4/21	170.68	50	825	−2,538
1990	3/21	156.56	4/23	162.00	3,400	4,238	−100
1991	3/21	177.20	4/23	168.72	−5,300	563	−6,125
1992	3/20	168.12	4/22	174.18	3,788	4,638	−500
1993	3/19	148.16	4/21	153.44	3,300	4,525	−1,313
1994	3/21	147.76	4/20	148.04	175	1,338	−1,263
1995	3/21	158.12	4/21	160.20	1,300	3,150	−283
1996	3/21	153.52	4/22	151.14	−1,488	63	−2,013
1997	3/21	159.90	4/23	163.02	1,950	3,413	−150
1998	3/20	165.76	4/22	167.00	775	2,013	−563
1999	3/19	162.52	4/21	160.56	−1,225	1,338	−2,638
2000	3/21	157.02	4/20	158.12	688	2,425	−513
2001	3/21	142.66	4/23	144.00	838	1,375	−875
2002	3/21	142.10	4/23	144.22	1,325	1,563	−388
2003	3/21	155.02	4/23	157.36	1,088	1,225	−1,075
2004	3/19	181.94	4/21	176.15	−3,619	1,850	−3,619
2005	3/21	189.16	4/21	190.32	725	1,500	−2,413
2006	3/21	175.15	4/21	178.13	1,863	2,700	−1,425
2007	3/21	195.77	4/20	200.28	2,819	3,050	−200
2008	3/24	196.65	4/23	197.80	719	2,363	−888
				34-Year Gain $20,981		**Up 24**	**Down 10**

YEAR	ENTRY DATE	ENTRY CLOSE	EXIT DATE	EXIT CLOSE	PROFIT/ LOSS	PROFIT AT HIGH	LOSS AT LOW
APRIL LONG CRUDE OIL – TRADING DAY: 7 – HOLD: 25 DAYS								
1983	4/12	30.50	5/17	29.85	–$650	$500	–$1,150
1984	4/10	30.50	5/16	31.70	1,200	1,200	–400
1985	4/10	28.72	5/15	26.92	–1,800	60	–2,310
1986	4/9	12.30	5/14	15.15	2,850	3,600	–1,020
1987	4/9	18.20	5/15	19.14	940	1,080	–750
1988	4/12	17.75	5/17	17.92	170	1,090	–640
1989	4/11	20.75	5/16	19.20	–1,550	850	–2,150
1990	4/10	18.90	5/16	19.62	720	850	–1,550
1991	4/9	20.35	5/14	21.05	700	1,760	–190
1992	4/9	20.52	5/15	20.62	100	680	–770
1993	4/12	20.17	5/17	19.45	–720	560	–780
1994	4/12	15.87	5/18	17.55	1,680	2,670	–230
1995	4/11	19.80	5/17	20.02	220	960	–770
1996	4/10	23.18	5/15	21.30	–1,880	2,520	–2,880
1997	4/9	19.60	5/14	20.93	1,330	1,950	–640
1998	4/9	15.65	5/15	15.75	100	650	–880
1999	4/12	16.48	5/17	17.75	1,270	2,570	–360
2000	4/11	24.15	5/17	29.40	5,250	6,100	–340
2001	4/10	28.00	5/16	29.50	1,500	1,500	–1,200
2002	4/9	26.25	5/14	28.80	2,550	2,550	–2,940
2003	4/9	27.95	5/15	29.10	1,150	2,700	–2,870
2004	4/12	37.35	5/17	41.35	4,000	4,210	–2,000
2005	4/11	52.60	5/16	48.00	–4,600	3,300	–4,850
2006	4/11	69.00	5/17	69.50	500	6,350	–1,050
2007	4/11	61.95	5/16	62.80	850	4,750	–1,200
2008	4/9	108.60	5/14	125.40	16,800	17,900	–120
				26-Year Gain $32,680		Up 20	Down 6
MAY SHORT COPPER – TRADING DAY: 8 – HOLD: 13 DAYS								
1973	5/10	66.65	5/30	71.40	–$1,188	$538	–$1,525
1974	5/10	129.50	5/30	111.00	4,625	6,625	–325
1975	5/12	55.70	5/30	54.30	350	350	–475
1976	5/12	71.20	6/1	70.30	225	975	–175
1977	5/11	66.50	5/31	60.00	1,625	1,750	–225
1978	5/10	59.30	5/30	65.60	–1,575	75	–1,775
1979	5/10	88.30	5/30	78.00	2,575	2,575	–38
1980	5/12	88.00	5/30	94.50	–1,625	50	–2,175
1981	5/12	81.90	6/1	81.65	63	750	–213
1982	5/12	73.75	6/1	63.50	2,563	2,563	N/A
1983	5/11	81.80	5/31	79.20	650	1,200	N/A
1984	5/10	63.25	5/30	64.75	–375	213	–563
1985	5/10	65.30	5/30	62.15	788	863	–175
1986	5/12	64.00	5/30	63.30	175	525	–13
1987	5/12	67.65	6/1	65.50	538	763	–225
1988	5/11	95.70	5/31	90.40	1,325	1,825	–375
1989	5/10	122.60	5/30	114.20	2,100	3,400	–575
1990	5/10	117.50	5/30	111.00	1,625	1,625	–438
1991	5/10	100.80	5/30	96.50	1,075	1,075	–500
1992	5/12	101.45	6/1	101.00	113	325	–38
1993	5/12	81.10	6/1	79.75	338	600	–750
1994	5/11	98.20	5/31	103.30	–1,275	300	–2,388
1995	5/10	123.60	5/30	131.10	–1,875	75	–2,163
1996	5/10	124.95	5/30	116.20	2,188	4,113	–388
1997	5/12	112.40	5/30	119.10	–1,675	100	–1,900
1998	5/12	79.10	6/1	76.95	538	1,400	–175
1999	5/12	71.75	6/1	62.80	2,238	2,663	–63
2000	5/10	83.90	5/30	82.80	275	325	–400
2001	5/10	76.75	5/30	76.80	–13	500	–938
2002	5/10	73.05	5/30	76.30	–813	200	–875
2003	5/12	73.65	5/30	77.25	–900	63	–1,138
2004	5/12	119.10	6/1	129.20	–2,525	1,350	–2,525
2005	5/11	144.40	5/31	142.80	400	2,850	–350
2006	5/10	364.50	5/30	380.00	–3,875	7,000	–9,875
2007	5/10	362.75	5/30	327.25	8,875	11,313	–63
2008	5/12	370.75	5/30	358.75	3,000	3,725	–3,675
				36-Year Gain $20,550		Up 24	Down 12

126

YEAR	ENTRY DATE	ENTRY CLOSE	EXIT DATE	EXIT CLOSE	PROFIT/ LOSS	PROFIT AT HIGH	LOSS AT LOW
		MAY SHORT CORN – TRADING DAY: 9 – HOLD: 46 DAYS					
1968	5/13	126 1/2	7/16	117 1/2	$450	$538	N/A
1969	5/13	128 3/4	7/17	125 3/4	150	363	−$138
1970	5/13	129	7/20	128 1/2	25	163	−450
1971	5/13	144 1/4	7/20	142	113	300	−938
1972	5/11	127	7/18	125 1/2	75	450	−50
1973	5/11	173 3/4	7/18	211	−1,863	138	−2,613
1974	5/13	263	7/18	305	−2,100	1,650	−2,250
1975	5/13	274 1/2	7/18	260 1/2	700	2,100	−875
1976	5/13	281 1/2	7/20	281	25	438	−1,650
1977	5/13	247	7/20	218	1,450	1,650	−225
1978	5/11	252 1/4	7/18	240 3/4	575	613	−963
1979	5/11	272	7/18	321	−2,450	563	−2,888
1980	5/13	278 3/4	7/18	332	−2,663	288	−3,125
1981	5/13	351	7/20	350	50	638	−1,300
1982	5/13	279 1/4	7/20	260 1/4	950	963	−213
1983	5/12	303 3/4	7/19	303	38	1,650	−338
1984	5/11	347 1/4	7/18	287 1/2	2,988	3,050	−488
1985	5/13	279	7/18	241	1,900	2,000	−25
1986	5/13	238	7/18	176	3,100	3,325	−263
1987	5/13	189 1/2	7/20	177	625	900	−1,325
1988	5/12	205 3/4	7/19	317 1/2	−5,588	75	−8,213
1989	5/11	274 1/4	7/18	238 3/4	1,775	1,775	−188
1990	5/11	290 3/4	7/18	259 1/2	1,563	1,638	−288
1991	5/13	244 3/4	7/18	238	338	1,238	−388
1992	5/13	260 1/2	7/20	231 1/2	1,450	1,450	−663
1993	5/13	233 1/2	7/20	250	−825	1,100	−1,375
1994	5/12	258 3/4	7/19	223	1,788	1,788	−1,350
1995	5/11	257 3/4	7/18	296	−1,913	238	−2,125
1996	5/13	492	7/18	350	7,100	7,975	−1,075
1997	5/13	281 3/4	7/18	253	1,438	2,713	−200
1998	5/13	246 3/4	7/20	235	588	800	−1,288
1999	5/13	224	7/20	203	1,050	1,488	−188
2000	5/11	245	7/10	181	3,200	3,338	−75
2001	5/11	198	7/18	216	−900	700	−1,875
2002	5/13	210	7/18	241	−1,550	300	−2,125
2003	5/13	252 1/4	7/18	211 1/2	2,038	2,050	−263
2004	5/13	295 3/4	7/21	239 1/4	2,825	2,825	−1,413
2005	5/12	205	7/19	267 1/2	−3,125	100	−3,400
2006	5/11	242 3/4	7/18	268 1/4	−1,275	738	−2,088
2007	5/11	359	7/18	335 1/2	1,175	1,375	−3,600
					40-Year Gain $15,288	Up 29	Down 11
		MAY SHORT SILVER – TRADING DAY: 10 – HOLD: 29 DAYS					
1972	5/12	162.5	6/23	161.5	$50	$275	−$150
1973	5/14	245.5	6/25	265.0	−975	525	1,800
1974	5/14	622.5	6/25	458.0	8,225	8,225	N/A
1975	5/14	470.0	6/25	460.0	500	1,700	−850
1976	5/14	450.5	6/25	487.0	−1,825	625	−2,575
1977	5/13	485.0	6/24	446.5	1,925	2,500	−25
1978	5/12	510.0	6/23	533.0	−1,150	150	−2,075
1979	5/14	845.0	6/25	880.0	−1,750	975	−2,750
1980	5/14	1315.0	6/25	1600.0	−14,250	11,250	−22,500
1981	5/14	1105.0	6/25	988.0	5,850	5,850	−1,100
1982	5/14	677.0	6/25	515.0	8,100	9,950	−750
1983	5/13	1310.0	6/24	1235.0	3,750	10,400	−3,900
1984	5/14	898.0	6/25	843.0	2,750	2,750	−3,200
1985	5/14	659.0	6/25	611.0	2,400	3,150	−950
1986	5/14	514.0	6/25	511.5	125	1,350	−1,725
1987	5/14	884.0	6/25	685.0	9,950	11,200	−3,900
1988	5/13	665.0	6/24	687.0	−1,100	500	−4,100
1989	5/12	573.5	6/23	533.0	2,025	3,075	−25
1990	5/14	510.0	6/25	485.0	1,260	1,676	1,225
1991	5/14	402.0	6/25	435.0	−1,650	125	−3,100
1992	5/14	411.5	6/25	402.0	475	625	−250
1993	5/14	445.0	6/25	441.0	200	1,450	−1,500
1994	5/13	545.0	6/24	542.0	150	1,175	−1,750
1995	5/12	541.0	6/23	535.0	300	1,450	−1,100
1996	5/14	538.0	6/25	515.5	1,125	2,100	−325
1997	5/14	487.5	6/25	475.5	600	1,250	−225
1998	5/14	555.0	6/25	527.0	1,400	3,125	−700
1999	5/14	550.5	6/25	513.5	1,850	3,275	−125
2000	5/12	505.0	6/23	497.0	400	700	−700
2001	5/14	434.0	6/25	430.5	175	300	−1,750
2002	5/14	460.5	6/25	483.5	−1,150	125	−2,725
2003	5/14	483.0	6/25	451.5	1,575	2,000	−300
2004	5/14	559.0	6/28	617.0	−2,900	150	−3,150
2005	5/13	692.5	6/24	729.0	−1,825	225	−3,525
2006	5/12	1488.0	6/23	1000.0	24,400	26,400	N/A
2007	5/14	1328.0	6/25	1301.0	1,350	2,575	−2,950
					36-Year Gain $52,325	Up 26	Down 10

YEAR	ENTRY DATE	ENTRY CLOSE	EXIT DATE	EXIT CLOSE	PROFIT/ LOSS	PROFIT AT HIGH	LOSS AT LOW
		MAY SHORT LEAN HOGS – TRADING DAY: 15 – HOLD: 60 DAYS					
1970	5/21	26.700	8/17	19.400	$2,920	$3,000	–$40
1971	5/21	21.350	8/17	18.950	960	1,040	–380
1972	5/19	27.225	8/15	27.150	30	560	–460
1973	5/21	39.000	8/15	54.050	–6,020	100	–7,400
1974	5/21	29.100	8/15	37.325	–3,290	2,030	–4,940
1975	5/21	48.900	8/15	48.850	20	660	–3,520
1976	5/21	48.800	8/17	39.250	3,820	4,900	–1,840
1977	5/20	47.550	8/17	35.500	4,820	5,580	–220
1978	5/19	55.025	8/15	45.150	3,950	4,970	–850
1979	5/21	44.950	8/15	35.200	3,900	5,380	–560
1980	5/21	35.250	8/15	45.250	–4,000	800	–4,180
1981	5/21	53.750	8/17	50.650	1,240	2,170	–1,590
1982	5/21	62.000	8/17	60.500	600	3,280	–500
1983	5/20	50.850	8/16	44.550	2,520	3,770	–20
1984	5/21	57.850	8/15	48.900	3,580	4,140	–740
1985	5/21	47.650	8/15	37.900	3,900	4,400	–1,720
1986	5/21	48.850	8/15	54.900	–2,420	900	–4,940
1987	5/21	56.400	8/17	48.700	3,080	3,780	–1,510
1988	5/20	53.500	8/15	40.750	5,100	5,970	–580
1989	5/19	48.000	8/15	40.150	3,140	3,560	–630
1990	5/21	66.825	8/15	49.650	6,870	7,280	–250
1991	5/21	56.800	8/15	42.800	5,600	5,900	–440
1992	5/21	46.950	8/17	40.250	2,680	3,700	–350
1993	5/21	53.400	8/17	45.350	3,220	3,600	–30
1994	5/20	49.400	8/16	40.000	3,760	3,760	–210
1995	5/19	43.800	8/15	43.350	180	680	–2,000
1996	5/21	66.200	8/15	55.150	4,420	5,270	–70
1997	5/21	80.950	8/15	73.000	3,180	3,720	–720
1998	5/21	61.650	8/17	44.300	6,940	7,580	–600
1999	5/21	56.500	8/18	43.950	5,020	5,530	–240
2000	5/19	70.200	8/15	54.300	6,360	6,360	–580
2001	5/21	68.200	8/15	61.250	2,780	3,840	–1,140
2002	5/21	49.175	8/15	36.600	5,030	5,030	–1,390
2003	5/21	65.900	8/15	52.100	5,520	6,060	–1,300
2004	5/21	74.550	8/18	64.600	3,980	4,070	–1,620
2005	5/20	72.850	8/16	60.500	4,940	6,660	–100
2006	5/19	67.250	8/15	64.550	1,080	3,540	–2,740
2007	5/21	74.550	8/15	69.200	2,140	2,140	–1,260
				38-Year Gain $101,550		Up 334	Down 4
		MAY SHORT COFFEE – TRADING DAY: 16 – HOLD: 54 DAYS					
1974	5/22	73.50	8/8	62.10	$4,275	$4,275	–$1,613
1975	5/22	53.70	8/8	83.30	–11,100	394	–13,144
1976	5/24	138.90	8/10	138.60	113	6,956	–7,313
1977	5/23	299.00	8/10	190.00	40,875	47,063	–4,688
1978	5/22	162.00	8/8	115.50	17,438	20,775	–9,188
1979	5/22	153.50	8/8	187.50	–12,750	1,969	–25,519
1980	5/22	200.00	8/8	152.50	17,813	26,063	–3,469
1981	5/22	116.50	8/10	113.50	1,125	12,281	–6,000
1982	5/24	126.90	8/10	120.50	2,400	2,719	–5,756
1983	5/23	132.30	8/9	126.30	2,250	3,056	–1,200
1984	5/22	154.75	8/8	140.40	5,381	6,244	–281
1985	5/22	145.70	8/9	135.10	3,975	5,419	–1,688
1986	5/22	215.25	8/11	171.25	16,500	22,594	–94
1987	5/22	123.10	8/10	105.50	6,600	8,850	–525
1988	5/23	133.40	8/9	118.50	5,588	9,525	–3,656
1989	5/22	134.00	8/8	83.00	19,125	20,813	–806
1990	5/22	97.00	8/8	91.90	1,913	4,688	–488
1991	5/22	87.10	8/9	81.30	2,175	2,813	–900
1992	5/22	62.25	8/10	55.35	2,588	2,794	–938
1993	5/24	65.50	8/10	77.10	–4,350	3,188	–5,475
1994	5/23	128.25	8/9	175.00	–17,531	4,594	–54,656
1995	5/22	166.30	8/9	145.50	7,800	17,363	–150
1996	5/22	123.50	8/9	115.70	2,925	8,250	–563
1997	5/22	254.00	8/8	206.00	18,000	36,750	–24,000
1998	5/22	133.50	8/11	133.00	188	10,688	–1,688
1999	5/24	117.00	8/11	94.50	8,438	9,975	–3,750
2000	5/22	97.95	8/9	83.00	5,606	5,831	–9,019
2001	5/22	65.50	8/8	50.00	5,813	6,000	–113
2002	5/22	51.80	8/9	47.90	1,463	1,988	–900
2003	5/22	65.75	8/8	64.50	469	2,944	–656
2004	5/24	72.50	8/11	67.25	1,969	2,813	–5,250
2005	5/23	116.80	8/9	102.50	5,363	7,744	–3,731
2006	5/22	100.30	8/8	106.50	–2,325	2,381	–3,225
2007	5/22	111.90	8/8	117.00	–1,913	1,200	–2,850
				34-Year Gain $158,194		Up 28	Down 6

YEAR	ENTRY DATE	ENTRY CLOSE	EXIT DATE	EXIT CLOSE	PROFIT/ LOSS	PROFIT AT HIGH	LOSS AT LOW
MAY SHORT BRITISH POUND – TRADING DAY: 20 – HOLD: 8 DAYS							
1975	5/29	228.00	6/10	227.50	$313	$313	–$938
1976	5/28	175.80	6/10	174.55	781	3,938	–188
1977	5/27	171.15	6/9	169.90	781	1,094	–344
1978	5/26	180.95	6/8	180.85	63	906	–1,906
1979	5/29	205.10	6/8	206.10	–625	63	–1,563
1980	5/29	233.70	6/10	228.40	3,313	5,594	–844
1981	5/29	207.50	6/10	198.20	5,813	8,594	–250
1982	5/28	179.15	6/10	178.40	469	719	–1,000
1983	5/27	160.25	6/9	158.00	1,406	3,344	–250
1984	5/29	138.20	6/8	140.25	–1,281	N/A	–1,625
1985	5/29	125.40	6/10	124.65	469	469	–2,875
1986	5/29	149.75	6/10	149.55	125	1,906	–844
1987	5/29	162.45	6/10	166.05	–2,250	250	–2,281
1988	5/27	185.65	6/9	180.90	2,969	4,069	–156
1989	5/26	160.40	6/8	157.34	1,913	3,250	–113
1990	5/29	168.64	6/8	168.26	238	1,463	–825
1991	5/29	173.96	6/10	164.74	5,763	5,763	–238
1992	5/29	181.86	6/10	180.18	1,050	1,050	–1,150
1993	5/28	155.64	6/10	150.18	3,413	3,738	–500
1994	5/27	150.84	6/9	150.60	150	425	–713
1995	5/26	160.74	6/8	159.08	1,038	1,650	–200
1996	5/29	151.66	6/10	153.26	–1,000	13	–2,525
1997	5/29	163.74	6/10	163.44	188	1,113	–338
1998	5/29	162.96	6/10	162.62	213	463	–1,150
1999	5/28	160.02	6/10	160.20	–113	175	–788
2000	5/26	147.28	6/8	152.00	–2,950	138	–3,688
2001	5/29	141.56	6/8	138.26	2,063	2,113	–713
2002	5/29	146.02	6/10	145.30	450	513	–475
2003	5/29	163.98	6/10	164.54	–350	1,113	–1,613
2004	5/28	183.31	6/10	180.88	1,519	1,519	–788
2005	5/27	182.54	6/9	181.65	556	1,044	–469
2006	5/26	186.76	6/8	184.39	1,481	1,481	–1,231
2007	5/29	198.67	6/8	196.63	1,275	1,275	–613
2008	5/29	197.54	6/10	193.71	2,394	2,394	–238
				34-Year Gain $31,631		Up 27	Down 7
JUNE SHORT SOYBEANS – TRADING DAY: 1 – HOLD: 90 DAYS							
1968	6/3	266	10/9	255	$550	$725	N/A
1969	6/2	267 1/2	10/9	239 3/4	1,388	1,713	N/A
1970	6/1	258	10/7	292	–1,700	13	–$2,200
1971	6/1	311 1/2	10/7	309	125	488	–1,538
1972	6/1	350 1/2	10/9	336 1/2	700	1,713	–463
1973	6/1	660	10/12	641	950	5,250	–13,450
1974	6/3	543	10/9	900	–17,850	650	–20,650
1975	6/2	499	10/8	550	–2,550	1,000	–7,675
1976	6/1	578	10/7	653	–3,750	250	–9,963
1977	6/1	957	10/7	548	20,450	23,000	–1,200
1978	0/1	738	10/9	665	3,550	7,525	–200
1979	6/1	738	10/9	706	1,600	2,700	–4,750
1980	6/2	624	10/8	828	–10,200	700	–12,800
1981	6/1	767 1/2	10/7	669	4,925	6,550	–1,525
1982	6/1	633	10/7	530	5,150	5,750	–850
1983	6/1	606	10/7	858	–12,600	875	–18,125
1984	6/1	850	10/9	594	12,800	14,075	–100
1985	6/3	566	10/9	509	2,850	3,313	–1,600
1986	6/2	526	10/8	469	2,850	3,038	–400
1987	6/1	553	10/7	536 1/2	825	3,063	–3,575
1988	6/1	815	10/7	809	300	3,050	–11,550
1989	6/1	711	10/9	566	7,250	7,450	–475
1990	6/1	608 1/2	10/9	633	–1,225	1,275	–3,600
1991	6/3	583	10/9	569 1/2	675	3,300	–3,350
1992	6/1	626	10/7	531 1/2	4,725	5,075	–550
1993	6/1	607	10/7	606 1/2	25	1,325	–7,525
1994	6/1	694	10/7	532	8,100	8,250	–650
1995	6/1	585	10/9	639	–2,700	200	–4,375
1996	6/3	741	10/9	737 1/2	175	1,138	–4,200
1997	6/2	880 1/2	10/8	661 1/2	10,950	15,175	–100
1998	6/1	614 1/2	10/7	531 1/2	4,150	5,300	–2,125
1999	6/1	453 1/2	10/8	506	–2,625	2,413	–3,400
2000	6/1	524 1/2	10/9	483	2,075	3,950	–500
2001	6/1	456	10/11	448 1/2	375	850	–4,100
2002	6/3	507	10/9	533 1/2	–1,325	1,000	–4,200
2003	6/2	622	10/8	685 1/2	–3,175	5,725	–3,950
2004	6/1	862	10/8	526 3/4	16,763	17,150	–1,700
2005	6/1	676 1/2	10/7	564 1/2	5,600	6,000	–4,675
2006	6/1	576	10/9	566 1/2	475	1,925	–3,175
2007	6/1	806 1/4	10/9	935	–6,438	88	–10,563
				40-Year Gain $54,213		Up 28	Down 12

	ENTRY			EXIT		PROFIT/	PROFIT	LOSS
YEAR	DATE	CLOSE	DATE	CLOSE		LOSS	AT HIGH	AT LOW
JUNE LONG COCOA – TRADING DAY: 2 – HOLD: 24 DAYS								
1973	6/4	1206	7/9	1558		$3,520	$3,630	–$410
1974	6/4	1337	7/9	1427		900	1,820	–360
1975	6/3	1009	7/8	1089		800	800	–1,030
1976	6/2	2050	7/7	2199		1,490	1,580	–1,610
1977	6/2	4123	7/7	4211		880	4,900	–600
1978	6/2	2954	7/7	3009		550	3,020	–1,020
1979	6/4	3358	7/9	3048		–3,100	1,430	–3,100
1980	6/3	2271	7/8	2324		530	2,630	–830
1981	6/2	1569	7/7	1825		2,560	2,560	–1,700
1982	6/2	1428	7/7	1501		730	1,220	–610
1983	6/2	2060	7/7	2131		710	2,900	–930
1984	6/4	2627	7/9	2171		–4,560	100	–4,560
1985	6/4	2062	7/10	2148		860	1,200	–990
1986	6/3	1743	7/9	1835		920	1,770	–520
1987	6/2	1880	7/7	2030		1,500	1,610	–360
1988	6/2	1588	7/7	1628		400	430	–910
1989	6/2	1152	7/7	1230		780	1,080	–190
1990	6/4	1317	7/9	1330		130	490	–1,430
1991	6/4	1010	7/10	893		–1,170	350	–1,170
1992	6/2	872	7/7	982		1,100	1,250	–720
1993	6/2	880	7/7	975		950	1,130	–340
1994	6/2	1398	7/7	1321		–770	280	–1,360
1995	6/2	1344	7/10	1243		–1,010	130	–1,010
1996	6/4	1339	7/10	1381		420	1,300	–20
1997	6/3	1445	7/8	1548		1,030	2,920	–370
1998	6/2	1623	7/7	1618		–50	450	–670
1999	6/2	887	7/7	970		830	2,930	–20
2000	6/2	855	7/10	842		–130	830	–490
2001	6/4	916	7/9	955		390	630	–450
2002	6/4	1577	7/10	1760		1,830	1,920	–1,490
2003	6/3	1501	7/8	1655		1,540	1,790	–450
2004	6/2	1415	7/8	1470		550	550	–1,170
2005	6/2	1408	7/7	1402		–60	1,860	–110
2006	6/2	1483	7/7	1710		2,270	2,370	–260
2007	6/4	1879	7/9	2128		2,490	2,620	–630
				35-Year Gain $19,810			Up 27	Down 8
JUNE LONG CBOT WHEAT – TRADING DAY: 6 – HOLD: 105 DAYS								
1968	6/10	146 1/2	11/7	136 3/4		–$488	$38	–$1,138
1969	6/9	129 1/2	11/6	135 1/4		288	438	–500
1970	6/8	141 1/2	11/5	178 3/4		1,863	1,863	–38
1971	6/8	159 3/4	11/4	160 1/4		25	688	–888
1972	6/8	143 1/4	11/6	223 1/2		4,013	4,463	–100
1973	6/8	268 1/2	11/7	450		9,075	13,725	–825
1974	6/10	369	11/7	515		7,300	8,350	–700
1975	6/9	296	11/5	379 3/4		4,188	8,550	–150
1976	6/8	375	11/5	274 1/2		–5,025	1,500	–5,313
1977	6/8	241	11/4	264 1/4		1,163	1,400	–900
1978	6/8	324 1/2	11/6	365 1/2		2,050	2,175	–1,175
1979	6/8	384 1/2	11/6	417 1/2		1,650	6,350	–25
1980	6/9	394	11/6	532		6,900	7,525	N/A
1981	6/8	410 1/2	11/4	439		1,425	1,700	–1,350
1982	6/8	346 1/2	11/5	330		–825	1,425	–2,363
1983	6/8	345	11/4	357 1/2		625	4,175	–200
1984	6/8	355	11/6	362		350	1,038	–575
1985	6/10	319 1/2	11/6	323 1/2		200	525	–2,000
1986	6/9	251	11/5	289 1/2		1,925	2,188	–600
1987	6/8	264 1/2	11/4	281 3/4		863	2,525	–575
1988	6/8	371	11/4	419		2,400	3,350	–350
1989	6/8	382	11/6	406 1/2		1,225	1,700	–88
1990	6/8	335 1/2	11/6	265		–3,525	225	–3,775
1991	6/10	297 1/2	11/6	360 1/2		3,150	3,588	–1,950
1992	6/8	367	11/4	358		–450	500	–2,725
1993	6/8	288	11/4	333		2,250	2,600	–550
1994	6/8	336 1/2	11/4	387 1/2		2,550	4,113	–900
1995	6/8	377	11/6	484		5,350	6,725	–450
1996	6/10	510	11/6	372		–6,900	700	–7,100
1997	6/9	358 1/2	11/5	359 1/2		50	1,975	–1,850
1998	6/8	279 1/2	11/4	284		225	1,225	–1,425
1999	6/8	257	11/5	259 1/2		125	2,250	–813
2000	6/8	265 1/2	11/6	266		25	1,100	–1,325
2001	6/8	264	11/7	286		1,100	1,650	–938
2002	6/10	274	11/6	397		6,150	8,300	–63
2003	6/9	319 1/2	11/5	362		2,125	3,975	–1,013
2004	6/8	361 1/2	11/5	301 1/2		–3,000	275	–3,225
2005	6/8	317	11/4	313 1/2		–175	1,950	–350
2006	6/8	385	11/6	500		5,750	8,600	–1,238
2007	6/8	520	11/6	796		13,800	22,088	–200
				40-Year Gain $69,788			Up 32	Down 8

JUNE SHORT CORN — TRADING DAY: 12 — HOLD: 31 DAYS

YEAR	ENTRY DATE	ENTRY CLOSE	EXIT DATE	EXIT CLOSE	PROFIT/ LOSS	PROFIT AT HIGH	LOSS AT LOW
1968	6/18	121 3/4	7/31	110	$588	$588	−$13
1969	6/17	121 3/4	8/1	117	238	313	−313
1970	6/16	132 1/2	7/30	126 3/4	288	350	−275
1971	6/16	158 3/4	7/30	130 1/4	1,425	1,500	−213
1972	6/16	121	8/1	126 1/2	−275	150	−350
1973	6/18	195 1/2	8/1	270	−3,725	525	−3,725
1974	6/18	251	8/1	365	−5,700	238	−6,288
1975	6/17	284	7/31	279	250	2,575	−400
1976	6/16	297	7/30	269	1,400	1,500	−550
1977	6/16	238 3/4	8/1	202 3/4	1,800	1,813	−63
1978	6/16	255 3/4	8/1	234 1/2	1,063	1,163	−400
1979	6/18	301	8/1	283	900	1,188	−1,438
1980	6/17	295 1/2	7/31	336	−2,025	188	−2,375
1981	6/16	364	7/30	346	900	1,213	−650
1982	6/16	275	7/30	254 1/4	1,038	1,325	−50
1983	6/16	275	8/1	325 1/2	−2,525	213	−2,850
1984	6/18	347 1/4	8/1	282 3/4	3,225	3,600	−413
1985	6/18	276 1/2	8/1	227 1/2	2,450	2,513	−63
1986	6/17	189 1/2	7/31	170 3/4	938	950	−200
1987	6/16	211	7/30	173	1,900	2,125	−250
1988	6/16	314 3/4	8/1	298 3/4	800	2,113	−2,763
1989	6/16	260 3/4	8/1	220 1/2	2,013	2,088	−863
1990	6/18	272 1/2	8/1	255	875	1,138	−1,200
1991	6/18	239	8/1	266	−1,350	950	−1,350
1992	6/16	256 1/2	7/30	227 1/2	1,450	1,613	−425
1993	6/16	212 1/2	7/30	244	−1,575	50	−2,425
1994	6/16	284	8/1	220 1/2	3,175	3,350	−88
1995	6/16	285	8/1	282 1/2	125	900	−763
1996	6/18	347	8/1	320	1,350	1,600	−2,100
1997	6/17	268 1/2	7/31	262 1/2	300	2,050	−138
1998	6/16	234	7/30	226	400	463	−1,925
1999	6/16	214 1/2	7/30	210 1/4	213	1,013	−663
2000	6/16	207 3/4	8/1	181	1,338	1,513	−100
2001	6/18	191 1/2	8/1	217	−1,275	375	−2,200
2002	6/18	208 1/4	8/1	262	−2,688	125	−2,688
2003	6/17	238 3/4	7/31	213 3/4	1,250	1,463	−400
2004	6/17	288 1/4	8/2	226 3/4	3,075	3,163	−13
2005	6/16	227 1/2	8/1	247	−975	225	−2,275
2006	6/16	235	8/1	255 1/2	−1,025	350	−2,475
2007	6/18	431	8/1	342 1/2	4,425	5,325	N/A
				40-Year Gain $16,050		**Up 29**	**Down 11**

JUNE LONG LIVE CATTLE — TRADING DAY: 14 — HOLD: 160 DAYS

YEAR	ENTRY DATE	ENTRY CLOSE	EXIT DATE	EXIT CLOSE	PROFIT/ LOSS	PROFIT AT HIGH	LOSS AT LOW
1970	6/18	31.100	2/5	32.350	$500	$800	−$1,790
1971	6/18	31.250	2/4	34.500	1,300	2,320	−370
1972	6/20	36.350	2/12	43.750	2,960	3,200	−1,460
1973	6/20	47.025	2/7	52.100	2,030	5,500	−3,050
1974	6/20	35.900	2/7	36.000	40	6,100	−640
1975	6/19	52.500	2/6	38.850	−5,460	N/A	−6,600
1976	6/18	44.000	2/7	38.850	−2,060	N/A	−4,400
1977	6/20	39.650	2/7	43.475	1,530	1,800	−1,000
1978	6/20	51.000	2/8	65.000	5,600	5,960	−1,480
1979	6/20	66.000	2/7	71.600	2,240	4,000	−4,340
1980	6/19	67.050	2/9	68.100	420	2,920	−1,080
1981	6/18	68.800	2/4	64.050	−1,900	220	−5,990
1982	6/18	62.600	2/7	62.700	40	1,280	−3,090
1983	6/20	61.650	2/7	66.950	2,120	4,060	−2,520
1984	6/20	63.600	2/6	68.500	1,960	2,160	−1,100
1985	6/20	60.700	2/6	60.700	0	2,800	−3,990
1986	6/19	53.800	2/5	62.800	3,600	4,110	−160
1987	6/18	63.350	2/4	71.000	3,060	3,160	−1,690
1988	6/20	63.550	2/6	76.750	5,280	5,340	−690
1989	6/20	70.600	2/6	77.050	2,580	3,800	−590
1990	6/20	74.825	2/6	77.325	1,000	1,980	−1,040
1991	6/20	72.100	2/6	77.550	2,180	2,300	−1,390
1992	6/18	70.750	2/4	78.500	3,100	4,160	−200
1993	6/18	74.500	2/3	75.175	270	880	−960
1994	6/20	64.850	2/6	73.450	3,440	4,160	−1,280
1995	6/20	61.650	2/6	64.650	1,200	3,040	−600
1996	6/20	64.950	2/6	65.450	200	3,430	−1,100
1997	6/19	64.150	2/6	65.550	560	2,920	−540
1998	6/18	65.450	2/5	67.200	700	780	−3,320
1999	6/18	64.000	2/9	71.900	3,160	3,560	−1,060
2000	6/20	67.050	2/7	78.675	4,650	5,610	−320
2001	6/20	73.800	2/8	75.975	870	1,060	−4,820
2002	6/20	63.850	2/7	77.700	5,540	7,260	−490
2003	6/19	67.400	2/6	72.300	1,960	12,760	−160
2004	6/21	86.950	2/8	88.800	740	2,320	−1,960
2005	6/20	79.600	2/7	89.850	4,100	7,120	−620
2006	6/20	83.700	2/8	95.750	4,820	5,000	−500
2007	6/20	91.000	2/7	95.050	1,620	4,040	−1,100
				38-Year Gain $65,950		**Up 34**	**Down 4**

YEAR	ENTRY DATE	ENTRY CLOSE	EXIT DATE	EXIT CLOSE	PROFIT/ LOSS	PROFIT AT HIGH	LOSS AT LOW
				JUNE LONG BRITISH POUND – TRADING DAY: 20 – HOLD: 16 DAYS			
1975	6/27	221.50	7/22	217.00	–$2,813	N/A	–$3,938
1976	6/28	174.00	7/21	176.45	1,531	$2,563	N/A
1977	6/28	170.95	7/22	171.10	94	125	–281
1978	6/28	184.25	7/21	190.50	3,906	3,906	–1,094
1979	6/28	214.80	7/23	228.30	8,438	9,063	–313
1980	6/27	231.60	7/22	235.75	2,594	2,625	–688
1981	6/26	196.20	7/21	185.55	–6,656	1,031	–6,656
1982	6/28	172.80	7/21	174.60	1,125	1,813	–844
1983	6/28	152.65	7/21	152.95	188	1,375	–781
1984	6/28	135.20	7/23	131.90	–2,063	938	–3,063
1985	6/28	128.15	7/23	140.50	7,719	8,344	–31
1986	6/27	150.95	7/22	148.55	–1,500	2,125	–2,625
1987	6/26	160.75	7/21	159.60	–719	1,594	–1,344
1988	6/28	171.66	7/21	171.88	138	275	–4,125
1989	6/28	154.64	7/21	161.78	4,463	5,350	–1,213
1990	6/28	171.30	7/23	180.02	5,450	5,825	–63
1991	6/28	160.40	7/23	166.20	3,625	4,900	–1,350
1992	6/26	186.52	7/21	187.66	713	4,363	–238
1993	6/28	147.98	7/21	151.08	1,938	2,388	–913
1994	6/28	154.36	7/21	154.76	250	2,050	–663
1995	6/28	158.04	7/21	159.14	688	1,413	–963
1996	6/28	154.72	7/23	155.20	300	1,138	–338
1997	6/27	166.34	7/22	167.40	663	2,038	–1,088
1998	6/26	165.90	7/21	164.22	–1,050	338	–2,313
1999	6/28	158.30	7/21	157.16	–713	213	–2,213
2000	6/28	150.76	7/21	151.48	450	988	–963
2001	6/28	140.64	7/23	141.94	813	1,638	–788
2002	6/28	152.70	7/23	156.14	2,150	3,125	–1,025
2003	6/27	164.48	7/22	159.58	–3,063	1,363	–4,238
2004	6/29	180.99	7/22	183.57	1,613	3,500	–1,088
2005	6/28	181.43	7/21	174.88	–4,094	38	–5,613
2006	6/28	182.42	7/21	186.03	2,256	2,256	–669
2007	6/28	200.14	7/23	205.70	3,475	3,475	–163
					33-Year Gain $31,906	Up 24	Down 9
				JULY LONG NATURAL GAS – TRADING DAY: 17 – HOLD: 62 DAYS			
1990	7/25	1.427	10/23	2.390	$9,630	$11,880	–$170
1991	7/24	1.200	10/21	2.175	9,750	9,950	–50
1992	7/24	1.705	10/21	2.405	7,000	9,250	
1993	7/26	2.090	10/21	2.265	1,750	3,850	–300
1994	7/26	1.855	10/21	1.805	–500	650	–3,700
1995	7/27	1.490	10/24	1.815	3,250	4,250	–1,000
1996	7/25	2.325	10/22	2.520	1,950	2,650	–5,900
1997	7/25	2.105	10/22	3.470	13,650	14,050	–250
1998	7/24	1.960	10/21	2.200	2,400	5,900	–3,300
1999	7/27	2.550	10/25	3.120	5,700	6,950	–1,400
2000	7/27	3.830	10/24	5.090	12,600	19,500	–600
2001	7/25	3.040	10/26	3.115	750	5,600	–10,100
2002	7/25	3.070	10/22	4.230	11,600	13,500	–4,300
2003	7/24	4.880	10/21	4.910	300	9,200	–4,900
2004	7/26	6.110	10/21	7.560	14,500	16,400	–15,900
2005	7/26	7.310	10/21	13.050	57,400	74,400	–100
2006	7/27	7.060	10/24	7.830	7,700	14,850	–24,600
2007	7/25	5.910	10/22	7.015	11,050	16,800	–5,700
					18-Year Gain $170,480	Up 17	Down 1
				JULY LONG GOLD – TRADING DAY: 18 – HOLD: 26 DAYS			
1975	7/25	172.5	9/2	152.8	–$1,970	$510	–$1,970
1976	7/27	116.0	9/1	104.3	–1,170	90	–1,600
1977	7/28	147.3	9/2	148.5	120	290	–330
1978	7/27	200.2	9/1	212.0	1,180	2,130	–90
1979	7/26	317.5	8/31	324.0	650	1,250	–2,950
1980	7/25	651.0	9/2	656.0	500	2,850	–3,100
1981	7/27	410.0	9/1	441.0	3,100	5,300	–1,200
1982	7/27	349.0	9/1	413.5	6,450	9,200	–1,470
1983	7/27	426.0	9/1	426.3	30	1,500	–1,600
1984	7/26	344.2	8/31	357.5	1,330	2,480	–1,220
1985	7/26	317.5	9/3	335.0	1,750	3,270	–90
1986	7/28	352.7	9/3	412.5	5,980	6,030	–120
1987	7/27	454.0	9/1	462.0	800	3,620	–190
1988	7/27	430.9	9/1	439.0	810	1,590	–110
1989	7/27	375.5	9/1	365.0	–1,050	700	–1,090
1990	7/26	371.0	8/31	394.4	2,340	5,400	–520
1991	7/26	364.4	9/3	351.2	–1,320	720	–1,440
1992	7/27	357.8	9/1	345.3	–1,250	420	–2,280
1993	7/27	393.1	9/1	374.4	–1,870	2,090	–2,610
1994	7/27	387.1	9/1	390.5	340	690	–690
1995	7/28	383.4	9/5	383.5	10	1,010	–180
1996	7/26	385.5	9/3	391.3	580	1,070	–150
1997	7/25	325.2	9/2	327.7	250	820	–420
1998	7/27	290.5	9/1	282.0	–850	330	–1,500
1999	7/28	254.8	9/2	255.7	90	970	–100
2000	7/28	278.7	9/5	280.8	210	630	–340
2001	7/26	267.1	8/31	277.6	1,050	1,670	–300
2002	7/26	307.3	9/3	315.0	770	1,240	–700
2003	7/25	360.7	9/2	375.0	1,430	1,830	–1,470
2004	7/27	392.2	9/1	411.5	1,930	2,460	–720
2005	7/27	422.5	9/1	440.0	1,750	3,090	–70
2006	7/28	627.0	9/5	640.0	1,300	4,120	–1,150
2007	7/26	671.0	8/31	682.4	1,140	1,700	–1,900
					33-Year Gain $26,410	Up 26	Down 7

132

YEAR	ENTRY DATE	ENTRY CLOSE	EXIT DATE	EXIT CLOSE	PROFIT/ LOSS	PROFIT AT HIGH	LOSS AT LOW
JULY SHORT COCOA – TRADING DAY: 18 – HOLD: 70 DAYS							
1973	7/26	1834	11/7	1166	$6,680	$7,090	N/A
1974	7/25	1598	11/4	1896	−2,980	880	−$3,840
1975	7/25	1386	11/5	1301	850	2,990	−180
1976	7/27	1962	11/5	2960	−9,980	1,220	−9,980
1977	7/28	4498	11/7	3439	10,590	10,970	−1,650
1978	7/27	3265	11/6	3803	−5,380	890	−7,920
1979	7/26	2883	11/2	2773	1,100	2,600	−4,130
1980	7/25	2298	11/3	2125	1,730	2,610	−1,020
1981	7/27	2030	11/3	1993	370	1,820	−2,450
1982	7/27	1410	11/4	1360	500	740	−2,440
1983	7/27	2371	11/3	1985	3,860	5,000	−900
1984	7/26	2196	11/2	2320	−1,240	2,360	−2,280
1985	7/26	2145	11/6	2127	180	830	−1,840
1986	7/28	1970	11/4	1882	880	990	−2,350
1987	7/27	2040	11/3	1861	1,790	2,550	N/A
1988	7/27	1488	11/3	1358	1,300	3,850	−460
1989	7/27	1287	11/3	978	3,090	3,340	−710
1990	7/26	1269	11/2	1170	990	1,580	−1,220
1991	7/26	968	11/4	1211	−2,430	N/A	−3,370
1992	7/27	1031	11/3	954	770	1,130	−1,060
1993	7/27	950	11/3	1099	−1,490	520	−2,710
1994	7/27	1447	11/3	1326	1,210	2,070	−780
1995	7/28	1255	11/6	1313	−580	220	−1,180
1996	7/26	1359	11/4	1332	270	590	−850
1997	7/25	1516	11/3	1595	−790	710	−2,440
1998	7/27	1588	11/3	1509	790	1,030	−470
1999	7/27	1050	11/4	856	1,940	2,200	−430
2000	7/28	841	11/6	750	910	940	−50
2001	7/26	941	11/8	1065	−1,240	560	−1,890
2002	7/26	1800	11/4	1795	50	1,050	−6,050
2003	7/25	1450	11/3	1430	200	900	−3,200
2004	7/27	1606	11/3	1462	1,440	2,160	−1,590
2005	7/27	1442	11/3	1373	690	1,140	−1,330
2006	7/27	1487	11/3	1495	−80	910	−1,280
2007	7/26	2060	11/2	1974	860	2,940	−80
				35-Year Gain $16,850		**Up 25**	**Down 10**
AUGUST SHORT BRITISH POUND – TRADING DAY: 1 – HOLD: 28 DAYS							
1975	8/1	213.70	9/11	208.70	$3,125	$3,250	−$63
1976	8/2	177.00	9/10	171.05	3,719	4,625	−656
1977	8/1	173.65	9/9	174.10	−281	250	−313
1978	8/1	192.50	9/11	191.50	625	813	−3,688
1979	8/1	225.10	9/11	223.35	1,094	3,625	−1,188
1980	8/1	231.50	9/11	239.00	−4,688	406	−4,969
1981	8/3	183.25	9/11	181.80	906	3,875	−4,813
1982	8/2	175.40	9/10	171.70	2,313	3,813	−1,625
1983	8/1	151.50	9/9	149.70	1,125	2,375	−1,438
1984	8/1	130.00	9/11	127.80	1,375	1,563	−2,250
1985	8/1	139.00	9/11	130.30	5,438	6,656	−1,188
1986	8/1	148.65	9/11	146.60	1,281	1,844	−1,250
1987	8/3	159.10	9/11	163.65	−2,844	2,063	−4,375
1988	8/1	171.10	9/9	169.94	725	3,025	−1,813
1989	8/1	164.72	9/11	152.06	7,913	7,913	−513
1990	8/1	183.88	9/11	180.62	2,038	2,038	−7,063
1991	8/1	167.38	9/11	170.78	−2,125	3,650	−2,813
1992	8/3	190.68	9/11	190.64	25	1,175	−6,088
1993	8/2	147.70	9/10	153.42	−3,575	1,563	−4,250
1994	8/1	154.18	9/9	154.04	88	1,013	−1,013
1995	8/1	159.52	9/11	154.76	2,975	4,113	−988
1996	8/1	155.64	9/11	155.50	88	1,438	−950
1997	8/1	163.30	9/11	158.24	3,163	4,000	−200
1998	8/3	161.04	9/11	100.00	−3,788	613	−4,350
1999	8/2	161.78	9/10	162.88	−688	2,075	−1,200
2000	8/1	150.18	9/11	141.78	5,250	5,250	−725
2001	8/1	142.98	9/11	145.04	−1,288	1,188	−2,100
2002	8/1	155.00	9/11	154.72	175	2,188	−1,400
2003	8/1	160.06	9/11	158.42	1,025	2,513	−925
2004	8/2	181.92	9/10	177.59	2,706	3,888	−1,488
2005	8/1	176.60	9/9	183.77	−4,481	613	−4,969
2006	8/1	186.88	9/11	186.75	81	344	−2,956
2007	8/1	202.55	9/11	202.71	−100	3,025	−1,188
				33-Year Gain $23,394		**Up 23**	**Down 10**

YEAR	ENTRY DATE	ENTRY CLOSE	EXIT DATE	EXIT CLOSE	PROFIT/ LOSS	PROFIT AT HIGH	LOSS AT LOW
AUGUST LONG SWISS FRANC – TRADING DAY: 6 – HOLD: 48 DAYS							
1975	8/8	37.40	10/16	38.10	$875	$1,100	-$1,100
1976	8/9	40.81	10/15	41.05	300	613	-388
1977	8/8	41.85	10/14	44.28	3,038	3,038	-1,075
1978	8/8	59.50	10/16	66.40	8,625	12,513	-275
1979	8/8	60.85	10/16	62.39	1,925	7,038	-675
1980	8/8	60.80	10/16	61.57	963	2,450	-1,438
1981	8/10	45.73	10/16	53.69	9,950	11,825	-88
1982	8/9	46.69	10/15	46.95	325	3,313	-775
1983	8/8	46.14	10/14	47.46	1,650	3,075	-625
1984	8/8	41.00	10/16	39.27	-2,163	1,925	-2,313
1985	8/8	42.74	10/16	45.67	3,663	5,675	-1,950
1986	8/8	59.96	10/16	62.16	2,750	3,400	-1,175
1987	8/10	63.77	10/16	67.53	4,700	5,725	-475
1988	8/8 ·	63.23	10/14	65.56	2,913	3,425	-1,350
1989	8/8	61.48	10/16	61.93	563	863	-4,463
1990	8/8	74.38	10/16	77.56	3,975	6,713	-425
1991	8/8	66.53	10/16	66.86	413	2,700	-3,263
1992	8/10	75.56	10/16	76.14	725	8,163	-1,200
1993	8/9	66.42	10/15	69.90	4,350	7,125	-1,850
1994	8/8	74.83	10/14	78.96	5,163	5,275	-750
1995	8/8	85.91	10/16	87.54	2,038	4,338	-6,188
1996	8/8	82.79	10/16	79.30	-4,363	1,763	-4,375
1997	8/8	65.98	10/17	68.55	3,213	5,288	-450
1998	8/10	67.10	10/19	76.47	11,713	14,025	-1,150
1999	8/9	67.18	10/19	68.55	1,713	2,575	-2,913
2000	8/8	58.80	10/17	56.49	-2,888	288	-3,688
2001	8/8	58.23	10/17	60.81	3,225	6,975	-50
2002	8/8	66.29	10/17	66.64	438	2,663	-925
2003	8/8	73.79	10/17	74.73	1,175	3,613	-4,550
2004	8/9	79.69	10/18	81.37	2,100	2,125	-2,288
2005	8/8	79.62	10/17	77.83	-2,238	2,388	-3,050
2006	8/8	81.95	10/17	79.25	-3,375	500	-3,950
2007	8/8	83.97	10/17	84.98	1,263	3,113	-2,250
				33-Year Gain $68,713		Up 28	Down 5
AUGUST LONG COFFEE – TRADING DAY: 12 – HOLD: 13 DAYS							
1974	8/16	60.75	9/5	58.50	-$844	$4,031	-$1,500
1975	8/18	85.40	9/5	81.60	-1,425	600	-2,025
1976	8/17	149.75	9/3	154.45	1,763	2,531	-2,063
1977	8/16	186.00	9/2	183.25	-1,031	4,500	-2,438
1978	8/16	125.25	9/5	155.50	11,344	11,344	-656
1979	8/16	194.60	9/5	208.00	5,025	5,119	-225
1980	8/18	154.75	9/5	133.00	-8,156	844	-9,281
1981	8/18	119.00	9/4	106.25	-4,781	113	-8,906
1982	8/17	123.75	9/3	126.00	844	1,481	-244
1983	8/16	129.00	9/2	129.90	338	1,275	-94
1984	8/16	141.90	9/5	145.70	1,425	2,963	-113
1985	8/16	137.10	9/5	136.25	-319	1,350	-319
1986	8/18	177.75	9/5	201.75	9,000	11,344	N/A
1987	8/18	107.75	9/4	116.20	3,169	4,294	-731
1988	8/16	118.70	9/2	122.40	1,388	3,788	N/A
1989	8/16	79.50	9/5	87.25	2,906	3,038	-488
1990	8/16	99.60	9/5	101.25	619	1,744	-1,256
1991	8/16	82.60	9/5	88.25	2,119	2,775	-450
1992	8/18	51.70	9/4	54.60	1,088	1,688	-150
1993	8/17	75.00	9/3	76.80	675	1,838	-656
1994	8/16	196.25	9/2	212.70	6,169	9,375	-5,719
1995	8/16	148.00	9/5	149.75	656	3,506	-1,594
1996	8/16	110.90	9/5	112.10	450	6,600	-225
1997	8/18	160.00	9/5	193.00	12,375	13,500	-2,063
1998	8/18	110.75	9/4	112.00	469	3,844	-938
1999	8/17	91.50	9/3	93.90	900	1,856	-1,219
2000	8/16	76.00	9/5	80.00	1,500	3,000	-150
2001	8/16	49.50	9/5	51.50	750	3,375	-188
2002	8/16	46.75	9/5	57.20	3,919	4,294	-244
2003	8/18	62.50	9/5	65.40	1,088	1,088	-169
2004	8/17	69.00	9/3	75.00	2,250	2,288	-263
2005	8/16	96.50	9/2	104.00	2,813	3,375	-600
2006	8/16	104.50	9/5	110.10	2,100	3,563	-244
2007	8/16	118.50	9/5	114.25	-1,594	150	-2,831
				34-Year Gain $58,988		Up 27	Down 7

YEAR	ENTRY		EXIT		PROFIT/ LOSS	PROFIT AT HIGH	LOSS AT LOW
	DATE	CLOSE	DATE	CLOSE			
AUGUST LONG COCOA – TRADING DAY: 14 – HOLD: 24 DAYS							
1973	8/20	1329	9/24	1396	$670	$670	-$2,020
1974	8/20	1673	9/24	1684	110	1,660	-1,060
1975	8/20	1185	9/24	1218	330	610	-980
1976	8/19	2183	9/23	2427	2,440	3,920	-760
1977	8/18	3814	9/22	4084	2,700	4,190	-1,980
1978	8/18	3379	9/22	3759	3,800	4,960	-2,030
1979	8/20	3071	9/24	3042	-290	1,210	-1,810
1980	8/20	2140	9/24	2318	1,780	2,600	-280
1981	8/20	2137	9/24	2140	30	1,380	-770
1982	8/19	1445	9/23	1540	950	2,090	-160
1983	8/18	2140	9/22	2174	340	490	-2,690
1984	8/20	2180	9/24	2385	2,050	2,050	-1,320
1985	8/20	2155	9/24	2318	1,630	1,740	-340
1986	8/20	1945	9/24	1993	480	2,600	-50
1987	8/20	1932	9/24	1933	10	830	-850
1988	8/18	1375	9/22	1237	-1,380	160	-2,100
1989	8/18	1195	9/22	1063	-1,320	70	-1,640
1990	8/20	1135	9/24	1299	1,640	2,560	N/A
1991	8/20	1020	9/24	1190	1,700	2,280	-130
1992	8/20	1091	9/24	973	-1,180	460	-1,340
1993	8/19	1038	9/23	1156	1,180	1,660	-260
1994	8/18	1448	9/22	1337	-1,110	230	-1,450
1995	8/18	1317	9/22	1319	20	560	-510
1996	8/20	1416	9/24	1357	-590	280	-870
1997	8/20	1555	9/24	1666	1,110	2,050	-20
1998	8/20	1583	9/24	1525	-580	520	-800
1999	8/19	960	9/23	970	100	320	-600
2000	8/18	800	9/22	815	150	400	-240
2001	8/20	1005	9/28	1077	720	720	-1,200
2002	8/20	1897	9/24	2110	2,130	2,410	-50
2003	8/20	1510	9/24	1582	720	2,600	-430
2004	8/19	1698	9/23	1527	-1,710	670	-2,560
2005	8/18	1390	9/22	1354	-360	1,850	-390
2006	8/18	1562	9/22	1528	-340	N/A	-1,470
2007	8/20	1792	9/24	1979	1,870	2,060	-260
				35-Year Gain $19,800		Up 25	Down 10
SEPTEMBER LONG SILVER – TRADING DAY: 1 – HOLD: 16 DAYS							
1972	9/1	193.0	9/26	171.0	-$1,300	$75	-$1,300
1973	9/4	270.0	9/26	289.0	950	950	-875
1974	9/3	422.5	9/25	431.0	425	425	-2,275
1975	9/2	450.0	9/24	453.0	150	1,225	-350
1976	9/1	417.0	9/24	441.5	1,225	1,600	-75
1977	9/1	453.5	9/26	465.5	600	725	-300
1978	9/1	561.5	9/26	577.5	800	900	-550
1979	9/4	1124.5	9/26	1540.0	20,775	26,275	-475
1980	9/2	1693.0	9/24	2393.0	35,000	36,250	-1,300
1981	0/1	950.0	9/24	997.0	2,350	11,500	-250
1982	9/1	794.0	9/24	912.0	5,900	10,150	-1,200
1983	9/1	1252.0	9/26	1232.0	-1,000	1,100	-3,600
1984	9/4	740.0	9/26	780.0	2,000	2,500	-1,375
1985	9/3	628.0	9/25	624.0	-200	200	-1,600
1986	9/2	527.5	9/24	600.0	3,625	4,225	-175
1987	9/1	760.0	9/24	780.0	1,000	3,200	-1,150
1988	9/1	668.5	9/26	623.0	-2,275	475	-2,275
1989	9/1	518.0	9/26	536.0	900	1,250	-350
1990	9/4	487.0	9/26	488.0	50	700	-425
1991	9/3	388.0	9/25	424.5	1,825	2,225	N/A
1992	9/1	377.0	9/24	382.0	250	750	-425
1993	9/1	488.0	9/24	416.5	-3,575	75	-4,800
1994	9/1	548.0	9/26	567.0	950	1,500	-350
1995	9/1	539.0	9/26	549.0	500	1,150	-950
1996	9/3	524.5	9/25	494.0	-1,525	25	-2,025
1997	9/2	471.5	9/24	473.0	75	675	-725
1998	9/1	472.5	9/24	507.0	1,725	2,125	N/A
1999	9/1	523.0	9/24	528.0	250	500	-625
2000	9/1	503.5	9/26	497.5	-300	75	-750
2001	9/4	419.0	9/28	461.5	2,125	2,850	-75
2002	9/3	450.0	9/25	465.0	750	1,100	-225
2003	9/2	513.0	9/24	525.0	600	1,250	-800
2004	9/1	679.0	9/24	646.5	-1,625	300	-3,600
2005	9/1	691.0	9/26	728.5	1,875	2,950	-100
2006	9/1	1299.0	9/26	1122.0	-8,850	1,900	-12,200
2007	9/4	1221.0	9/26	1358.0	6,850	7,800	-250
				36-Year Gain $73,075		Up 27	Down 9

YEAR	ENTRY DATE	ENTRY CLOSE	EXIT DATE	EXIT CLOSE	PROFIT/ LOSS	PROFIT AT HIGH	LOSS AT LOW
SEPTEMBER LONG SUGAR – TRADING DAY: 1 – HOLD: 62 DAYS							
1972	9/1	8.36	12/5	8.78	$470	$470	–$1,635
1973	9/4	8.45	12/5	10.20	1,960	2,677	–672
1974	9/3	36.00	12/4	47.20	12,544	33,600	–10,416
1975	9/2	16.70	12/4	12.80	–4,368	112	–4,760
1976	9/1	11.30	12/3	8.45	–3,192	34	–3,763
1977	9/1	9.12	12/5	9.33	235	291	–1,299
1978	9/1	8.23	12/5	8.34	123	1,848	–11
1979	9/4	10.90	11/30	16.60	6,384	6,384	–448
1980	9/2	33.05	12/1	33.50	504	14,224	–2,184
1981	9/1	12.14	11/30	13.10	1,075	1,635	–1,579
1982	9/1	6.62	12/1	8.24	1,814	1,915	–414
1983	9/1	11.75	12/1	9.41	–2,621	235	–3,282
1984	9/4	4.68	11/30	5.26	650	1,781	–448
1985	9/3	4.81	12/3	6.49	1,882	1,960	N/A
1986	9/2	5.22	12/1	6.71	1,669	2,330	–482
1987	9/1	5.69	12/1	7.96	2,542	2,722	–123
1988	9/1	10.25	12/1	11.14	997	1,221	–1,747
1989	9/1	13.26	12/1	14.19	1,042	2,374	–146
1990	9/4	10.45	12/3	9.95	–560	1,064	–1,534
1991	9/3	8.78	12/2	8.84	67	594	–739
1992	9/1	9.19	12/1	8.40	–885	571	–986
1993	9/1	9.07	12/1	10.40	1,490	2,195	–34
1994	9/1	12.06	12/1	14.56	2,800	3,573	–202
1995	9/1	10.95	12/1	11.00	56	146	–1,064
1996	9/3	11.75	12/2	10.63	–1,254	504	–1,725
1997	9/2	11.60	12/1	12.27	750	941	–381
1998	9/1	7.45	12/1	8.23	874	1,176	–952
1999	9/1	6.73	12/2	5.75	–1,098	672	–1,243
2000	9/1	10.65	12/1	9.73	–1,030	840	–2,218
2001	9/4	7.82	12/7	7.81	–11	280	–1,915
2002	9/3	6.00	12/2	7.50	1,680	1,982	–45
2003	9/2	6.20	12/1	6.29	101	314	–470
2004	9/1	8.15	12/1	8.80	728	1,366	–661
2005	9/1	10.02	12/1	12.50	2,778	2,867	–11
2006	9/1	11.75	12/1	12.50	840	1,680	–1,221
2007	9/4	9.46	12/3	9.73	302	1,165	–560
					36-Year Gain $31,338	**Up 27**	**Down 9**
SEPTEMBER LONG YEN – TRADING DAY: 1 – HOLD: 14 DAYS							
1976	9/1	34.62	9/22	34.83	$218	$230	–$45
1977	9/1	37.39	9/22	37.66	293	305	–58
1978	9/1	53.18	9/22	53.88	830	1,268	–870
1979	9/4	45.84	9/24	45.50	–470	493	–895
1980	9/2	46.45	9/22	46.83	430	1,243	–1,033
1981	9/1	43.51	9/22	45.05	1,880	2,818	–270
1982	9/1	38.68	9/22	38.45	–333	1,143	–895
1983	9/1	40.67	9/22	41.56	1,068	1,280	–283
1984	9/4	41.18	9/24	41.57	443	693	–595
1985	9/3	41.82	9/23	43.60	2,180	2,180	–1,195
1986	9/2	64.88	9/22	65.20	355	1,455	–1,120
1987	9/1	70.64	9/22	69.95	–908	1,155	–1,458
1988	9/1	73.30	9/22	74.97	2,043	3,168	–470
1989	9/1	69.02	9/22	69.27	268	1,493	–1,770
1990	9/4	69.51	9/24	73.77	5,280	5,280	–83
1991	9/3	73.22	9/23	74.64	1,730	1,818	–70
1992	9/1	81.38	9/22	82.35	1,168	1,168	–2,645
1993	9/1	94.87	9/22	94.45	–570	2,268	–2,033
1994	9/1	99.97	9/22	102.68	3,343	3,968	–158
1995	9/1	102.69	9/22	102.30	–533	2,093	–7,208
1996	9/3	91.58	9/23	92.12	630	1,843	–195
1997	9/2	82.36	9/22	82.54	180	4,255	–158
1998	9/1	72.97	9/22	74.49	1,855	6,118	–845
1999	9/1	91.60	9/22	97.20	6,955	7,705	–1,295
2000	9/1	94.19	9/22	94.20	–33	2,268	–145
2001	9/4	83.85	9/25	85.82	2,418	3,743	–1,758
2002	9/3	85.39	9/23	81.53	–4,870	268	–5,358
2003	9/2	85.53	9/22	89.46	4,868	4,868	–433
2004	9/1	91.46	9/22	90.81	–858	843	–1,395
2005	9/1	90.56	9/22	90.73	168	1,855	–520
2006	9/1	85.48	9/22	87.12	2,005	2,005	–270
2007	9/4	86.74	9/24	87.77	1,243	3,343	–695
					32-Year Gain $33,273	**Up 24**	**Down 8**
SEPTEMBER LONG EURO – TRADING DAY: 5 – HOLD: 16 DAYS							
1999	9/8	106.94	9/30	107.24	$375	$375	–$4,200
2000	9/8	87.34	10/2	88.39	1,313	2,638	–3,200
2001	9/10	90.20	10/3	91.92	2,150	3,525	–950
2002	9/9	97.56	10/1	98.30	925	1,400	–2,050
2003	9/8	110.42	9/30	116.31	7,363	7,363	–313
2004	9/8	120.26	9/30	124.10	4,800	4,800	–113
2005	9/8	124.24	9/30	120.94	–4,125	513	–4,950
2006	9/8	127.13	10/2	127.41	350	2,188	–688
2007	9/10	138.38	10/2	141.84	4,325	5,750	–200
					9-Year Gain $17,475	**Up 8**	**Down 1**

136

	ENTRY			EXIT		PROFIT/	PROFIT	LOSS
YEAR	DATE	CLOSE	DATE	CLOSE		LOSS	AT HIGH	AT LOW
SEPTEMBER SHORT CRUDE OIL – TRADING DAY: 8 – HOLD: 62 DAYS								
1983	9/13	30.87	12/12	29.03		$1,840	$2,370	–$670
1984	9/13	29.55	12/12	27.24		2,310	2,620	–300
1985	9/12	27.95	12/11	25.00		2,950	2,950	–3,220
1986	9/11	15.07	12/10	15.03		40	1,550	–860
1987	9/11	19.55	12/10	18.10		1,450	2,100	–970
1988	9/13	14.44	12/12	15.67		–1,230	2,310	–1,360
1989	9/13	19.74	12/11	20.65		–910	740	–930
1990	9/13	31.30	12/11	26.65		4,650	6,050	–9,850
1991	9/12	21.67	12/10	19.58		2,090	2,370	–2,360
1992	9/11	21.95	12/10	18.98		2,970	3,300	–470
1993	9/13	16.68	12/10	14.64		2,040	2,280	–2,410
1994	9/13	17.30	12/12	17.01		290	880	–1,890
1995	9/13	18.75	12/12	18.60		150	1,920	–390
1996	9/12	25.20	12/11	24.10		1,100	2,710	–600
1997	9/11	19.49	12/10	18.67		820	1,020	–3,660
1998	9/11	14.90	12/10	11.00		3,900	4,080	–1,460
1999	9/13	23.42	12/13	25.50		–2,080	2,870	–3,730
2000	9/13	34.00	12/12	29.60		4,400	6,150	–2,950
2001	9/19	27.39	12/18	19.50		7,890	10,270	–60
2002	9/12	29.83	12/11	27.68		2,150	5,020	–1,370
2003	9/11	29.46	12/10	32.10		–2,640	2,740	–3,390
2004	9/13	43.60	12/10	43.05		550	2,900	–12,050
2005	9/13	63.60	12/12	60.25		3,350	7,600	–4,500
2006	9/13	64.25	12/12	61.55		2,700	8,100	–950
2007	9/13	79.85	12/11	88.15		–8,300	1,450	–18,850
					25-Year Gain $32,480		**Up 20**	**Down 5**
SEPTEMBER SHORT COCOA – TRADING DAY: 10 – HOLD: 33 DAYS								
1972	9/15	710	11/6	702		$35	$385	–$405
1973	9/17	1301	11/5	1147		1,495	1,715	–1,135
1974	9/16	1609	11/1	1938		–3,335	375	–3,775
1975	9/15	1204	10/31	1356		–1,565	535	–1,815
1976	9/15	2513	11/3	2805		–2,965	1,605	–4,015
1977	9/15	4233	11/2	3465		7,635	8,275	–45
1978	9/15	3826	11/2	3792		295	2,705	–2,355
1979	9/17	3086	11/1	2822		2,595	4,585	–2,145
1980	9/15	2315	10/30	2070		2,405	2,735	–895
1981	9/15	2242	10/30	1950		2,875	3,895	–55
1982	9/15	1645	11/1	1370		2,705	3,005	–135
1983	9/15	2000	11/1	1970		255	755	–1,975
1984	9/17	2348	11/1	2292		515	2,085	–805
1985	9/16	2170	11/4	2199		–335	885	–1,635
1986	9/15	2175	10/30	1940		2,305	2,585	–95
1987	9/15	1920	10/30	1835		805	1,305	–495
1988	9/15	1222	11/1	1317		–995	1,145	–1,665
1989	9/15	1098	11/1	965		1,285	1,375	–115
1990	9/17	1312	11/1	1162		1,455	1,825	–285
1991	9/16	1192	10/31	1185		25	$445	–1,175
1992	9/15	1010	10/30	932		735	875	–435
1993	9/15	1153	11/1	1116		325	585	–725
1994	9/15	1346	11/1	1311		305	1,015	–465
1995	9/15	1295	11/1	1306		–155	455	–535
1996	9/16	1375	10/31	1363		75	295	–475
1997	9/15	1630	10/30	1605		205	515	–1,135
1998	9/15	1565	10/30	1512		485	755	–95
1999	9/15	974	11/2	868		1,015	1,115	–1,235
2000	9/15	816	11/1	752		595	595	–345
2001	9/21	1002	11/7	1011		–135	225	–1,325
2002	9/16	2013	10/31	1935		735	1,665	–3,965
2003	9/15	1500	10/30	1431		645	1,355	–2,125
2004	9/15	1486	11/1	1469		125	915	–615
2005	9/15	1411	11/1	1360		465	785	–375
2006	9/15	1482	11/1	1475		25	815	–575
2007	9/17	1836	11/1	1941		–1,095	215	–2,225
					36-Year Gain $21,840		**Up 28**	**Down 8**
SEPTEMBER LONG BRITISH POUND – TRADING DAY: 12 – HOLD: 33 DAYS								
1975	9/17	205.80	11/3	206.20		$250	$563	–$2,813
1976	9/17	169.50	11/4	160.60		–5,563	188	–10,375
1977	9/19	174.50	11/3	180.00		3,438	6,688	–375
1978	9/19	194.85	11/3	197.00		1,344	9,375	–438
1979	9/19	213.50	11/5	206.25		–4,531	4,313	–4,781
1980	9/17	237.25	11/3	244.00		4,219	4,625	–656
1981	9/17	186.10	11/3	187.15		656	3,500	–5,594
1982	9/17	171.50	11/4	166.85		–2,906	969	–2,906
1983	9/19	150.20	11/3	148.90		–813	1,156	–1,813
1984	9/19	123.95	11/5	126.45		1,563	1,563	–3,469
1985	9/18	132.25	11/4	143.80		7,219	7,500	–156
1986	9/17	146.10	11/3	140.60		–3,438	250	–4,656
1987	9/17	163.55	11/3	174.30		6,719	6,719	–1,875
1988	9/19	166.12	11/3	177.28		6,975	7,450	–975
1989	9/19	154.90	11/3	155.90		625	3,825	–1,800
1990	9/19	187.20	11/5	195.14		4,963	5,738	–3,563
1991	9/18	171.08	11/4	176.26		3,238	3,238	–2,113
1992	9/17	173.50	11/3	153.20		–12,688	1,750	–13,550
1993	9/17	151.62	11/3	147.60		–2,513	1,025	–3,200
1994	9/19	157.08	11/3	162.08		3,125	4,550	–625
1995	9/19	154.16	11/3	157.60		2,150	3,400	–50
1996	9/18	155.94	11/4	163.74		4,875	5,000	–775
1997	9/17	159.22	11/4	168.04		5,513	5,800	–25
1998	9/17	168.48	11/4	165.04		–2,150	2,425	–2,238
1999	9/17	161.90	11/5	162.68		488	3,800	–150
2000	9/19	140.58	11/6	144.66		2,550	4,763	–63
2001	9/20	145.80	11/7	146.14		213	1,125	–2,675
2002	9/18	153.20	11/5	155.96		1,725	2,238	–25
2003	9/17	159.24	11/4	167.14		4,938	6,750	–163
2004	9/17	178.35	11/4	184.25		3,688	3,844	–1,156
2005	9/19	180.14	11/4	176.19		–2,469	550	–3,756
2006	9/19	188.17	11/6	189.66		931	2,050	–1,800
2007	9/19	199.53	11/6	208.40		5,544	5,681	–281
					33-Year Gain $39,875		**Up 24**	**Down 9**

YEAR	ENTRY DATE	ENTRY CLOSE	EXIT DATE	EXIT CLOSE	PROFIT/ LOSS	PROFIT AT HIGH	LOSS AT LOW
OCTOBER SHORT GOLD – TRADING DAY: 2 – HOLD: 25 DAYS							
1975	10/2	145.0	11/10	144.5	$50	$650	–$410
1976	10/4	114.0	11/9	130.8	–1,680	110	–1,910
1977	10/4	157.3	11/8	164.6	–730	190	–1,120
1978	10/3	223.5	11/8	223.2	30	1,450	–2,590
1979	10/2	444.5	11/6	388.5	5,600	7,950	N/A
1980	10/2	689.0	11/7	593.0	9,600	9,600	–1,950
1981	10/2	445.0	11/6	430.5	1,450	1,850	–2,400
1982	10/4	400.0	11/9	411.0	–1,100	1,000	–6,500
1983	10/4	399.0	11/8	384.3	1,470	2,180	–980
1984	10/2	351.8	11/6	347.5	430	1,830	–400
1985	10/2	327.0	11/6	326.5	50	250	–870
1986	10/2	432.0	11/6	407.5	2,450	3,200	–1,450
1987	10/2	460.3	11/6	460.0	30	430	–3,570
1988	10/4	401.3	11/8	423.7	–2,240	250	–2,590
1989	10/3	371.3	11/7	388.0	–1,670	700	–1,670
1990	10/2	392.5	11/6	382.0	1,050	3,100	–1,090
1991	10/2	360.1	11/6	355.3	480	480	–730
1992	10/2	349.3	11/6	337.3	1,200	1,280	–410
1993	10/4	356.9	11/8	378.6	–2,170	690	–2,430
1994	10/4	395.5	11/8	384.5	1,100	1,240	–230
1995	10/3	384.9	11/7	383.8	110	230	–380
1996	10/2	381.7	11/6	379.2	250	390	–480
1997	10/2	334.5	11/6	313.0	2,150	2,620	–270
1998	10/2	303.1	11/6	294.9	820	1,440	–250
1999	10/4	315.0	11/9	292.0	2,300	2,700	–2,250
2000	10/3	275.7	11/7	267.5	820	1,220	–360
2001	10/2	293.0	11/6	279.7	1,330	1,720	–180
2002	10/2	321.6	11/6	317.2	440	1,250	–300
2003	10/2	385.2	11/6	382.4	280	1,870	–780
2004	10/4	417.5	11/8	432.8	–1,530	700	–1,750
2005	10/4	471.8	11/8	460.1	1,170	1,570	–1,040
2006	10/3	595.0	11/7	627.5	–3,250	3,150	–3,640
2007	10/2	737.0	11/6	820.8	–8,380	1,050	–8,380
				33-Year Gain $11,910		**Up 24**	**Down 9**
OCTOBER SHORT SILVER – TRADING DAY: 4 – HOLD: 17 DAYS							
1972	10/5	179.0	11/1	185.0	–$300	$125	–$450
1973	10/4	279.0	10/31	285.0	–300	225	–1,500
1974	10/4	494.0	10/30	508.5	–725	2,275	–1,775
1975	10/6	449.5	10/30	427.0	1,125	1,725	–175
1976	10/6	431.5	10/29	427.5	200	1,025	–25
1977	10/6	468.0	10/31	486.5	–925	25	–1,275
1978	10/5	588.0	10/30	628.0	–2,000	275	–2,000
1979	10/4	1691.0	10/29	1665.0	1,300	5,000	–6,100
1980	10/6	2085.0	10/29	1960.0	6,250	11,550	–7,150
1981	10/6	930.0	10/29	915.0	750	1,500	–3,750
1982	10/6	835.0	10/29	1004.0	–8,450	250	–11,750
1983	10/6	1047.0	10/31	875.0	8,600	8,950	–1,550
1984	10/4	772.0	10/29	728.0	2,200	3,000	–200
1985	10/4	643.0	10/29	624.0	950	1,400	–500
1986	10/6	577.0	10/29	561.5	775	1,500	–650
1987	10/6	774.0	10/29	717.0	2,850	5,200	–4,400
1988	10/6	640.0	10/31	635.0	250	875	–725
1989	10/5	534.0	10/30	531.0	150	1,300	–175
1990	10/4	476.0	10/29	405.5	3,525	3,525	–125
1991	10/4	419.0	10/29	406.5	625	800	–175
1992	10/6	376.5	10/29	375.0	75	350	–325
1993	10/6	414.0	10/29	440.0	–1,300	75	–2,300
1994	10/6	562.5	10/31	535.0	1,375	1,625	–475
1995	10/5	536.5	10/30	531.5	250	525	–725
1996	10/4	491.5	10/29	490.5	50	225	–900
1997	10/6	528.0	10/29	477.0	2,550	3,250	–200
1998	10/6	507.5	10/29	502.5	250	1,550	–675
1999	10/7	558.0	11/1	519.5	1,925	2,150	–450
2000	10/5	494.0	10/30	480.0	700	1,000	–225
2001	10/4	464.0	10/29	424.0	2,000	2,275	–450
2002	10/4	448.0	10/29	444.0	200	1,000	–75
2003	10/6	484.0	10/29	508.5	–1,225	475	–1,900
2004	10/6	721.0	10/29	718.0	150	2,000	–1,225
2005	10/6	749.0	10/31	783.0	–1,700	125	–2,325
2006	10/5	1103.0	10/30	1223.0	–6,000	800	–6,250
2007	10/4	1332.0	10/29	1448.0	–5,800	600	–5,800
				36-Year Gain $10,350		**Up 25**	**Down 11**

YEAR	ENTRY DATE	ENTRY CLOSE	EXIT DATE	EXIT CLOSE	PROFIT/ LOSS	PROFIT AT HIGH	LOSS AT LOW
		OCTOBER SHORT YEN – TRADING DAY: 12 – HOLD: 78 DAYS					
1976	10/18	34.08	2/8	34.84	–$995	$768	–$995
1977	10/18	39.88	2/8	41.54	–2,120	743	–3,620
1978	10/17	55.45	2/9	50.92	5,618	7,330	–2,420
1979	10/16	43.50	2/7	41.92	1,930	4,393	–608
1980	10/16	48.29	2/10	49.39	–1,420	2,580	–3,783
1981	10/16	43.80	2/8	43.14	780	1,268	–4,745
1982	10/18	37.53	2/9	42.40	–6,133	1,918	–8,608
1983	10/18	43.38	2/9	42.97	468	1,318	–483
1984	10/16	40.49	2/6	38.60	2,318	2,368	–1,833
1985	10/16	46.16	2/6	52.63	–8,133	55	–8,133
1986	10/16	65.02	2/6	64.85	168	5,318	–2,145
1987	10/16	70.70	2/8	77.70	–8,795	1,618	–15,670
1988	10/18	79.15	2/8	77.60	1,893	2,580	–4,708
1989	10/17	70.58	2/7	68.97	1,968	2,743	–1,183
1990	10/16	77.80	2/6	77.58	230	6,330	–3,370
1991	10/16	76.66	2/6	79.59	–3,708	1,568	–5,958
1992	10/16	82.95	2/8	80.40	3,143	4,705	–1,008
1993	10/18	93.35	2/7	91.99	1,655	6,118	–1,870
1994	10/18	102.71	2/8	101.46	1,518	4,268	–2,183
1995	10/17	100.34	2/7	94.82	6,855	8,230	–1,245
1996	10/16	89.88	2/7	80.88	11,205	11,205	–1,170
1997	10/17	83.82	2/11	81.01	3,468	10,555	–1,270
1998	10/19	88.15	2/10	87.10	1,268	9,018	–6,345
1999	10/20	94.90	2/11	91.60	4,080	4,080	–6,195
2000	10/18	93.43	2/9	85.52	9,843	10,655	–1,320
2001	10/16	82.55	2/8	74.54	9,968	10,330	–1,458
2002	10/17	80.68	2/11	82.39	–2,183	1,268	–5,895
2003	10/17	91.23	2/11	94.86	–4,583	1,755	–4,845
2004	10/19	92.42	2/10	94.16	–2,220	130	–7,583
2005	10/19	87.14	2/13	85.02	2,605	5,593	–2,120
2006	10/18	85.01	2/9	82.75	2,780	3,105	–3,158
2007	10/17	86.04	2/11	93.71	–9,633	–20	–11,770
				32-Year Gain $23,835		**Up 21**	**Down 11**
		OCTOBER LONG SOYBEANS – TRADING DAY: 16 – HOLD: 12 DAYS					
1968	10/22	255	11/8	259 1/4	$213	$213	–$13
1969	10/22	243 3/4	11/7	249 1/2	288	313	–100
1970	10/22	299	11/10	306 1/2	375	600	–13
1971	10/22	326 1/4	11/9	323	–163	63	–688
1972	10/23	340 1/2	11/9	357 1/2	850	1,050	–88
1973	10/23	541	11/8	545	200	1,700	–1,150
1974	10/22	855	11/8	858	150	650	–4,750
1975	10/22	507	11/7	504	–150	300	–1,600
1976	10/22	621 1/2	11/10	667	2,275	3,225	N/A
1977	10/24	518	11/9	599	4,050	4,700	N/A
1978	10/23	670	11/9	674	200	3,050	–100
1979	10/22	652	11/7	665	650	1,125	–1,350
1980	10/22	892	11/10	916	1,200	3,300	–450
1981	10/22	655	11/9	670	750	1,150	–675
1982	10/22	527 1/2	11/10	580	2,625	2,750	–200
1983	10/24	828	11/9	868	2,000	2,650	–900
1984	10/22	631 1/2	11/7	638	325	900	–1,050
1985	10/22	505	11/7	528	1,150	1,525	–375
1986	10/22	485	11/7	499	700	988	–75
1987	10/22	530	11/9	555	1,250	1,250	–125
1988	10/24	773 1/2	11/9	807	1,675	2,275	–1,125
1989	10/23	563	11/8	578	750	1,075	–325
1990	10/22	613	11/7	592 1/2	–1,025	175	–1,150
1991	10/22	547 1/2	11/7	560 1/2	650	1,363	–425
1992	10/22	541	11/9	553	600	888	–125
1993	10/22	623 1/2	11/9	638 1/2	750	1,463	–525
1994	10/24	545 1/2	11/9	569 1/2	1,200	1,250	–125
1995	10/23	674	11/8	688 1/2	725	1,175	–650
1996	10/22	680 1/2	11/7	686	275	1,325	–875
1997	10/22	698	11/7	724	1,300	1,650	–900
1998	10/22	550	11/9	570	1,000	1,125	–238
1999	10/25	472 1/2	11/10	473 1/2	50	825	–375
2000	10/23	468	11/8	486	900	1,150	–600
2001	10/22	424	11/7	437	650	950	–175
2002	10/22	548 1/2	11/7	574	1,275	1,550	–175
2003	10/22	740	11/7	758	900	3,275	–75
2004	10/22	527	11/9	505 1/2	–1,075	900	–1,200
2005	10/24	580	11/9	582	100	1,200	–350
2006	10/23	618 1/4	11/8	674	2,788	3,188	–88
2007	10/22	980	11/7	1047	3,350	3,375	N/A
				40-Year Gain $35,775		**Up 36**	**Down 4**

OCTOBER LONG CORN – TRADING DAY: 20 – HOLD: 133 DAYS

YEAR	ENTRY DATE	ENTRY CLOSE	EXIT DATE	EXIT CLOSE	PROFIT/ LOSS	PROFIT AT HIGH	LOSS AT LOW
1968	10/28	114	5/1	127 1/2	$675	$713	-$13
1969	10/28	117 3/4	5/12	129 1/4	575	600	-63
1970	10/28	150 1/4	5/11	143	-363	375	-450
1971	10/28	115 3/4	5/9	127	563	650	-75
1972	10/27	135 1/4	5/14	173	1,888	2,600	-100
1973	10/29	242	5/13	263	1,050	5,350	-650
1974	10/28	363	5/9	271	-4,600	1,325	-5,488
1975	10/28	275	5/10	279	200	450	-925
1976	10/28	257 1/2	5/12	242	-775	400	-1,350
1977	10/28	210	5/10	251	2,050	2,888	N/A
1978	10/27	236 1/2	5/11	272	1,775	2,013	-588
1979	10/26	263	5/12	278	750	1,650	-363
1980	10/28	371 1/2	5/12	355	-825	1,938	-1,125
1981	10/28	286 1/4	5/10	281 1/4	-250	463	-1,663
1982	10/28	217 3/4	5/11	313	4,763	5,188	-138
1983	10/28	347	5/10	347 1/4	13	763	-1,550
1984	10/26	277 3/4	5/8	278 1/4	25	413	-813
1985	10/28	220 1/4	5/8	234	688	1,588	-163
1986	10/28	178	5/8	190 1/4	613	700	-1,800
1987	10/28	182	5/9	210	1,400	1,625	-350
1988	10/28	272 1/2	5/10	275	125	1,013	-775
1989	10/27	243 3/4	5/9	288	2,213	2,500	-550
1990	10/26	229 1/4	5/8	252	1,138	1,788	-688
1991	10/28	249 1/2	5/11	259	475	1,513	-588
1992	10/28	205 1/2	5/10	228 1/2	1,150	1,700	-50
1993	10/28	254	5/11	256 1/2	125	2,888	-75
1994	10/28	217 1/2	5/10	258	2,025	2,125	-350
1995	10/27	328 3/4	5/8	463 1/2	6,738	7,763	-238
1996	10/28	276 1/2	5/8	285	425	2,175	-1,025
1997	10/28	284 1/2	5/11	250	-1,725	250	-2,038
1998	10/28	218	5/11	221 1/4	163	813	-700
1999	10/29	200	5/11	245	2,250	2,913	-650
2000	10/27	201 3/4	5/10	202 1/2	38	1,513	-275
2001	10/26	206 1/2	5/10	207 1/2	50	825	-663
2002	10/28	249 1/4	5/12	250	38	188	-1,100
2003	10/28	236	5/10	303 1/2	3,375	4,963	-350
2004	10/28	206 1/4	5/11	207	38	1,238	-600
2005	10/28	198	5/11	242 3/4	2,238	2,763	-375
2006	10/27	331 1/2	5/11	359	1,375	5,875	-575
2007	10/26	369 1/2	5/8	617	12,375	12,725	-125
				40-Year Gain $44,838		Up 34	Down 6

NOVEMBER LONG LEAN HOGS – TRADING DAY: 2 – HOLD: 13 DAYS

YEAR	ENTRY DATE	ENTRY CLOSE	EXIT DATE	EXIT CLOSE	PROFIT/ LOSS	PROFIT AT HIGH	LOSS AT LOW
1969	11/4	25.600	11/21	26.850	$500	$520	-$60
1970	11/4	16.500	11/23	16.750	100	220	-60
1971	11/2	21.300	11/19	21.950	260	540	-80
1972	11/2	29.475	11/22	29.950	190	250	-130
1973	11/2	44.550	11/21	49.300	1,900	2,180	-310
1974	11/4	42.500	11/22	43.200	280	1,140	-1,120
1975	11/4	51.975	11/21	54.250	910	1,450	-370
1976	11/3	30.700	11/22	33.550	1,140	1,480	-360
1977	11/2	39.700	11/21	41.100	560	560	-680
1978	11/2	49.400	11/22	53.350	1,580	1,580	-260
1979	11/2	37.600	11/21	45.800	3,280	3,280	-100
1980	11/5	50.700	11/24	55.850	2,060	2,480	-360
1981	11/3	46.700	11/20	47.800	440	760	-230
1982	11/3	53.750	11/22	56.000	900	1,860	-20
1983	11/2	43.500	11/21	46.300	1,120	1,160	-780
1984	11/2	48.800	11/21	52.550	1,500	1,660	-130
1985	11/4	46.750	11/21	47.475	290	400	-620
1986	11/4	51.900	11/21	54.350	980	1,360	-220
1987	11/3	41.600	11/20	44.050	980	1,300	-40
1988	11/2	41.550	11/21	40.200	-540	340	-690
1989	11/2	48.100	11/21	49.400	520	780	-560
1990	11/2	52.050	11/21	53.200	460	1,060	-80
1991	11/4	40.950	11/21	42.450	600	700	-230
1992	11/3	42.900	11/20	44.850	780	860	-140
1993	11/2	49.350	11/19	45.700	-1,460	N/A	-1,670
1994	11/2	34.000	11/21	32.650	-540	220	-800
1995	11/2	42.150	11/21	46.675	1,810	2,020	-100
1996	11/4	55.600	11/21	57.800	880	1,480	-60
1997	11/4	62.300	11/21	63.600	520	630	-660
1998	11/3	34.900	11/20	30.850	-1,620	920	-1,760
1999	11/2	44.900	11/19	50.800	2,360	2,830	-150
2000	11/2	51.200	11/21	53.600	960	1,400	N/A
2001	11/2	52.700	11/21	48.800	-1,560	180	-2,100
2002	11/4	43.350	11/21	46.100	1,100	1,480	-300
2003	11/4	52.600	11/21	54.350	700	1,760	-1,100
2004	11/2	69.700	11/19	73.550	1,540	2,340	-340
2005	11/2	61.400	11/21	66.250	1,940	2,400	-80
2006	11/2	63.800	11/21	66.650	1,140	1,140	-1,220
2007	11/2	52.800	11/21	62.400	3,840	4,120	-740
				39-Year Gain $32,400		Up 34	Down 5

YEAR	ENTRY DATE	ENTRY CLOSE	EXIT DATE	EXIT CLOSE	PROFIT/ LOSS	PROFIT AT HIGH	LOSS AT LOW
NOVEMBER LONG COCOA – TRADING DAY: 4 – HOLD: 34 DAYS							
1972	11/6	702	12/27	733	$310	$630	-$230
1973	11/7	1166	12/28	1249	830	1,130	-1,170
1974	11/7	2004	12/30	1479	-5,250	30	-5,930
1975	11/7	1235	12/31	1415	1,800	2,090	-660
1976	11/5	2960	12/28	3020	600	2,970	-1,950
1977	11/4	3472	12/28	3059	-4,130	1,880	-4,250
1978	11/6	3803	12/28	3834	310	3,690	-1,190
1979	11/6	2844	12/27	3147	3,030	3,620	-380
1980	11/7	1972	12/30	2090	1,180	2,180	-670
1981	11/5	1925	12/28	2000	750	1,600	-1,090
1982	11/5	1353	12/27	1608	2,550	2,680	-80
1983	11/4	2030	12/27	2620	5,900	6,090	-190
1984	11/6	2295	12/27	2051	-2,440	50	-2,610
1985	11/6	2127	12/27	2235	1,080	1,460	-100
1986	11/6	1906	12/30	1906	0	970	-690
1987	11/5	1830	12/28	1801	-290	1,000	-1,030
1988	11/4	1342	12/27	1525	1,830	1,940	-50
1989	11/6	973	12/27	920	-530	410	-770
1990	11/6	1137	12/28	1153	160	2,480	-10
1991	11/6	1225	12/27	1327	1,020	1,120	-390
1992	11/5	943	12/28	967	240	1,230	-200
1993	11/4	1089	12/27	1173	840	2,310	-200
1994	11/4	1317	12/27	1311	-60	300	-1,110
1995	11/6	1313	12/28	1259	-540	1,020	-590
1996	11/6	1320	12/30	1351	310	1,050	N/A
1997	11/6	1613	12/30	1620	70	1,530	-540
1998	11/5	1508	12/28	1390	-1,180	210	-1,400
1999	11/4	856	12/27	870	140	790	-560
2000	11/6	750	12/27	770	200	230	-430
2001	11/6	990	1/2	1310	3,200	3,750	50
2002	11/6	1777	12/30	2010	2,330	3,430	-1,220
2003	11/6	1475	12/30	1547	720	3,150	-600
2004	11/4	1520	12/27	1570	500	3,100	-20
2005	11/4	1360	12/27	1464	1,040	1,370	-410
2006	11/6	1485	12/27	1615	1,300	2,090	-140
2007	11/6	1929	12/28	2066	1,370	2,180	-630
				36-Year Gain $19,190		**Up 27**	**Down 9**
NOVEMBER LONG SILVER – TRADING DAY: 11 – HOLD: 13 DAYS							
1972	11/16	182.0	12/7	194.5	$625	$825	-$200
1973	11/16	280.5	12/7	313.5	1,650	1,650	-350
1974	11/19	437.5	12/9	429.0	-425	1,325	-1,700
1975	11/19	435.5	12/10	405.5	-1,500	25	-2,125
1976	11/16	437.0	12/7	441.5	225	425	-775
1977	11/15	482.0	12/6	484.5	125	250	-925
1978	11/16	567.0	12/8	598.0	1,550	2,075	N/A
1979	11/15	1602.0	12/5	1930.0	16,400	20,650	-600
1980	11/18	1870.0	12/8	1823.0	-2,350	6,250	-3,000
1981	11/16	835.0	12/4	902.0	3,350	3,350	-1,900
1982	11/16	957.0	12/6	1072.0	5,750	5,850	-3,100
1983	11/15	908.0	12/6	972.0	3,200	5,000	-3,800
1984	11/15	761.0	12/5	723.0	-1,900	350	-3,300
1985	11/15	615.0	12/5	619.0	200	850	-400
1986	11/17	568.0	12/5	546.0	-1,100	N/A	-2,400
1987	11/16	660.0	12/4	700.0	2,000	3,600	-550
1988	11/15	644.5	12/6	629.5	-750	275	-2,325
1989	11/15	539.5	12/5	564.5	1,250	2,475	-200
1990	11/15	417.0	12/5	425.0	400	475	-625
1991	11/15	399.0	12/5	407.5	425	925	-25
1992	11/16	374.5	12/4	378.5	200	275	-200
1993	11/15	451.5	12/6	487.0	1,775	1,875	-675
1994	11/15	521.5	12/6	469.0	-2,625	300	-3,125
1995	11/15	533.5	12/6	528.5	-250	175	-1,075
1996	11/15	483.5	12/6	491.0	375	675	-725
1997	11/17	510.5	12/8	543.0	1,625	1,950	-225
1998	11/16	503.0	12/7	477.0	-1,300	100	-1,750
1999	11/15	507.5	12/6	512.0	225	1,175	-100
2000	11/15	469.0	12/6	479.0	500	675	-450
2001	11/15	411.0	12/6	421.0	500	700	-475
2002	11/15	457.0	12/6	467.0	500	500	-775
2003	11/17	542.0	12/8	553.5	575	750	-1,400
2004	11/15	761.0	12/6	805.0	2,200	3,125	-650
2005	11/15	780.0	12/6	866.0	4,300	4,700	-500
2006	11/15	1272.0	12/6	1383.0	5,550	8,250	-1,100
2007	11/15	1485.0	12/5	1434.0	-2,550	100	-4,850
				36-Year Gain $40,725		**Up 26**	**Down 10**

YEAR	ENTRY DATE	ENTRY CLOSE	EXIT DATE	EXIT CLOSE	PROFIT/ LOSS	PROFIT AT HIGH	LOSS AT LOW
			NOVEMBER LONG GOLD – TRADING DAY: 13 – HOLD: 10 DAYS				
1975	11/21	141.8	12/8	138.2	–$360	N/A	–$530
1976	11/18	129.0	12/3	131.5	250	$620	–100
1977	11/17	159.0	12/2	159.8	80	390	–430
1978	11/20	198.5	12/6	198.8	30	500	–650
1979	11/19	393.0	12/4	441.0	4,800	5,150	–470
1980	11/20	634.0	12/5	635.0	100	2,300	–2,600
1981	11/18	406.0	12/3	425.0	1,900	2,350	–1,350
1982	11/18	408.0	12/3	450.0	4,200	4,840	–300
1983	11/17	377.5	12/5	406.0	2,850	3,150	–450
1984	11/19	344.3	12/4	335.8	–850	40	–1,910
1985	11/19	325.2	12/4	329.0	380	820	–240
1986	11/19	393.8	12/4	395.0	120	970	–1,730
1987	11/18	464.6	12/3	494.3	2,970	3,500	–130
1988	11/17	425.0	12/5	435.8	1,080	1,300	–900
1989	11/17	394.0	12/4	415.0	2,100	2,750	–180
1990	11/19	378.2	12/4	380.3	210	1,200	–190
1991	11/19	361.3	12/4	369.0	770	1,110	N/A
1992	11/18	335.1	12/3	336.8	170	260	–230
1993	11/17	373.5	12/3	374.0	50	690	–550
1994	11/17	386.9	12/5	379.7	–720	80	–810
1995	11/17	387.1	12/5	387.6	50	340	–560
1996	11/19	379.1	12/5	370.5	–860	130	–1,140
1997	11/19	306.6	12/5	289.4	–1,720	160	–1,840
1998	11/18	296.2	12/4	294.2	–200	290	–520
1999	11/17	296.8	12/3	283.5	–1,330	360	–1,330
2000	11/17	267.2	12/5	273.4	620	780	–160
2001	11/19	274.0	12/5	275.9	190	470	–210
2002	11/19	320.4	12/5	322.5	210	410	–490
2003	11/19	396.7	12/5	402.9	620	930	–720
2004	11/17	443.5	12/3	452.5	900	1,420	–330
2005	11/17	483.0	12/5	510.0	2,700	2,700	–250
2006	11/17	616.5	12/5	650.0	3,350	3,930	–200
2007	11/19	787.8	12/4	800.8	1,300	4,420	–1,180
					33-Year Gain $25,960	**Up 26**	**Down 7**
			NOVEMBER SHORT CBOT WHEAT – TRADING DAY: 17 – HOLD: 118 DAYS				
1968	11/26	133 3/4	5/19	132 3/4	50	$425	–$150
1969	11/25	142 1/4	5/19	137 3/4	225	375	–425
1970	11/25	170 1/4	5/17	150	1,013	1,075	–200
1971	11/23	154 1/4	5/12	144 1/4	500	588	–738
1972	11/27	239 3/4	5/18	251 1/2	–588	1,563	–1,688
1973	11/26	467	5/17	363	5,200	6,850	–8,450
1974	11/26	491	5/16	309	9,100	9,225	–1,125
1975	11/25	374	5/17	358	800	2,300	–1,500
1976	11/24	273	5/17	253	1,000	1,238	–1,525
1977	11/23	281 1/2	5/15	314 3/4	–1,663	950	–2,775
1978	11/28	361 1/2	5/17	361	25	2,100	–800
1979	11/26	456	5/19	417	1,950	3,575	–1,325
1980	11/26	536	5/19	418	5,900	6,300	–325
1981	11/24	439 1/2	5/14	359	4,025	4,725	–275
1982	11/24	361 1/2	5/16	352 1/2	450	2,150	–825
1983	11/23	347	5/15	341	300	1,375	–1,025
1984	11/26	359	5/15	320 3/4	1,913	2,013	–38
1985	11/25	331	5/15	283	2,400	4,500	–850
1986	11/25	281	5/15	304	–1,150	1,300	–1,775
1987	11/24	312 1/2	5/13	309 1/2	150	850	–1,325
1988	11/23	419	5/15	412	350	1,950	–1,500
1989	11/24	410 1/2	5/15	344 3/4	3,288	3,925	–300
1990	11/26	264 1/2	5/15	292 1/2	–1,400	1,000	–1,950
1991	11/25	368 1/2	5/18	351 1/2	850	1,025	–4,738
1992	11/24	375	5/14	293 3/4	4,063	4,225	–900
1993	11/23	352 1/2	5/16	321 1/2	1,550	2,063	–2,100
1994	11/23	379 3/4	5/15	365	738	2,113	–1,500
1995	11/24	497	5/14	582	–4,250	2,925	–6,950
1996	11/25	393	5/15	385 1/2	375	2,150	–3,300
1997	11/25	354 3/4	5/18	303 1/2	2,563	2,763	–513
1998	11/24	276	5/17	261 1/2	725	1,900	–1,550
1999	11/23	241	5/15	280 1/2	–1,975	225	–2,250
2000	11/24	259	5/16	277	–900	250	–1,775
2001	11/26	286 1/2	5/17	275 1/2	550	1,100	–1,338
2002	11/25	372	5/19	336	1,800	4,725	–675
2003	11/25	386 1/2	5/17	361	1,275	1,488	–1,875
2004	11/23	312 1/2	5/16	305	375	1,275	–2,825
2005	11/23	314 1/2	5/16	398	–4,175	375	–4,825
2006	11/24	506 1/2	5/17	491	775	4,725	–1,175
2007	11/26	862	5/15	761	5,050	5,050	–24,375
					40-Year Gain $43,225	**Up 32**	**Down 8**

YEAR	ENTRY DATE	ENTRY CLOSE	EXIT DATE	EXIT CLOSE	PROFIT/ LOSS	PROFIT AT HIGH	LOSS AT LOW
NOVEMBER SHORT SUGAR – TRADING DAY: 17 – HOLD: 50 DAYS							
1972	11/27	7.56	2/13	9.00	−$1,613	$101	−$3,293
1973	11/27	9.30	2/8	17.35	−9,016	78	−10,696
1974	11/27	56.00	2/13	36.80	21,504	25,760	−840
1975	11/28*	13.30	2/5	13.10	179	907	−1,535
1976	11/26	8.65	2/8	8.85	−224	1,366	−806
1977	11/28	9.06	2/10	9.00	67	202	−605
1978	11/28	8.42	2/8	8.28	157	571	−694
1979	11/26	15.85	2/7	22.60	−7,560	1,120	−9,688
1980	11/26	36.20	2/11	27.85	9,352	13,104	−280
1981	11/24	11.95	2/8	13.48	−1,714	22	−2,408
1982	11/24	7.63	2/7	6.56	1,198	1,770	−784
1983	11/23	9.62	2/7	7.20	2,710	2,710	−414
1984	11/26	5.10	2/7	4.08	1,142	1,221	−381
1985	11/25	6.25	2/7	5.84	459	1,434	−347
1986	11/25	6.56	2/11	7.82	−1,411	885	−1,971
1987	11/24	7.64	2/8	8.55	−1,019	11	−3,573
1988	11/23	10.64	2/7	10.30	381	1,546	−1,523
1989	11/27	15.13	2/7	14.45	762	2,632	−134
1990	11/27	9.94	2/11	8.52	1,590	1,646	−101
1991	11/25	8.63	2/7	8.17	515	750	−717
1992	11/24	8.35	2/8	8.03	358	437	−381
1993	11/23	10.21	2/7	11.06	−952	123	−1,042
1994	11/23	14.45	2/7	13.85	672	941	−1,546
1995	11/27	10.96	2/12	11.88	−1,030	291	−1,725
1996	11/25	10.63	2/10	10.56	78	594	−549
1997	11/25	12.16	2/12	10.97	1,333	1,736	−437
1998	11/24	8.12	2/9	6.78	1,501	1,725	−784
1999	11/23	6.00	2/8	5.68	358	896	−314
2000	11/27	10.15	2/8	9.87	314	1,086	−381
2001	11/27	7.55	2/13	6.18	1,534	1,848	−560
2002	11/25	7.47	2/11	9.03	−1,747	358	−1,747
2003	11/25	6.11	2/12	5.35	851	862	−762
2004	11/23	8.88	2/8	8.90	−22	493	−504
2005	11/23	12.05	2/8	18.10	−6,776	34	−8,624
2006	11/27	11.90	2/9	10.32	1,770	2,139	−750
2007	11/27	9.74	2/11	12.71	−3,326	123	−3,752
					36-Year Gain $12,376	Up 23	Down 13

* 16th trading day selected

YEAR	ENTRY DATE	ENTRY CLOSE	EXIT DATE	EXIT CLOSE	PROFIT/ LOSS	PROFIT AT HIGH	LOSS AT LOW
NOVEMBER LONG SWISS FRANC – TRADING DAY: 18 – HOLD: 24 DAYS							
1975	11/26	37.47	1/5	38.70	$1,538	$1,538	−$163
1976	11/26	41.02	1/3	41.25	288	450	−63
1977	11/25	46.40	12/30	50.60	5,250	5,250	−13
1978	11/29	59.66	1/4	61.90	2,800	5,250	−538
1979	11/27	62.40	1/3	64.87	3,088	4,500	−288
1980	11/28	57.75	1/6	58.55	1,000	1,850	−1,725
1981	11/25	56.35	12/31	56.20	−188	800	−2,863
1982	11/26	46.20	1/3	50.45	5,313	5,838	−38
1983	11/28	46.08	1/3	46.00	−100	825	−475
1984	11/27	39.72	1/2	38.40	−1,650	663	−1,650
1985	11/26	47.56	1/2	49.08	1,900	2,150	−388
1986	11/26	60.56	1/2	62.53	2,463	2,463	−2,200
1987	11/25	73.03	12/31	79.20	7,713	7,713	−213
1988	11/25	69.51	12/30	67.20	−2,888	488	−3,888
1989	11/27	62.50	1/2	64.23	2,163	3,600	−463
1990	11/27	79.08	1/2	79.00	−100	1,013	−4,650
1991	11/26	70.51	1/2	73.25	3,425	4,288	−1,475
1992	11/25	69.84	12/31	67.95	−2,363	2,475	−3,050
1993	11/24	66.98	12/30	67.58	750	3,388	−888
1994	11/25	75.90	12/30	76.60	875	2,000	−1,675
1995	11/27	87.26	1/2	87.69	538	1,238	−2,925
1996	11/26	77.45	1/2	74.79	−3,325	538	−3,738
1997	11/20	70.09	1/5	68.42	2,338	060	2,338
1998	11/25	71.43	12/31	72.89	1,825	6,013	−825
1999	11/26	63.20	12/31	63.24	50	2,225	−675
2000	11/27	55.57	1/2	62.34	8,463	8,463	N/A
2001	11/28	60.55	1/3	60.84	363	1,163	−2,063
2002	11/27	67.26	1/3	71.55	5,363	6,550	−625
2003	11/28	77.50	1/5	81.32	4,775	4,775	−800
2004	11/26	87.40	12/31	88.71	1,638	1,888	−1,525
2005	11/28	75.01	1/3	76.92	1,263	3,775	−275
2006	11/27	82.93	1/2	83.01	100	1,650	−963
2007	11/28	89.68	1/3	90.12	550	688	−3,600
					33-Year Gain $50,538	Up 25	Down 8

	ENTRY		EXIT		PROFIT/	PROFIT	LOSS
YEAR	DATE	CLOSE	DATE	CLOSE	LOSS	AT HIGH	AT LOW

DECEMBER LONG COPPER – TRADING DAY: 10 – HOLD 47 DAYS

YEAR	DATE	CLOSE	DATE	CLOSE	PROFIT/LOSS	PROFIT AT HIGH	LOSS AT LOW
1972	12/14	48.95	2/27	61.60	$3,163	$3,163	-$188
1973	12/13	78.50	2/26	114.90	9,100	9,100	-50
1974	12/13	56.80	2/24	59.20	600	600	-1,375
1975	12/12	54.30	2/23	59.50	1,300	1,300	-250
1976	12/14	59.20	2/22	66.40	1,800	2,125	-25
1977	12/14	60.00	2/24	56.40	-800	450	-975
1978	12/14	69.30	2/22	91.70	5,600	5,800	-125
1979	12/14	98.50	2/25	121.00	5,625	12,475	-225
1980	12/12	81.30	2/23	84.00	675	2,600	-575
1981	12/14	73.70	2/22	74.00	75	838	-663
1982	12/14	68.25	2/22	79.00	2,688	2,938	-588
1983	12/14	65.35	2/22	65.45	25	438	-1,025
1984	12/14	58.10	2/25	59.90	450	1,463	-650
1985	12/13	64.15	2/21	64.35	50	813	-425
1986	12/12	60.45	2/23	63.30	713	788	-100
1987	12/14	112.50	2/23	90.10	-5,600	3,825	-6,250
1988	12/14	132.50	2/22	135.50	750	4,850	-2,550
1989	12/14	105.00	2/22	114.90	2,475	2,525	-2,500
1990	12/14	107.80	2/25	110.70	725	2,575	-1,375
1991	12/13	96.90	2/21	101.60	1,175	1,525	-800
1992	12/14	99.20	2/22	98.60	-150	2,200	-475
1993	12/14	79.65	2/22	86.70	1,763	2,913	-388
1994	12/14	132.30	2/22	133.20	225	2,650	-1,200
1995	12/14	124.40	2/23	115.40	-2,250	825	-3,288
1996	12/13	99.70	2/21	112.70	3,250	3,250	-975
1997	12/12	82.40	2/23	72.80	-2,400	275	-2,400
1998	12/14	66.70	2/23	61.60	-1,275	725	-1,388
1999	12/14	80.15	2/24	84.40	1,063	2,088	-63
2000	12/14	88.35	2/23	80.30	-2,013	275	-2,163
2001	12/14	67.40	2/26	70.90	875	2,000	-438
2002	12/13	74.35	2/24	78.05	925	1,288	-1,238
2003	12/12	98.35	2/25	134.80	9,113	9,238	-125
2004	12/14	135.70	2/25	148.20	3,125	3,700	-838
2005	12/13	202.30	2/23	223.50	5,300	7,800	-1,563
2006	12/14	308.00	2/26	284.00	-6,000	425	-17,375
2007	12/14	294.80	2/25	376.00	20,300	22,325	-1,925
				36-Year Gain $62,338		**Up 28**	**Down 8**

DECEMBER SHORT BRITISH POUND – TRADING DAY: 19 – HOLD: 56 DAYS

YEAR	DATE	CLOSE	DATE	CLOSE	PROFIT/LOSS	PROFIT AT HIGH	LOSS AT LOW
1975	12/29	200.05	3/18	189.90	$6,344	$7,594	-$1,563
1976	12/28	166.40	3/18	169.15	-1,719	406	-3,500
1977	12/28	190.50	3/20	190.40	63	1,594	-4,500
1978	12/28	203.65	3/20	202.80	531	4,250	-500
1979	12/31	221.30	3/20	220.10	750	1,719	-6,188
1980	12/29	238.50	3/19	228.00	6,563	13,156	-3,906
1981	12/28	188.50	3/18	181.75	4,219	5,313	-3,063
1982	12/28	160.90	3/18	148.50	7,750	7,813	-1,375
1983	12/28	143.85	3/18	144.70	-531	2,906	-3,688
1984	12/28	116.30	3/20	113.30	1,875	8,031	-63
1985	12/27	142.05	3/19	146.30	-2,656	3,781	-4,531
1986	12/26	144.90	3/19	159.30	-9,000	500	-9,000
1987	12/28	185.15	3/17	184.20	594	7,719	-2,063
1988	12/28	177.54	3/20	170.32	4,513	4,775	-2,663
1989	12/28	159.88	3/20	159.48	250	1,788	-6,938
1990	12/28	188.60	3/20	174.06	9,088	10,188	-6,488
1991	12/27	185.28	3/18	170.40	9,300	11,038	-438
1992	12/28	150.90	3/18	145.90	3,125	6,125	-2,750
1993	12/28	149.98	3/17	149.28	438	2,975	-575
1994	12/28	154.76	3/20	158.22	-2,163	325	-6,438
1995	12/28	155.20	3/19	152.74	1,538	3,563	-325
1996	12/27	168.04	3/20	159.46	5,363	6,100	-2,025
1997	12/26	166.26	3/19	165.90	225	3,650	-713
1998	12/28	167.00	3/19	162.52	2,800	4,750	-788
1999	12/28	161.68	3/17	157.40	2,675	2,963	-2,563
2000	12/28	149.10	3/21	142.46	4,025	4,500	-1,188
2001	12/28	144.02	3/21	142.10	1,200	1,450	-600
2002	12/27	159.12	3/20	155.52	2,250	2,700	-3,563
2003	12/26	176.29	3/19	181.94	-3,531	188	-8,838
2004	12/28	192.92	3/18	190.62	1,438	5,113	-75
2005	12/28	173.40	3/21	175.15	-1,094	1,250	-3,500
2006	12/28	196.42	3/21	195.77	406	2,813	-1,619
2007	12/28	199.33	3/20	196.63	1,688	3,706	-1,856
				33-Year Gain $58,313		**Up 26**	**Down 7**

DECEMBER SHORT SWISS FRANC – TRADING DAY: 19 – HOLD: 41 DAYS

YEAR	DATE	CLOSE	DATE	CLOSE	PROFIT/LOSS	PROFIT AT HIGH	LOSS AT LOW
1975	12/29	38.30	2/26	39.50	-$1,500	$25	-$1,713
1976	12/28	41.17	2/25	39.56	2,013	2,113	-138
1977	12/28	49.89	2/27	55.39	-6,875	475	-9,125
1978	12/28	63.33	2/27	62.12	1,513	5,463	-663
1979	12/31	64.00	2/28	62.00	2,500	3,088	-1,450
1980	12/29	58.00	2/26	61.77	7,788	10,200	-813
1981	12/28	55.85	2/25	53.41	3,050	4,325	-1,125
1982	12/28	50.79	2/25	49.28	1,888	2,513	-2,513
1983	12/28	46.35	2/27	46.10	313	2,063	-375
1984	12/28	39.04	2/27	35.49	4,438	6,200	-38
1985	12/27	48.29	2/26	53.00	-5,888	625	-6,413
1986	12/26	61.10	2/25	65.05	-4,938	88	-8,038
1987	12/28	77.90	2/25	71.70	7,750	9,500	-2,063
1988	12/28	66.64	2/27	64.74	2,375	5,050	-1,363
1989	12/28	65.31	2/27	67.11	-2,250	2,938	-3,425
1990	12/28	77.15	2/27	76.04	1,388	1,388	-4,913
1991	12/27	73.44	2/26	66.30	8,925	9,075	-675
1992	12/28	68.58	2/25	65.86	3,400	5,013	-838
1993	12/28	69.14	2/24	68.80	425	2,913	-463
1994	12/28	75.44	2/27	81.00	-6,950	163	-6,950
1995	12/28	87.33	2/27	84.85	3,100	6,588	-538
1996	12/27	74.61	2/27	67.77	8,550	9,238	-1,013
1997	12/26	70.35	2/26	68.13	2,775	4,113	-188
1998	12/28	73.25	2/26	69.46	4,738	5,625	-2,500
1999	12/28	63.39	2/25	61.08	2,888	3,738	-2,325
2000	12/28	61.23	2/28	60.02	1,513	2,863	-2,263
2001	12/28	59.42	2/28	58.63	988	1,675	-2,163
2002	12/27	71.37	2/27	73.91	-3,175	375	-3,888
2003	12/26	80.31	2/26	79.10	1,513	1,850	-2,538
2004	12/28	88.62	2/25	85.43	3,988	8,650	-363
2005	12/28	77.02	2/28	75.97	1,313	1,625	-3,688
2006	12/28	82.62	2/28	82.01	763	3,400	-563
2007	12/28	88.82	2/28	94.39	-6,963	575	-6,963
				33-Year Gain $41,350		**Up 25**	**Down 8**

CRUDE OIL CYCLE, SEASONAL PATTERN & TRADING GUIDE

Crude oil is one of the most actively traded commodities in the futures industry. The contract for light sweet crude oil is traded at the New York Mercantile Exchange. However, it migrated its products for trade execution to the CME Groups Globex® platform for electronic trading in January 2008. One futures contract is 1,000 barrels (42,000 gallons) and every dollar move represents a $1,000 change in value per contract position. The contract symbol is CL, it has a tradable contract for each month of the year.

This commodity is now traded both electronically and through the open outcry session; the pit-traded hours are from 9:00 AM until 1:30 PM (CT). The daily price limits are $10.00 per barrel ($10,000 per contract) for all months. If any contract is traded, bid, or offered at the limit for five minutes, trading is halted for five minutes. When trading resumes, the limit is expanded by $10.00 per barrel in either direction. If another halt were triggered, the market would continue to be expanded by $10.00 per barrel in either direction after each successive five-minute trading halt. There will be no maximum price fluctuation limits during any one trading session.

Crude oil has shown strong seasonal bottoms in December and has a strong tendency to peak in September. One explanation for this is that refiners are building inventories ahead of the summer driving season and there is still a demand for heating oil as well as the competition for diesel and jet fuels. As the summer driving season ends, refiners focus more on increasing inventories for heating oil and there is less demand for gasoline so we have seen price weakness through the end of December. One of the many aspects that have resulted in the unprecedented price increase in crude oil is the insatiable demand from China, India, and other developing nations. In addition, it is valued in terms of the U.S. dollar, so when we have periods when the dollar is weak, this has helped support the value of crude oil prices, as has occurred through late 2007 into mid-2008.

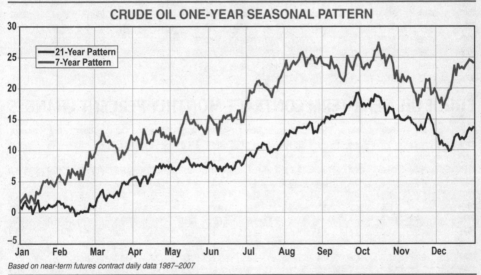

CRUDE OIL ONE-YEAR SEASONAL PATTERN

- 21-Year Pattern
- 7-Year Pattern

Based on near-term futures contract daily data 1987–2007

CRUDE OIL NEAR-TERM CONTRACT ANNUAL HIGHS, LOWS & CLOSES SINCE 1984

YEAR	HIGH DATE	HIGH CLOSE	LOW DATE	LOW CLOSE	YEAR CLOSE	YEAR	HIGH DATE	HIGH CLOSE	LOW DATE	LOW CLOSE	YEAR CLOSE
1984	05/16	31.22	12/20	26.33	26.41	1997	01/08	26.62	12/30	17.60	17.64
1985	11/25	31.01	12/17	25.09	26.30	1998	01/29	17.82	12/10	10.72	12.05
1986	01/06	26.57	03/31	10.42	17.94	1999	11/22	27.07	02/16	11.48	25.60
1987	08/03	22.16	12/18	15.40	16.70	2000	10/12	35.72	04/11	23.39	26.80
1988	04/26	18.60	10/05	12.60	17.24	2001	02/08	31.59	11/15	17.84	19.84
1989	12/26	21.91	02/14	16.81	21.82	2002	12/27	32.72	01/17	18.63	31.20
1990	10/09	40.40	07/06	16.47	28.44	2003	03/07	37.78	04/29	25.24	32.52
1991	01/16	30.29	02/22	17.91	19.12	2004	10/22	55.17	02/06	32.48	43.45
1992	06/24	22.89	01/09	17.86	19.50	2005	08/30	69.81	01/03	42.12	61.04
1993	03/04	21.07	12/28	14.11	14.17	2006	07/14	78.71	11/02	57.88	61.05
1994	08/01	20.55	03/28	14.08	17.76	2007	11/23	98.18	01/18	51.81	95.98
1995	05/01	20.50	07/20	16.77	19.55	2008*	05/21	133.17	01/23	86.99	*AT PRESS-TIME*
1996	12/31	25.92	01/29	17.45	25.92						

*Through May 30, 2008

CRUDE OIL NEAR-TERM CONTRACT MONTHLY CLOSING PRICES

	Jan	Feb	Mar	Apr	May	Jun	Jul	Aug	Sep	Oct	Nov	Dec
1984	29.98	30.55	30.85	30.26	30.83	29.75	27.60	29.23	29.66	28.46	27.31	26.41
1985	26.41	26.73	28.29	27.63	27.84	26.87	27.12	28.08	29.08	30.38	29.75	26.30
1986	18.83	13.26	10.42	13.34	14.30	12.78	11.15	15.90	14.77	15.27	15.00	17.94
1987	18.75	16.60	18.83	18.73	19.38	20.29	21.37	19.73	19.59	19.96	18.51	16.70
1988	16.94	16.01	17.08	17.99	17.51	15.16	16.31	15.18	13.37	13.58	15.32	17.24
1989	17.03	18.15	20.19	20.42	19.90	20.27	18.31	18.83	20.13	19.94	19.89	21.82
1990	22.68	21.54	20.28	18.54	17.40	17.07	20.69	27.32	39.51	35.23	28.85	28.44
1991	21.54	19.16	19.63	20.96	21.13	20.56	21.68	22.26	22.23	23.37	21.48	19.12
1992	18.90	18.68	19.44	20.85	22.11	21.60	21.87	21.48	21.71	20.62	19.89	19.50
1993	20.26	20.60	20.44	20.53	20.02	18.85	17.88	18.29	18.79	16.92	15.43	14.17
1994	15.19	14.48	14.79	16.90	18.31	19.37	20.30	17.56	18.39	18.19	18.05	17.76
1995	18.39	18.49	19.17	20.38	18.89	17.40	17.56	17.84	17.54	17.64	18.18	19.55
1996	17.74	19.54	21.47	21.20	19.76	20.92	20.42	22.25	24.38	23.35	23.75	25.92
1997	24.15	20.30	20.41	20.21	20.88	19.80	20.14	19.61	21.18	21.08	19.15	17.64
1998	17.21	15.44	15.61	15.39	15.20	14.18	14.21	13.34	16.14	14.42	11.22	12.05
1999	12.75	12.27	16.76	18.66	16.84	19.29	20.53	22.11	24.51	21.75	24.59	25.60
2000	27.64	30.43	26.90	25.74	29.01	32.50	27.43	33.12	30.84	32.70	33.82	26.80
2001	28.66	27.39	26.29	28.46	28.37	26.25	26.35	27.20	23.43	21.18	19.44	19.84
2002	19.48	21.74	26.31	27.29	25.31	26.86	27.02	28.98	30.45	27.22	26.89	31.20
2003	33.51	36.60	31.04	25.80	29.56	30.19	30.54	31.57	29.20	29.11	30.41	32.52
2004	33.05	36.16	35.76	37.38	39.88	37.05	43.80	42.12	49.64	51.76	49.13	43.45
2005	48.20	51.75	55.40	49.72	51.97	56.50	60.57	68.94	66.24	59.76	57.32	61.04
2006	67.92	61.41	66.63	71.88	71.29	73.93	74.40	70.26	62.91	58.73	63.13	61.05
2007	58.14	61.79	65.87	65.71	64.01	70.68	78.21	74.04	81.66	94.53	88.71	95.98
2008	91.75	101.84	101.58	113.46	127.35							

CRUDE OIL NEAR-TERM CONTRACT MONTHLY PERCENT CHANGES

	Jan	Feb	Mar	Apr	May	Jun	Jul	Aug	Sep	Oct	Nov	Dec	Year's Change
1984	1.3	1.9	1.0	−1.9	1.9	−3.5	−7.2	5.9	1.5	−4.0	−4.0	−3.3	−10.8
1985	N/C	1.2	5.8	−2.3	0.8	−3.5	0.9	3.5	3.6	4.5	−2.1	−11.6	−0.4
1986	−28.4	−29.6	−21.4	28.0	7.2	−10.6	−12.8	42.6	−7.1	3.4	−1.8	19.6	−31.8
1987	4.5	−11.5	13.4	−0.5	3.5	4.7	5.3	−7.7	−0.7	1.9	−7.3	−9.8	−6.9
1988	1.4	−5.5	6.7	5.3	−2.7	−13.4	7.6	−6.9	−11.9	1.6	12.8	12.5	3.2
1989	−1.2	6.6	11.2	1.1	−2.5	1.9	−9.7	2.8	6.9	−0.9	−0.3	9.7	26.6
1990	3.9	−5.0	−5.8	−8.6	−6.1	−1.9	21.2	32.0	44.6	−10.8	−18.1	−1.4	30.3
1991	−24.3	−11.0	2.5	6.8	0.8	−2.7	5.4	2.7	−0.1	5.1	−8.1	−11.0	−32.8
1992	−1.2	−1.2	4.1	7.3	6.0	−2.3	1.3	−1.8	1.1	−5.0	−3.5	−2.0	2.0
1993	3.9	1.7	−0.8	0.4	−2.5	−5.8	−5.1	2.3	2.7	−10.0	−8.8	−8.2	−27.3
1994	7.2	−4.7	2.1	14.3	8.3	5.8	4.8	−13.5	4.7	−1.1	−0.8	−1.6	25.3
1995	3.5	0.5	3.7	6.3	−7.3	−7.9	0.9	1.6	−1.7	0.6	3.1	7.5	10.1
1996	−9.3	10.1	9.9	−1.3	−6.8	5.9	−2.4	9.0	9.6	−4.2	1.7	9.1	32.6
1997	−6.8	−15.9	0.5	−1.0	3.3	−5.2	1.7	−2.6	8.0	−0.5	−9.2	−7.9	−31.9
1998	−2.4	−10.3	1.1	−1.4	−1.2	−6.7	0.2	−6.1	21.0	−10.7	−22.2	7.4	−31.7
1999	5.8	−3.8	36.6	11.3	−9.8	14.5	6.4	7.7	10.9	−11.3	13.1	4.1	112.4
2000	8.0	10.1	−11.6	−4.3	12.7	12.0	−15.6	20.7	−6.9	6.0	3.4	−20.8	4.7
2001	6.9	−4.4	−4.0	8.3	−0.3	−7.5	0.4	3.2	−13.9	−9.6	−8.2	2.1	−26.0
2002	−1.8	11.6	21.0	3.7	−7.3	6.1	0.6	7.3	5.1	−10.6	−1.2	16.0	57.3
2003	7.4	9.2	−15.2	−16.9	14.6	2.1	1.2	3.4	−7.5	−0.3	4.5	6.9	4.2
2004	1.6	9.4	−1.1	4.5	6.7	−7.1	18.2	−3.8	17.9	4.3	−5.1	−11.6	33.6
2005	10.9	7.4	7.1	−10.3	4.5	8.7	7.2	13.8	−3.9	−9.8	−4.1	6.5	40.5
2006	11.3	−9.6	8.5	7.9	−0.8	3.7	0.6	−5.6	−10.5	−6.6	7.5	−3.3	0.02
2007	−4.8	6.3	6.6	−0.2	−2.6	10.4	10.7	−5.3	10.3	15.8	−6.2	8.2	57.2
2008	−4.4	11.0	−0.3	11.7	12.2								
TOTALS	−7.0	−25.5	81.6	68.2	32.6	−2.3	41.8	105.2	83.7	−52.2	−64.9	17.1	
AVG.	−0.3	−1.0	3.3	2.7	1.3	−0.1	1.7	4.4	3.5	−2.2	−2.7	0.7	
# Up	14	13	17	14	13	11	18	15	14	9	7	12	
# Down	10	12	8	11	12	13	6	9	10	15	17	12	

NATURAL GAS CYCLE, SEASONAL PATTERN & TRADING GUIDE

Natural gas is traded at the New York Mercantile Exchange. However, it migrated its products for trade execution to the CME Groups Globex® platform for electronic trading in January 2008. One futures contract is 10,000 million British thermal units (mmbtu) and every dollar move represents a $10,000 change in value per contract position. The contract symbol is NG, it has a tradable contract for each month of the year.

This commodity is now traded both electronically and through the open outcry session; the pit-traded hours are from 9:00 AM until 1:30 PM (CT). The daily maximum price fluctuation is $3.00 per mmbtu ($30,000 per contract) for all months. If any contract is traded, bid, or offered at the limit for five minutes, trading is halted for five minutes. When trading resumes, the limit is expanded by $3.00 per mmbtu in either direction. If another halt were triggered, the market would continue to be expanded by $3.00 per mmbtu in either direction after each successive five-minute trading halt. There will be no maximum price fluctuation limits during any one trading session.

Natural gas is really a fascinating energy source. It accounts for almost a quarter of total U.S. energy consumption. Its market share is likely to expand because of the favorable competitive position of gas in relation to other fuels, and the tightening environmental standards for fuel combustion. Industrial users and electric utilities together account for 59% of the market; commercial and residential users combined are 42%. It is primarily methane, the lightest hydrocarbon molecule. It is burned to drive turbines in electrical-power-generation plants, to heat homes and businesses across the nation, and as a feedstock to produce the agricultural fertilizer ammonia. It is one of the most important economic commodities in the U.S. today after crude oil.

This market has a strong seasonal tendency to bottom in July and then peak in December. The main reason for this can be explained by the fact that in cold weather it is used to heat homes and business and production companies are building inventories ahead of this season. Then as production companies anticipate the needs for utility companies to produce electricity for spikes in electricity demands for air conditioning we see prices rise in early summer and then rise through yearend, where we begin the winter heating cycle.

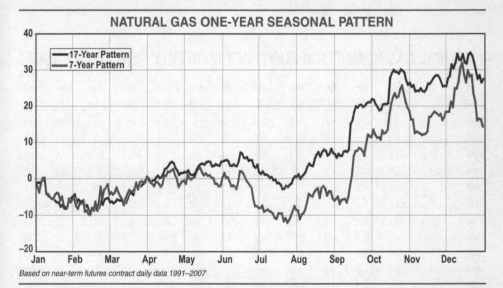

NATURAL GAS ONE-YEAR SEASONAL PATTERN

— 17-Year Pattern
— 7-Year Pattern

Based on near-term futures contract daily data 1991–2007

NATURAL GAS NEAR-TERM CONTRACT ANNUAL HIGHS, LOWS & CLOSES SINCE 1991

YEAR	HIGH DATE	HIGH CLOSE	LOW DATE	LOW CLOSE	YEAR CLOSE	YEAR	HIGH DATE	HIGH CLOSE	LOW DATE	LOW CLOSE	YEAR CLOSE
1991	10/17	2.186	06/24	1.118	1.343	2000	12/29	9.775	01/05	2.168	9.775
1992	09/23	2.593	02/14	1.079	1.687	2001	01/09	9.819	10/01	2.208	2.570
1993	04/23	2.514	01/19	1.508	1.997	2002	12/16	5.297	01/28	1.984	4.789
1994	02/01	2.639	09/02	1.560	1.725	2003	02/28	8.101	09/26	4.621	6.189
1995	12/27	2.868	01/13	1.323	2.619	2004	10/26	9.363	09/10	4.570	6.149
1996	12/20	3.920	09/04	1.764	2.757	2005	12/13	15.378	01/03	5.790	11.225
1997	10/27	3.836	03/03	1.803	2.264	2006	01/03	10.626	09/14	4.892	6.299
1998	04/08	2.689	09/02	1.652	1.945	2007	11/01	8.637	08/31	5.468	7.483
1999	10/27	3.223	02/26	1.628	2.329	2008*	05/28	11.995	01/23	7.581	*AT PRESS-TIME*

*Through May 30, 2008

NATURAL GAS NEAR-TERM CONTRACT MONTHLY CLOSING PRICES

	Jan	Feb	Mar	Apr	May	Jun	Jul	Aug	Sep	Oct	Nov	Dec
1991	1.380	1.373	1.405	1.375	1.333	1.208	1.260	1.564	1.935	2.046	2.090	1.343
1992	1.180	1.171	1.357	1.422	1.625	1.518	1.892	2.112	2.515	2.295	2.087	1.687
1993	1.597	1.856	2.069	2.365	2.141	2.181	2.220	2.375	2.291	2.368	2.243	1.997
1994	2.554	2.208	2.075	2.067	1.917	2.184	1.893	1.586	1.657	1.950	1.695	1.725
1995	1.354	1.483	1.685	1.662	1.718	1.530	1.614	1.748	1.750	1.866	2.018	2.619
1996	2.658	2.236	2.336	2.224	2.406	2.911	2.163	1.859	2.214	2.728	3.497	2.757
1997	2.385	1.821	1.926	2.184	2.239	2.139	2.177	2.714	3.082	3.552	2.578	2.264
1998	2.257	2.321	2.522	2.221	2.170	2.469	1.844	1.752	2.433	2.275	1.976	1.945
1999	1.777	1.628	2.013	2.253	2.358	2.394	2.543	2.825	2.744	2.961	2.304	2.329
2000	2.662	2.761	2.945	3.141	4.356	4.476	3.774	4.782	5.186	4.490	6.589	9.775
2001	5.707	5.236	5.025	4.695	3.914	3.096	3.296	2.380	2.244	3.291	2.701	2.570
2002	2.138	2.357	3.283	3.795	3.217	3.245	2.954	3.296	4.138	4.156	4.200	4.789
2003	5.605	8.101	5.060	5.385	6.251	5.411	4.718	4.731	4.830	4.893	4.925	6.189
2004	5.397	5.416	5.933	5.862	6.442	6.155	6.112	5.074	6.795	8.725	7.620	6.149
2005	6.321	6.730	7.653	6.585	6.379	6.981	7.885	11.472	13.921	12.205	12.587	11.225
2006	9.316	6.714	7.210	6.555	6.384	6.104	8.211	6.048	5.620	7.534	8.844	6.299
2007	7.667	7.300	7.730	7.863	7.935	6.773	6.191	5.468	6.870	8.330	7.302	7.483
2008	8.074	9.366	10.101	10.843	11.703							

NATURAL GAS NEAR-TERM CONTRACT MONTHLY PERCENT CHANGES

	Jan	Feb	Mar	Apr	May	Jun	Jul	Aug	Sep	Oct	Nov	Dec	Year's Change
1991	−29.2	−0.5	2.3	−2.1	−3.1	−9.4	4.3	24.1	23.7	5.7	2.2	−35.7	−31.1
1992	−12.1	−0.8	15.9	4.8	14.3	−6.6	24.6	11.6	19.1	−8.7	−9.1	−19.2	25.6
1993	−5.3	16.2	11.5	14.3	−9.5	1.9	1.8	7.0	−3.5	3.4	−5.3	−11.0	18.4
1994	27.9	−13.5	−6.0	−0.4	−7.3	13.9	−13.3	−16.2	4.5	17.7	−13.1	1.8	−13.6
1995	−21.5	9.5	13.6	−1.4	3.4	−10.9	5.5	8.3	0.1	6.6	8.1	29.8	51.8
1996	1.5	−15.9	4.5	−4.8	8.2	21.0	−25.7	−14.1	19.1	23.2	28.2	−21.2	5.3
1997	−13.5	−23.6	5.8	13.4	2.5	−4.5	1.8	24.7	13.6	15.2	−27.4	−12.2	−17.9
1998	−0.3	2.8	8.7	−11.9	−2.3	13.8	−25.3	−5.0	38.9	−6.5	−13.1	−1.6	−14.1
1999	−8.6	−8.4	23.6	11.9	4.7	1.5	6.2	11.1	−2.9	7.9	−22.2	1.1	19.7
2000	14.3	3.7	6.7	6.7	38.7	2.8	−15.7	26.7	8.4	−13.4	46.7	48.4	319.7
2001	−41.6	−8.3	−4.0	−6.6	−16.6	−20.9	6.5	−27.8	−5.7	46.7	−17.9	−4.9	−73.7
2002	−16.8	10.2	39.3	15.6	−15.2	0.9	−9.0	11.6	25.5	0.4	1.1	14.0	86.3
2003	17.0	44.5	−37.5	6.4	16.1	−13.4	−12.8	0.3	2.1	1.3	0.7	25.7	29.2
2004	−12.8	0.4	9.5	−1.2	9.9	−4.5	−0.7	−17.0	33.9	28.4	−12.7	−19.3	−0.6
2005	2.8	6.5	13.7	−14.0	−3.1	9.4	12.9	45.5	21.3	−12.3	3.1	−10.8	82.6
2006	−17.0	−27.9	7.4	−9.1	−2.6	−4.4	34.5	−26.3	−7.1	34.1	17.4	−28.8	−43.9
2007	21.7	−4.8	5.9	1.7	0.9	−14.6	−8.6	−11.7	25.6	21.3	−12.3	2.5	18.8
2008	7.9	16.0	7.8	7.3	7.9								
TOTALS	−85.6	6.1	128.7	30.6	46.9	−24.0	−13.0	52.8	216.6	171.0	−25.6	−41.4	
AVG.	−4.8	0.3	7.2	1.7	2.6	−1.4	−0.8	3.1	12.7	10.1	−1.5	−2.4	
# Up	7	9	15	9	10	8	9	10	13	13	8	7	
# Down	11	9	3	9	8	9	8	7	4	4	9	10	

COPPER CYCLE, SEASONAL PATTERN & TRADING GUIDE

Copper is also traded at the New York Mercantile Exchange; however, it migrated its products for trade execution to the CME Groups Globex® platform for electronic trading in January 2008. One futures contract is 25,000 pounds, and every penny move represents a $250 change in value per contract position. The contract symbol is HG, and it has several tradable contract months, beginning with March, then May, July, September, and the December contract.

This commodity is now traded both electronically and through the open outcry session; the pit-traded hours are from 7:10 AM until 2:00 PM (CT) but most trades are electronic which closes at 4 PM (CT). Initial daily price limit, based upon the preceding day's settlement price, is $0.20 per pound. Two minutes after the two most active month's trade at the limit, trading in all months of futures and options will cease for a 15-minute period. Trading will also cease if either of the two active months is bid at the upper limit or offered at the lower limit for two minutes without trading. Trading will not cease if the limit is reached during the final 20 minutes of a day's trading. If the limit is reached during the final half-hour of trading, trading will resume no later than 10 minutes before the normal closing time. When trading resumes after a cessation of trading, the price limits will be expanded by increments of 100%.

Copper does have a tendency to make a major seasonal bottom in December and then has a tendency to post major seasonal peaks in May. This is perhaps due to mines and manufacturers building inventories up into the construction building season in the late winter and early spring time and ahead of the new car model year that begins in late summer. Copper is used in automobiles for air conditioning and due to the fact it is highly resistant to corrosion from salt water it is also used to line interior hulls of cargo ships.

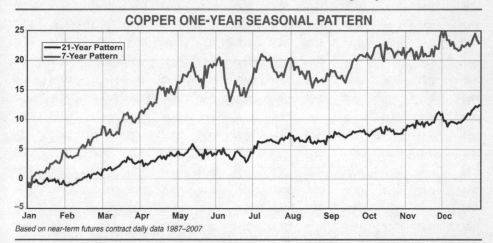

COPPER ONE-YEAR SEASONAL PATTERN

— 21-Year Pattern
— 7-Year Pattern

Based on near-term futures contract daily data 1987–2007

COPPER NEAR-TERM CONTRACT ANNUAL HIGHS, LOWS & CLOSES SINCE 1973

	HIGH		LOW		YEAR		HIGH		LOW		YEAR
YEAR	DATE	CLOSE	DATE	CLOSE	CLOSE	YEAR	DATE	CLOSE	DATE	CLOSE	CLOSE
1973	11/20	105.85	01/02	50.20	84.80	1991	01/02	119.30	12/10	96.60	97.55
1974	05/03	136.10	12/31	53.60	53.60	1992	07/16	116.35	01/09	94.35	103.60
1975	08/25	63.30	06/11	51.70	55.30	1993	01/08	107.60	10/26	72.60	83.30
1976	07/06	78.30	01/26	53.80	63.20	1994	12/01	138.85	01/07	78.60	138.60
1977	03/18	72.40	08/12	52.60	60.30	1995	06/22	145.75	12/06	119.05	120.55
1978	12/27	71.15	02/23	56.10	71.05	1996	05/13	125.55	06/25	83.25	100.25
1979	10/01	113.00	01/02	70.05	105.20	1997	06/16	122.20	12/29	77.70	78.10
1980	02/12	145.20	12/11	81.10	86.55	1998	04/28	85.95	12/23	66.10	67.20
1981	01/05	90.90	12/10	72.55	75.70	1999	12/30	86.30	02/22	61.35	86.30
1982	01/04	75.90	06/18	54.40	69.65	2000	09/12	93.60	04/17	74.35	84.30
1983	05/10	81.50	11/07	61.10	67.00	2001	01/18	86.15	11/07	60.60	65.90
1984	03/30	71.75	10/17	55.50	57.20	2002	06/04	78.60	01/02	65.80	70.25
1985	04/12	65.90	01/02	56.40	64.15	2003	12/31	104.55	04/03	71.10	104.55
1986	03/21	68.60	08/18	56.95	61.15	2004	10/08	146.95	01/07	106.65	145.25
1987	12/31	127.40	01/20	60.20	127.40	2005	12/28	206.90	01/04	134.30	204.20
1988	11/28	154.80	02/26	84.70	135.50	2006	05/11	392.30	01/03	204.85	287.10
1989	01/23	149.55	07/06	98.80	106.40	2007	10/03	376.35	02/05	241.65	304.10
1990	08/15	133.55	01/30	95.65	116.85	2008*	04/09	400.00	01/02	306.40	AT PRESS-TIME

*Through May 30, 2008

COPPER NEAR-TERM CONTRACT MONTHLY CLOSING PRICES

	Jan	Feb	Mar	Apr	May	Jun	Jul	Aug	Sep	Oct	Nov	Dec
1973	54.50	64.20	67.35	67.50	71.45	78.30	87.60	81.40	80.90	92.50	86.70	84.80
1974	97.60	109.00	129.60	135.00	107.40	93.80	89.30	74.20	68.20	63.60	60.50	53.60
1975	52.40	59.50	62.90	56.70	54.70	56.50	57.90	60.00	56.50	56.90	54.30	55.30
1976	54.90	59.80	63.40	71.70	69.90	75.60	74.50	69.60	63.80	56.30	58.10	63.20
1977	64.70	68.90	70.60	64.10	60.40	60.80	56.30	55.40	56.40	55.00	57.90	60.30
1978	58.00	56.50	60.60	60.10	65.30	60.10	63.00	65.25	67.20	70.20	68.40	71.05
1979	78.90	92.70	94.60	93.60	79.50	81.30	81.30	92.10	107.00	90.90	102.70	105.20
1980	130.50	123.00	87.10	90.30	93.40	92.90	95.80	90.10	93.45	93.90	94.25	86.55
1981	84.20	82.55	86.40	83.55	81.45	77.85	83.75	81.30	76.70	77.05	75.65	75.70
1982	74.45	71.15	67.55	72.40	64.60	61.00	63.15	64.40	60.00	65.90	68.00	69.65
1983	75.25	75.20	75.15	78.75	78.35	76.30	76.95	73.85	66.95	62.95	67.80	67.00
1984	64.40	66.10	71.75	65.70	63.95	62.00	57.00	63.10	57.55	59.95	58.85	57.20
1985	62.60	59.60	62.60	61.90	60.65	59.55	61.10	61.85	59.35	60.25	61.85	64.15
1986	65.70	64.80	66.15	62.65	63.10	60.35	58.50	58.45	61.20	58.80	61.05	61.15
1987	60.40	63.40	62.45	62.15	65.90	71.45	78.15	75.10	79.75	82.15	102.20	127.40
1988	95.75	86.30	105.30	89.70	91.30	98.00	93.00	101.00	109.60	141.15	133.00	135.50
1989	142.90	131.20	132.60	138.70	114.35	103.90	111.50	128.95	122.90	114.00	109.15	106.40
1990	98.60	113.85	122.40	116.90	110.85	114.00	124.60	124.80	118.80	115.75	107.10	116.85
1991	106.40	111.50	106.20	105.10	96.85	101.00	101.30	103.15	104.80	106.60	101.00	97.55
1992	98.60	103.20	101.65	100.45	101.10	109.70	112.50	110.85	104.75	101.40	97.60	103.60
1993	98.95	95.95	96.20	84.50	79.85	86.50	88.30	86.00	74.90	73.15	75.00	83.30
1994	86.80	86.65	86.75	91.50	103.75	108.25	111.40	115.75	112.55	122.60	137.15	138.60
1995	136.30	130.10	136.70	127.10	131.00	136.70	135.30	131.95	131.65	124.75	132.25	120.55
1996	114.80	115.30	116.50	119.15	115.00	90.40	93.20	95.25	90.10	91.30	110.30	100.25
1997	103.75	110.90	113.00	111.35	119.10	112.15	108.90	99.30	97.00	90.75	84.05	78.10
1998	79.30	77.05	79.85	83.70	77.50	73.80	76.95	71.35	73.75	72.40	70.05	67.20
1999	64.50	63.25	62.75	72.75	62.80	76.65	76.25	79.20	82.65	80.55	81.80	86.30
2000	84.95	79.80	80.50	79.60	81.45	82.40	87.45	89.50	92.05	84.85	84.55	84.30
2001	84.55	81.60	76.40	77.70	75.75	71.35	68.25	68.70	65.20	62.50	73.20	65.90
2002	73.35	72.05	76.35	73.90	76.40	77.45	68.10	69.55	66.60	71.70	74.95	70.25
2003	79.45	78.10	71.45	73.10	78.25	75.30	82.05	81.05	81.85	93.85	91.40	104.55
2004	114.55	134.60	136.00	120.75	127.75	120.80	130.80	128.10	139.60	133.75	143.40	145.25
2005	143.50	149.85	150.25	146.40	145.65	151.00	164.45	161.95	172.75	181.10	192.60	204.20
2006	222.85	217.85	246.30	322.05	362.40	335.50	357.00	345.60	346.05	334.55	319.55	287.10
2007	259.45	275.20	314.60	355.65	339.55	345.05	364.85	339.70	364.00	347.30	318.45	304.10
2008	329.80	385.50	383.10	390.45	360.60							

150

COPPER NEAR-TERM CONTRACT MONTHLY PERCENT CHANGES

	Jan	Feb	Mar	Apr	May	Jun	Jul	Aug	Sep	Oct	Nov	Dec	Year's Change
1973	8.5	17.8	4.9	0.2	5.9	9.6	11.9	−7.1	−0.6	14.3	−6.3	−2.2	68.8
1974	15.1	11.7	18.9	4.2	−20.4	−12.7	−4.8	−16.9	−8.1	−6.7	−4.9	−11.4	−36.8
1975	−2.2	13.5	5.7	−9.9	−3.5	3.3	2.5	3.6	−5.8	0.7	−4.6	1.8	3.2
1976	−0.7	8.9	6.0	13.1	−2.5	8.2	−1.5	−6.6	−8.3	−11.8	3.2	8.8	14.3
1977	2.4	6.5	2.5	−9.2	−5.8	0.7	−7.4	−1.6	1.8	−2.5	5.3	4.1	−4.6
1978	−3.8	−2.6	7.3	−0.8	8.7	−8.0	4.8	3.6	3.0	4.5	−2.6	3.9	17.8
1979	11.0	17.5	2.0	−1.1	−15.1	2.3	N/C	13.3	16.2	−15.0	13.0	2.4	48.1
1980	24.0	−5.7	−29.2	3.7	3.4	−0.5	3.1	−5.9	3.7	0.5	0.4	−8.2	−17.7
1981	−2.7	−2.0	4.7	−3.3	−2.5	−4.4	7.6	−2.9	−5.7	0.5	−1.8	0.1	−12.5
1982	−1.7	−4.4	−5.1	7.2	−10.8	−5.6	3.5	2.0	−6.8	9.8	3.2	2.4	−8.0
1983	8.0	−0.1	−0.1	4.8	−0.5	−2.6	0.9	−4.0	−9.3	−6.0	7.7	−1.2	−3.8
1984	−3.9	2.6	8.5	−8.4	−2.7	−3.0	−8.1	10.7	−8.8	4.2	−1.8	−2.8	−14.6
1985	9.4	−4.8	5.0	−1.1	−2.0	−1.8	2.6	1.2	−4.0	1.5	2.7	3.7	12.2
1986	2.4	−1.4	2.1	−5.3	0.7	−4.4	−3.1	−0.1	4.7	−3.9	3.8	0.2	−4.7
1987	−1.2	5.0	−1.5	−0.5	6.0	8.4	9.4	−3.9	6.2	3.0	24.4	24.7	108.3
1988	−24.8	−9.9	22.0	−14.8	1.8	7.3	−5.1	8.6	8.5	28.8	−5.8	1.9	6.4
1989	5.5	−8.2	1.1	4.6	−17.6	−9.1	7.3	15.7	−4.7	−7.2	−4.3	−2.5	−21.5
1990	−7.3	15.5	7.5	−4.5	−5.2	2.8	9.3	0.2	−4.8	−2.6	−7.5	9.1	9.8
1991	−8.9	4.8	−4.8	−1.0	−7.8	4.3	0.3	1.8	1.6	1.7	−5.3	−3.4	−16.5
1992	1.1	4.7	−1.5	−1.2	0.6	8.5	2.6	−1.5	−5.5	−3.2	−3.7	6.1	6.2
1993	−4.5	−3.0	0.3	−12.2	−5.5	8.3	2.1	−2.6	−12.9	−2.3	2.5	11.1	−19.6
1994	4.2	−0.2	0.1	5.5	13.4	4.3	2.9	3.9	−2.8	8.9	11.9	1.1	66.4
1995	−1.7	−4.5	5.1	−7.0	3.1	4.4	−1.0	−2.5	−0.2	−5.2	6.0	−0.8	−13.0
1996	−4.8	0.4	1.0	2.3	−3.5	−21.4	3.1	2.2	−5.4	1.3	20.8	−9.1	−16.8
1997	3.5	6.9	1.9	−1.5	7.0	−5.8	−2.9	−8.8	−2.3	−6.4	−7.4	−7.1	−22.1
1998	1.5	−2.8	3.6	4.8	−7.4	−4.8	4.3	−7.3	3.4	−1.8	−3.2	−4.1	−14.0
1999	−4.0	−1.9	−0.8	15.9	−13.7	22.1	−0.5	3.9	4.4	−2.5	1.6	5.5	28.4
2000	−1.6	−6.1	0.9	−1.1	2.3	1.2	6.1	2.3	2.8	−7.8	−0.4	−0.3	−2.3
2001	0.3	−3.5	−6.4	1.7	−2.5	−5.8	−4.3	0.7	−5.1	−4.1	17.1	−10.0	−21.8
2002	11.3	−1.8	6.0	−3.2	3.4	1.4	−12.1	2.1	−4.2	7.7	4.5	−6.3	6.6
2003	13.1	−1.7	−8.5	2.3	7.0	−3.8	9.0	−1.2	1.0	14.7	−2.6	14.4	48.8
2004	9.6	17.5	1.0	−11.2	5.8	−5.4	8.3	−2.1	9.0	−4.2	7.2	1.3	38.9
2005	−1.2	4.4	0.3	−2.6	−0.5	3.7	8.9	−1.5	6.7	4.8	6.4	6.0	40.6
2006	9.1	−2.2	13.1	30.8	12.5	−7.4	6.4	−3.2	0.1	−3.3	−4.5	−10.2	40.6
2007	−9.6	6.1	14.3	13.0	−4.5	1.6	5.7	−6.9	7.2	−4.6	−8.3	−4.5	5.9
2008	8.5	16.9	−0.6	1.9	−7.6								
TOTALS	63.9	93.9	87.3	16.1	−60.0	−4.1	71.8	−10.8	−25.0	5.8	66.7	16.5	
AVG.	1.8	2.6	2.4	0.4	−1.7	−0.1	2.1	−0.3	−0.7	0.2	1.9	0.5	
# Up	19	17	26	16	15	18	23	16	16	16	18	19	
# Down	17	19	10	20	21	17	11	19	19	19	17	16	

GOLD CYCLE, SEASONAL PATTERN & TRADING GUIDE

Gold is traded at the New York Mercantile Exchange; however it migrated its products for trade execution to the CME Groups Globex® platform for electronic trading in January 2008. One futures contract is 100 troy ounces, and every dollar move represents a $100 change in value per contract position. The contract symbol is GC, and it has several tradable contract months, beginning with February, April, June, August, October, and the December contract.

This commodity is now traded both electronically and through the open outcry session; the pit-traded hours are from 7:20 AM until 12:30 PM (CT). There are no longer any daily price limits, but back in 1987, the daily limits had been $25 an ounce for gold. Gold has a seasonal tendency to peak in late January after the holiday season as jewelry demand starts to decline. Price increases can last into the first part of February as inventories are being replenished by dealers preparing for retail sales for Valentine's Day gifts.

Gold tends to post seasonal bottoms in late July or early August as demand increases as jewelers again stock up ahead of a the seasonal wedding event in India and also as investors return from summer vacations. Gold prices are also subject to spikes in demand from the investment community as a hedge or protection from concerns over inflation or times of economic instability or uncertainties. It is valued in terms of the U.S. dollar so periods of dollar weakness helps support Gold's value. Longer term cyclical forces can dramatically impact the seasonal price moves of this market like we saw in the July-August time period in 2007.

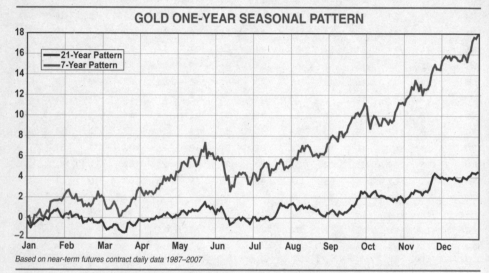

GOLD ONE-YEAR SEASONAL PATTERN

Based on near-term futures contract daily data 1987–2007

GOLD NEAR-TERM CONTRACT ANNUAL HIGHS, LOWS & CLOSES SINCE 1975

YEAR	HIGH DATE	HIGH CLOSE	LOW DATE	LOW CLOSE	YEAR CLOSE	YEAR	HIGH DATE	HIGH CLOSE	LOW DATE	LOW CLOSE	YEAR CLOSE
1975	02/20	187.7	09/23	131.2	141.0	1992	07/24	363.2	11/10	330.1	333.1
1976	01/02	141.2	08/30	102.8	135.7	1993	07/30	411.3	03/10	326.9	391.9
1977	11/11	168.9	01/10	127.6	167.5	1994	09/27	401.4	04/22	372.1	384.4
1978	10/30	247.0	01/04	168.0	229.0	1995	04/18	397.8	01/06	372.2	388.1
1979	12/31	541.0	01/11	218.6	541.0	1996	02/02	417.7	12/31	369.2	369.2
1980	01/21	834.0	03/17	480.0	599.5	1997	01/02	366.6	12/12	284.8	289.9
1981	01/06	605.0	12/28	397.2	402.8	1998	04/23	315.8	08/28	277.9	289.2
1982	09/08	497.0	06/22	301.5	453.0	1999	10/05	326.0	07/19	253.9	289.6
1983	01/31	518.2	11/16	376.3	388.0	2000	02/10	318.7	11/13	265.3	273.6
1984	03/05	407.3	12/27	309.2	309.7	2001	09/26	294.8	04/02	256.6	279.0
1985	08/28	347.3	02/25	284.1	331.1	2002	12/27	349.7	01/03	278.5	348.2
1986	09/22	445.2	01/02	328.9	406.9	2003	12/30	417.2	04/07	322.2	416.1
1987	12/11	502.0	02/17	394.9	488.9	2004	12/03	457.8	05/13	374.9	438.4
1988	01/14	488.2	09/30	399.2	412.3	2005	12/12	531.5	02/08	414.3	518.9
1989	11/24	425.0	06/09	362.0	405.2	2006	05/11	721.5	01/05	527.8	638.0
1990	02/05	427.5	06/14	349.8	396.2	2007	12/28	842.7	01/05	606.9	838.0

*Through May 30, 2008

152

GOLD NEAR-TERM CONTRACT MONTHLY CLOSING PRICES

	Jan	Feb	Mar	Apr	May	Jun	Jul	Aug	Sep	Oct	Nov	Dec
1975	178.0	183.0	179.5	166.8	169.0	167.8	173.4	162.8	142.2	142.8	138.8	141.0
1976	129.0	132.6	129.7	128.9	127.3	123.9	114.2	103.2	116.1	123.8	132.6	135.7
1977	134.0	144.6	151.0	148.0	144.3	143.6	147.1	148.1	156.4	162.7	162.3	167.5
1978	178.9	184.4	186.2	170.6	187.0	183.7	209.8	210.6	220.9	240.7	196.4	229.0
1979	236.6	252.9	243.8	249.2	281.1	283.8	297.3	326.7	404.5	385.7	430.5	541.0
1980	704.0	640.0	519.0	507.0	555.0	654.0	642.0	656.0	688.5	642.0	644.5	599.5
1981	512.5	486.5	525.5	489.0	492.5	428.5	423.2	443.5	443.0	431.2	413.3	402.8
1982	391.8	364.5	334.2	346.5	329.0	317.8	355.5	418.5	404.8	423.0	449.0	453.0
1983	518.2	423.7	422.0	433.5	418.5	418.5	427.4	424.8	407.8	378.8	409.0	388.0
1984	379.2	398.9	394.3	379.6	393.6	376.1	350.3	358.0	351.3	336.0	333.5	309.7
1985	307.4	288.7	334.1	316.5	319.5	317.7	335.2	339.8	327.1	326.7	327.3	331.1
1986	352.9	341.0	334.8	348.1	347.1	347.7	369.7	393.3	429.8	405.5	394.8	406.9
1987	408.9	407.4	422.7	456.5	456.0	452.2	475.1	458.7	458.8	471.2	497.2	488.9
1988	458.5	431.9	457.9	452.6	459.8	437.7	447.3	439.9	399.2	415.1	429.6	412.3
1989	395.8	390.4	390.0	380.5	366.5	377.3	378.7	365.4	372.0	377.6	417.5	405.2
1990	417.8	408.9	375.0	371.4	368.6	359.9	379.2	389.2	408.1	381.3	385.7	396.2
1991	368.5	369.0	359.4	357.7	364.8	370.0	370.8	352.9	357.3	359.5	371.1	355.2
1992	358.9	354.1	345.5	337.9	338.4	344.4	361.4	345.3	349.4	340.1	335.5	333.1
1993	330.7	329.1	339.3	357.2	380.3	379.2	411.3	375.7	357.1	369.6	371.9	391.9
1994	383.6	382.5	394.3	377.8	390.0	387.3	389.2	390.8	397.6	384.9	384.5	384.4
1995	377.7	378.3	394.3	388.5	387.6	385.6	388.4	386.9	386.5	384.3	388.6	388.1
1996	408.5	401.2	398.4	393.5	394.4	381.6	393.1	391.3	380.5	379.1	375.0	369.2
1997	346.0	365.1	354.0	341.2	347.5	335.3	328.6	327.4	336.9	312.1	298.6	289.9
1998	304.6	300.1	303.3	307.9	295.1	298.1	290.5	278.9	299.0	293.7	295.1	289.2
1999	288.2	288.3	281.9	287.8	272.0	263.6	258.8	257.3	299.5	300.3	293.0	289.6
2000	286.2	294.2	281.4	274.7	274.8	291.5	283.2	282.1	276.9	266.4	273.3	273.6
2001	268.0	267.8	259.2	264.4	266.9	271.3	269.2	276.5	294.0	280.5	274.9	279.0
2002	282.9	297.1	303.7	309.2	327.5	313.9	305.2	313.9	325.2	318.4	317.8	348.2
2003	369.1	350.3	336.9	339.4	365.6	346.3	355.8	376.8	386.1	384.6	398.0	416.1
2004	402.9	396.8	428.3	387.5	394.9	393.0	393.7	412.4	420.4	429.4	453.2	438.4
2005	424.1	437.6	431.1	436.3	418.9	437.1	435.8	438.1	472.3	466.9	498.7	518.9
2006	575.5	563.9	586.7	654.5	649.0	616.0	646.8	634.2	604.2	606.8	652.9	638.0
2007	657.9	672.5	669.0	683.5	666.7	650.9	679.3	681.9	750.0	795.3	789.1	838.0
2008	928.0	975.0	921.5	865.1	891.5							

GOLD NEAR-TERM CONTRACT MONTHLY PERCENT CHANGES

	Jan	Feb	Mar	Apr	May	Jun	Jul	Aug	Sep	Oct	Nov	Dec	Year's Change
1975	-3.2	2.8	-1.9	-7.1	1.3	-0.7	3.3	-6.1	-12.7	0.4	-2.8	1.6	-23.3
1976	-8.5	2.8	-2.2	-0.6	-1.2	-2.7	-7.8	-9.6	12.5	6.6	7.1	2.3	-3.8
1977	-1.3	7.9	4.4	-2.0	-2.5	-0.5	2.4	0.7	5.6	4.0	-0.2	3.2	23.4
1978	6.8	3.1	1.0	-8.4	9.6	-1.8	14.2	0.4	4.9	9.0	-18.4	16.6	36.7
1979	3.3	6.9	-3.6	2.2	12.8	1.0	4.8	9.9	23.8	-4.6	11.6	25.7	136.2
1980	30.1	-9.1	-18.9	-2.3	9.5	17.8	-1.8	2.2	5.0	-6.8	0.4	-7.0	10.8
1981	-14.5	-5.1	8.0	-6.9	0.7	-13.0	-1.2	4.8	-0.1	-2.7	-4.2	-2.5	-32.8
1982	-2.7	-7.0	-8.3	3.7	-5.1	-3.4	11.9	17.7	-3.3	4.5	6.1	0.9	12.5
1983	14.4	-18.2	-0.4	2.7	-3.5	N/C	2.1	-0.6	-4.0	-7.1	8.0	-5.1	-14.3
1984	-2.3	5.2	-1.2	-3.7	3.7	-4.4	-6.9	2.2	-1.9	-4.4	-0.7	-7.1	-20.2
1985	-0.7	-6.1	15.7	-5.3	0.9	-0.6	5.5	1.4	-3.7	-0.1	0.2	1.2	6.9
1986	6.6	-3.4	-1.8	4.0	-0.3	0.2	6.3	6.4	9.3	-5.7	-2.6	3.1	22.9
1987	0.5	-0.4	3.8	8.0	-0.1	-0.8	5.1	-3.5	0.0	2.7	5.5	-1.7	20.2
1988	-6.2	-5.8	6.0	-1.2	1.6	-4.8	2.2	-1.7	-9.3	4.0	3.5	-4.0	-15.7
1989	-4.0	-1.4	-0.1	-2.4	-3.7	2.9	0.4	-3.5	1.8	1.5	10.6	-2.9	-1.7
1990	3.1	-2.1	-8.3	-1.0	-0.8	-2.4	5.4	2.6	4.9	-6.6	1.2	2.7	-2.2
1991	-7.0	0.1	-2.6	-0.5	2.0	1.4	0.2	-4.8	1.2	0.6	3.2	-4.3	-10.3
1992	1.0	-1.3	-2.4	-2.2	0.1	1.8	4.9	-4.5	1.2	-2.7	-1.4	-0.7	-6.2
1993	-0.7	-0.5	3.1	5.3	6.5	-0.3	8.5	-8.7	-5.0	3.5	0.6	5.4	17.7
1994	-2.1	-0.3	3.1	-4.2	3.2	-0.7	0.5	0.4	1.7	-3.2	-0.1	0.0	-1.9
1995	-1.7	0.2	4.2	-1.5	-0.2	-0.5	0.7	-0.4	-0.1	-0.6	1.1	-0.1	1.0
1996	5.3	-1.8	-0.7	-1.2	0.2	-3.2	3.0	-0.5	-2.8	-0.4	-1.1	-1.5	-4.9
1997	-6.3	5.5	-3.0	-3.6	1.8	-3.5	-2.0	-0.4	2.9	-7.4	-4.3	-2.9	-21.5
1998	5.1	-1.5	1.1	1.5	-4.2	1.0	-2.5	-4.0	7.2	-1.8	0.5	-2.0	-0.2
1999	-0.3	0.0	-2.2	2.1	-5.5	-3.1	-1.8	-0.6	16.4	0.3	-2.4	-1.2	0.1
2000	-1.2	2.8	-4.4	-2.4	0.0	6.1	-2.8	-0.4	-1.8	-3.8	2.6	0.1	-5.5
2001	-2.0	-0.1	-3.2	2.0	0.9	1.6	-0.8	2.7	6.3	-4.6	-2.0	1.5	2.0
2002	1.4	5.0	2.2	1.8	5.9	-4.2	-2.8	2.9	3.6	-2.1	-0.2	9.6	24.8
2003	6.0	-5.1	-3.8	0.7	7.7	-5.3	2.7	5.9	2.5	-0.4	3.5	4.5	19.5
2004	-3.2	-1.5	7.9	-9.5	1.9	-0.5	0.2	4.7	1.9	2.1	5.5	-3.3	5.4
2005	-3.3	3.2	-1.5	1.2	-3.9	4.3	-0.3	0.5	7.8	-1.1	6.8	4.1	18.4
2006	10.9	-2.0	4.0	11.6	-0.8	-5.1	5.0	-1.9	-4.7	0.4	7.6	-2.3	23.0
2007	3.1	2.2	-0.5	2.2	-2.5	-2.4	4.4	0.4	10.0	6.0	-0.8	6.2	31.3
2008	10.7	5.1	-5.5	-6.1	3.1								
TOTALS	37.1	-19.9	-12.0	-23.1	39.1	-25.8	63.0	14.6	81.1	-20.5	44.4	40.1	
AVG.	1.1	-0.6	-0.4	-0.7	1.2	-0.8	1.9	0.4	2.5	-0.6	1.3	1.2	
# Up	15	15	13	14	20	10	22	17	21	14	19	16	
# Down	9	19	21	20	14	22	11	16	12	19	14	16	

SILVER CYCLE, SEASONAL PATTERN & TRADING GUIDE

Silver is also traded at the New York Mercantile Exchange; however, it migrated its products for trade execution to the CME Groups Globex® platform for electronic trading in January 2008. One futures contract is 5000 troy ounces, and every penny move represents a $50 change in value per contract position. The contract symbol is SI, and it has several tradable contract months, beginning with March, then May, July, September, and the December contract.

This commodity is now traded both electronically and through the open outcry session; the pit-traded hours are from 7:25 AM until 12:25 PM (CT) but most trades are electronic, which closes at 4 PM (CT). Initial price limit is $1.50 above or below the preceding day's settlement price. Two minutes after either of the two most active months trades at its limit, trades in all months and in silver options will cease for a 15-minute period. Trading will also cease if either of the two active months is bid at the upper limit or offered at the lower limit for two minutes without trading. Trading will not cease if the limit is reached during the final 20 minutes of a day's trading. Trading will resume no later than 10 minutes before the normal closing time.

Silver does have a tendency to make a major seasonal bottom in June, and then has a tendency to post major seasonal peaks in February. It does track the price moves of gold, but from a traders or investors perspective it is considered the poor's man gold. Due to technology and the age of digital imaging, silver has lost its industrial demand element as it once had a tremendous demand from the photo industry though it still is needed for film and X-ray processing. Silver prices are also subject to spikes in demand from the investment community as a hedge or protection from concerns over inflation or times of economic instability or uncertainties. Dollar weakness helps support silver's value. Longer-term cyclical forces can dramatically impact the seasonal price moves of this market like we saw in the June-August time period in 2007.

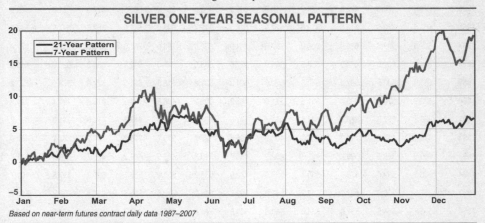

SILVER ONE-YEAR SEASONAL PATTERN

— 21-Year Pattern
— 7-Year Pattern

Based on near-term futures contract daily data 1987–2007

SILVER NEAR-TERM CONTRACT ANNUAL HIGHS, LOWS & CLOSES SINCE 1973

YEAR	HIGH DATE	HIGH CLOSE	LOW DATE	LOW CLOSE	YEAR CLOSE	YEAR	HIGH DATE	HIGH CLOSE	LOW DATE	LOW CLOSE	YEAR CLOSE
1973	12/31	329.7	01/22	196.1	329.7	1991	06/10	456.0	02/22	355.6	391.2
1974	02/26	624.2	01/04	329.0	447.0	1992	01/16	433.8	11/10	364.5	369.0
1975	08/07	528.5	01/21	398.5	423.6	1993	08/02	545.8	02/22	355.0	511.7
1976	07/06	518.8	01/26	385.3	439.0	1994	03/25	580.0	12/05	464.5	491.7
1977	03/21	500.8	08/15	432.6	484.9	1995	05/04	616.0	03/03	442.0	520.7
1978	10/30	636.5	02/08	484.8	613.7	1996	02/02	584.0	11/06	471.3	479.0
1979	12/31	2905.0	01/11	598.5	2905.0	1997	12/24	637.8	07/16	418.5	598.8
1980	01/21	4150.0	05/21	1140.0	1612.0	1998	02/05	728.0	08/31	467.8	502.0
1981	01/05	1670.0	11/19	816.0	829.0	1999	09/28	577.0	04/14	486.0	545.3
1982	12/29	1138.0	06/21	499.0	1110.0	2000	02/04	557.2	11/21	463.0	463.5
1983	02/16	1475.0	11/18	855.0	915.5	2001	01/18	482.5	11/21	403.5	458.8
1984	03/05	1021.0	12/31	638.0	638.0	2002	06/04	512.5	01/31	422.3	481.2
1985	04/08	673.5	03/11	558.5	590.5	2003	12/30	599.3	03/21	435.3	596.5
1986	01/24	633.5	05/19	489.5	546.0	2004	04/06	822.0	05/11	552.3	683.7
1987	05/15	950.0	02/17	540.5	677.0	2005	12/09	909.5	01/07	644.8	889.0
1988	07/20	790.0	11/21	602.5	613.0	2006	05/11	1493.5	01/05	887.2	1293.5
1989	01/23	625.5	10/10	510.0	527.3	2007	11/09	1554.5	08/16	1149.5	1492.0
1990	01/12	538.8	12/14	400.5	424.7	2008*	03/05	2078.5	01/02	1529.0	AT PRESS-TIME

*Through May 30, 2008

SILVER NEAR-TERM CONTRACT MONTHLY CLOSING PRICES

	Jan	Feb	Mar	Apr	May	Jun	Jul	Aug	Sep	Oct	Nov	Dec
1973	204.7	255.0	220.4	217.5	259.7	272.1	290.1	269.0	282.2	288.1	301.7	329.7
1974	406.0	587.0	536.9	574.0	493.5	480.0	500.2	429.5	442.5	484.5	474.0	447.0
1975	410.5	451.5	427.5	436.5	452.0	467.5	505.5	467.5	452.5	419.2	418.6	423.6
1976	397.0	424.5	405.3	450.0	471.0	489.0	451.2	414.2	437.2	433.2	433.6	439.0
1977	449.5	477.5	483.2	480.7	456.5	451.7	452.1	453.7	468.7	489.2	485.4	484.9
1978	499.8	502.8	549.0	503.0	543.0	528.5	569.2	559.7	571.5	621.5	609.0	613.7
1979	675.5	783.0	751.1	809.0	876.6	878.0	906.5	1086.0	1680.0	1679.0	1927.0	2905.0
1980	3575.0	3634.0	1905.0	1300.0	1395.0	1690.0	1555.0	1684.0	2125.0	1910.0	1945.0	1612.0
1981	1345.0	1250.0	1203.0	1138.0	1088.0	880.0	864.0	972.0	938.0	925.0	844.0	829.0
1982	828.0	794.0	723.0	702.0	629.5	616.0	674.0	804.0	824.0	1009.0	1033.0	1110.0
1983	1421.0	1187.0	1075.0	1224.0	1310.0	1176.0	1191.0	1241.0	1107.0	863.0	985.0	915.5
1984	866.0	981.0	990.0	911.0	934.0	855.0	708.5	766.0	762.0	728.0	717.5	638.0
1985	639.0	570.0	672.5	624.0	619.0	619.0	633.0	637.0	609.5	612.5	621.0	590.5
1986	607.5	570.5	516.5	519.0	527.0	516.5	512.7	523.0	562.5	568.0	547.5	546.0
1987	552.5	549.3	622.0	808.0	767.0	741.0	835.0	753.0	761.0	699.0	719.0	677.0
1988	654.5	632.0	678.5	658.5	665.0	677.5	685.5	671.0	622.5	634.8	629.0	613.0
1989	583.5	593.5	582.3	570.5	520.5	524.3	531.3	516.5	531.0	521.8	579.5	527.3
1990	522.8	520.5	498.0	501.5	511.0	496.3	482.2	486.8	483.2	418.0	421.7	424.7
1991	385.1	377.3	386.8	401.5	411.7	447.5	407.8	387.0	417.3	410.8	411.3	391.2
1992	418.0	413.5	414.3	401.5	402.2	405.8	393.7	376.7	376.2	376.2	377.2	369.0
1993	366.0	359.7	389.2	441.7	462.2	458.7	540.8	488.5	408.2	436.7	446.5	511.7
1994	513.5	539.0	578.5	538.3	555.0	542.5	533.2	551.2	565.7	526.2	497.5	491.7
1995	466.3	456.5	531.0	578.3	531.0	506.5	505.2	539.0	548.5	536.0	526.7	520.7
1996	558.8	554.5	554.0	534.0	540.3	503.5	514.8	525.0	487.7	480.8	478.5	479.0
1997	492.0	536.0	507.5	469.3	467.5	464.8	449.0	468.5	523.2	473.7	529.8	598.8
1998	612.5	648.0	646.7	623.0	508.5	553.5	545.8	467.8	536.0	504.3	488.5	502.0
1999	523.5	563.0	497.0	543.0	489.5	528.7	546.5	522.0	561.5	518.0	524.0	545.3
2000	531.7	510.8	504.5	501.5	496.5	508.3	503.8	504.5	494.8	477.8	475.8	463.5
2001	481.5	451.5	429.5	435.8	441.0	432.7	422.8	421.0	467.5	422.5	415.7	458.8
2002	422.3	451.7	465.0	455.5	504.2	485.5	459.8	446.8	454.8	450.5	443.5	481.2
2003	486.0	460.0	446.5	465.2	453.3	456.8	512.0	513.2	514.2	506.5	538.2	596.5
2004	625.0	671.5	794.5	609.0	611.0	579.5	656.0	681.2	693.8	730.5	777.7	683.7
2005	674.7	739.5	718.0	694.0	745.2	707.5	726.2	685.5	751.2	758.0	838.5	889.0
2006	988.5	980.5	1152.0	1363.0	1245.5	1092.0	1137.0	1303.0	1154.0	1227.0	1411.5	1293.5
2007	1357.0	1423.5	1345.0	1357.5	1347.0	1247.3	1301.7	1223.0	1392.0	1443.8	1416.5	1492.0
2008	1699.5	1991.5	1731.0	1659.3	1686.5							

SILVER NEAR-TERM CONTRACT MONTHLY PERCENT CHANGES

	Jan	Feb	Mar	Apr	May	Jun	Jul	Aug	Sep	Oct	Nov	Dec	Year's Change
1973	N/C	24.6	-13.6	-1.3	19.4	4.8	6.6	-7.3	4.9	2.1	4.7	9.3	61.1
1974	23.1	44.6	-8.5	6.9	-14.0	-2.7	4.2	-14.1	3.0	9.5	-2.2	-5.7	35.6
1975	-8.2	10.0	-5.3	2.1	3.6	3.4	8.1	-7.5	-3.2	-7.4	-0.1	1.2	-5.2
1976	-6.3	6.9	-4.5	11.0	4.7	3.8	-7.7	-8.2	5.6	-0.9	0.1	1.2	3.6
1977	2.4	6.2	1.2	-0.5	-5.0	-1.1	0.1	0.4	3.3	4.4	-0.8	-0.1	10.5
1978	3.1	0.6	9.2	-8.4	8.0	-2.7	7.7	-1.7	2.1	8.7	-2.0	0.8	26.6
1979	10.1	15.9	-4.1	7.7	8.4	0.2	3.2	19.8	54.7	-0.1	14.8	50.8	373.4
1980	23.1	1.7	-47.6	-31.8	7.3	21.1	-8.0	8.3	26.2	-10.1	1.8	-17.1	-44.5
1981	-16.6	-7.1	-3.8	-5.4	-4.4	-19.1	-1.8	12.5	-3.5	-1.4	-8.8	-1.8	-48.6
1982	-0.1	-4.1	-8.9	-2.9	-10.3	-2.1	9.4	19.3	2.5	22.5	2.4	7.5	33.9
1983	28.0	-16.5	-9.4	13.9	7.0	-10.2	1.3	4.2	-10.8	-22.0	14.1	-7.1	-17.5
1984	-5.4	13.3	0.9	-8.0	2.5	-8.5	-17.1	8.1	-0.5	-4.5	-1.4	-11.1	-30.3
1985	0.2	-10.8	18.0	-7.2	-0.8	N/C	2.3	0.6	-4.3	0.5	1.4	-4.9	-7.4
1986	2.9	-6.1	-9.5	0.5	1.5	-2.0	-0.7	2.0	7.6	1.0	-3.6	-0.3	-7.5
1987	1.2	-0.6	13.2	29.9	-5.1	-3.4	12.7	-9.8	1.1	-8.1	2.9	-5.8	24.0
1988	-3.3	-3.4	7.4	-2.9	1.0	1.9	1.2	-2.1	-7.2	2.0	-0.9	-2.5	-9.5
1989	-4.8	1.7	-1.9	-2.0	-8.8	0.7	1.3	-2.8	2.8	-1.7	11.1	-9.0	-14.0
1990	-0.9	-0.4	-4.3	0.7	1.9	-2.9	-2.8	1.0	-0.7	-13.5	0.9	0.7	-19.5
1991	-9.3	-2.0	2.5	3.8	2.5	8.7	-8.9	-5.1	7.8	-1.6	0.1	-4.9	-7.9
1992	6.9	-1.1	0.2	-3.1	0.2	0.9	-3.0	-4.3	-0.1	N/C	0.3	-2.2	-5.7
1993	-0.8	-1.7	8.2	13.5	4.6	-0.8	17.9	-9.7	-16.4	7.0	2.2	14.6	38.7
1994	0.4	5.0	7.3	-6.9	3.1	-2.3	-1.7	3.4	2.6	-7.0	-5.5	-1.2	-3.9
1995	-5.2	-2.1	16.3	8.9	-8.2	-4.6	-0.3	6.7	1.8	-2.3	-1.7	-1.1	5.9
1996	7.3	-0.8	-0.1	-3.6	1.2	-6.8	2.2	2.0	-7.1	-1.4	-0.5	0.1	-8.0
1997	2.7	8.9	-5.3	-7.5	-0.4	-0.6	-3.4	4.3	11.7	-9.5	11.8	13.0	25.0
1998	2.3	5.8	-0.2	-3.7	-18.4	8.8	-1.4	-14.3	14.6	-5.9	-3.1	2.8	-16.2
1999	4.3	7.5	-11.7	9.3	-9.9	8.0	3.4	-4.5	7.6	-7.7	1.2	4.1	8.6
2000	-2.5	-3.9	-1.2	-0.6	-1.0	2.4	-0.9	0.1	-1.9	-3.4	-0.4	-2.6	-15.0
2001	3.9	-6.2	-4.9	1.5	1.2	-1.9	-2.3	-0.4	11.0	-9.6	-1.6	10.4	-1.0
2002	-8.0	7.0	2.9	-2.0	10.7	-3.7	-5.3	-2.8	1.8	-0.9	-1.6	8.5	4.9
2003	1.0	-5.3	-2.9	4.2	-2.6	0.8	12.1	0.2	0.2	-1.5	6.3	10.8	24.0
2004	4.8	7.4	18.3	-23.3	0.3	-5.2	13.2	3.8	1.8	5.3	6.5	-12.1	14.6
2005	-1.3	9.6	-2.9	-3.3	7.4	-5.1	2.6	-5.6	9.6	0.9	10.6	6.0	30.0
2006	11.2	-0.8	17.5	18.3	-8.6	-12.3	4.1	14.6	-11.4	6.3	15.0	-8.4	45.5
2007	4.9	4.9	-5.5	0.9	-0.8	-7.4	4.4	-6.0	13.8	3.7	-1.9	5.3	15.3
2008	13.9	17.2	-13.1	-4.1	1.6								
TOTALS	85.0	125.9	-46.1	4.6	-0.2	-39.9	52.7	5.1	131.0	-46.6	72.1	49.2	
AVG.	2.4	3.5	-1.3	0.1	-0.01	-1.1	1.5	0.1	3.7	-1.3	2.1	1.4	
# Up	21	19	14	16	21	13	20	18	23	13	19	17	
# Down	14	17	22	20	15	21	15	17	12	21	16	18	

CORN CYCLE, SEASONAL PATTERN & TRADING GUIDE

Corn is traded at the CME Group, which was formerly the Chicago Board of Trade. One futures contract is 5,000 bushels, and every penny move represents a $50 change in value per contract position. The contract symbol is C and it has several tradable contract months, beginning with March, May, July, September, and then the December contract. December is considered a "new crop contract," as this is the first contract traded after the seasonal harvest period.

This commodity is now traded both electronically and through the open outcry session; the pit-traded hours are from 9:30 AM until 1:15 PM (CT). The daily price limit move is 20 cents from the previous day's settlement price, which represents a $1,000 move per contract. However, there are no price limits in the expiring contract during the delivery month or on the two business days prior to the first day of the delivery month.

Due to the push for ethanol production and increased demand for animal feed grain supplies corn prices made historic price gains in 2008. Expectations in 2008 for record acres planted were diminished Excess rains and flooding throughout much of the Midwest cut plantable acres down to around 86 million and created a slow start to the growing season. This threatened to reduce the yield and leaves the door open in 2009 for a strong floor of support as supplies may need to be rationed by higher prices.

We might see increased planting in the South American planting season in the fall of 2008, but not much can be done to alleviate a tight supply/demand outlook for the 2008/2009 season. In fact, ending stocks and stocks/usage levels are already projecting 2008/2009 season to be one of the tightest on record. However, despite this outlook the low in corn prices is typically set during the fall at harvest when there is an abundance of supply. Prices typically rise to higher levels prior to planting in the spring. Price levels are affected by weather, especially during the summer growing season around late June and July. Prices usually rise following harvest.

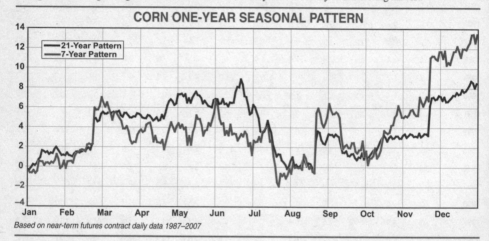

CORN ONE-YEAR SEASONAL PATTERN

Legend: 21-Year Pattern, 7-Year Pattern

Based on near-term futures contract daily data 1987–2007

CORN NEAR-TERM CONTRACT ANNUAL HIGHS, LOWS & CLOSES SINCE 1970

YEAR	HIGH DATE	HIGH CLOSE	LOW DATE	LOW CLOSE	YEAR CLOSE	YEAR	HIGH DATE	HIGH CLOSE	LOW DATE	LOW CLOSE	YEAR CLOSE
1970	09/14	157 1/4	01/27	120 1/8	155 1/2	1990	06/12	292 1/4	11/21	220 1/2	231 3/4
1971	06/16	160 3/8	09/30	112 7/8	123 3/8	1991	04/23	263 1/4	07/08	219 1/2	251 1/2
1972	12/12	163 1/4	02/15	119 1/8	154 3/4	1992	03/09	278 3/4	10/28	205	216 1/2
1973	08/14	347 3/4	02/07	150 7/8	268 3/4	1993	12/30	306	02/08	211 3/4	306
1974	10/03	395	04/05	251 3/4	341 3/4	1994	01/13	310	10/10	213 3/4	231
1975	01/06	350 3/4	06/30	249	261 1/2	1995	12/29	369 1/4	01/03	228 1/2	369 1/4
1976	06/10	309	11/15	232	256 1/2	1996	05/17	504 1/2	12/30	258 1/4	258 1/4
1977	02/24	265 1/4	08/19	183 1/4	223 3/4	1997	04/01	313	07/07	229 1/4	265
1978	05/30	270	08/11	213 1/2	231 3/4	1998	03/11	282	08/31	199 1/2	213 1/2
1979	06/22	320 1/2	01/05	228 1/4	289 1/4	1999	03/22	232 1/4	07/13	186	204 1/2
1980	11/28	409	03/31	258 1/4	378	2000	05/03	250 3/4	08/11	174 3/4	231 3/4
1981	01/02	381 3/4	12/15	263	270 1/2	2001	07/12	234 1/4	06/21	188 1/4	209
1982	04/26	289	10/25	214	244 3/4	2002	09/11	292 1/2	04/15	196	235 3/4
1983	08/23	371	01/04	242 3/4	337 1/4	2003	05/15	255 3/4	07/23	205 1/2	246
1984	04/04	361 3/4	12/21	265 1/4	269 1/4	2004	04/02	330 1/4	11/11	197 1/4	204 3/4
1985	04/19	285 1/2	09/09	215 1/4	248 1/4	2005	07/18	260	11/18	191 1/4	215 3/4
1986	01/15	249 1/4	12/30	160	160	2006	11/30	390 1/2	01/19	205	390 1/4
1987	06/16	202 1/4	02/13	142 3/4	184 3/4	2007	12/31	455 1/2	07/23	310	455 1/2
1988	06/27	357 1/2	01/04	187 1/2	284 1/2	2008*	05/08	630 1/4	01/02	462 1/2	AT PRESS-TIME
1989	01/10	289 1/2	08/03	217 1/4	239 3/4						

*Through May 30, 2008

CORN NEAR-TERM CONTRACT MONTHLY CLOSING PRICES

	Jan	Feb	Mar	Apr	May	Jun	Jul	Aug	Sep	Oct	Nov	Dec
1970	120 3/8	123 1/8	122 7/8	129 1/4	129 3/8	137 5/8	130 7/8	154 1/2	149 1/2	145 7/8	152 1/4	155 1/2
1971	153 7/8	152 1/2	146 1/8	144 1/2	149 7/8	150 1/4	132 1/2	118 5/8	112 7/8	115 3/4	119 3/4	123 3/8
1972	120 3/4	121 1/4	124 1/4	126 7/8	125 3/8	124 1/8	127 5/8	134 1/4	140 1/8	136 3/4	143 7/8	154 3/4
1973	161 1/2	158 5/8	155 1/2	164 7/8	218 3/8	199 3/4	288	250 1/2	252 1/4	238 1/2	265	268 3/4
1974	301 3/4	322 3/4	278	277 3/4	266	289 1/4	379 1/2	342 1/4	387 1/2	380 3/4	375 1/4	341 3/4
1975	311 1/4	262 1/4	298 3/4	285 1/4	270 1/2	249	287	302 3/4	303 1/4	277 3/4	279	261 1/2
1976	265	278	265 1/2	273 3/4	290 3/4	285 1/2	280 1/4	279 3/4	266 3/4	252 1/4	248 3/4	256 1/2
1977	253 1/2	262	251 3/4	252 1/2	249 1/2	225 3/4	194 1/4	191 3/4	203	214	228 3/4	223 3/4
1978	226 1/4	228 1/2	256 1/4	246 3/4	269 1/2	251 1/2	228	222 1/4	226 1/4	234 1/4	238 1/4	231 3/4
1979	234 1/4	246 3/4	251 1/2	265 3/4	268	299 1/2	281 1/2	286 3/4	282 1/2	264 1/2	291 1/4	289 1/4
1980	274 3/4	276 1/4	258 1/4	278 1/2	276 3/4	290 3/4	335 1/4	357 1/2	348 3/4	373 1/2	409	378
1981	355 1/2	369 3/4	364 3/4	367 1/2	351 3/4	334 1/2	338 1/2	306 1/4	288	287 1/2	280 1/4	270 1/2
1982	274	270	274 1/4	286 1/4	275	265 1/4	245 3/4	229 1/2	222	215 1/4	241	244 3/4
1983	267 3/4	281 1/2	312 3/4	318 1/4	304 1/2	297 1/4	320 1/4	359 1/2	354 3/4	344 3/4	340 3/4	337 1/4
1984	329 1/4	332 1/4	353 1/4	342 1/4	350 1/2	328 1/2	294 1/4	283 1/2	278 1/2	274 1/2	278 1/4	269 1/4
1985	272 1/2	271 1/4	281 1/4	279 3/4	274 1/2	255 1/2	231	218 3/4	224 3/4	232 3/4	243 3/4	248 1/4
1986	244	227	234 3/4	232 3/4	237	184	165 1/4	165 1/4	176 3/4	173 1/4	177 3/4	160
1987	157	153 3/4	162 1/2	184 1/4	188 3/4	186 1/2	163 1/2	166 1/2	179 3/4	179 1/2	196 1/2	184 3/4
1988	196 3/4	209 1/4	209 3/4	211 1/4	224 1/4	337 3/4	275	296 1/2	285 3/4	282 1/4	270 1/2	284 1/2
1989	274 3/4	278 1/2	268 1/2	270 1/2	260 3/4	255 1/2	222 1/2	236 3/4	233	237 1/2	241 3/4	239 3/4
1990	238 1/4	253 1/4	261 1/4	283	278	289 1/2	260 1/4	233 1/4	228	229 1/4	237 3/4	231 3/4
1991	244 1/4	251	252 3/4	254	245 3/4	224	258	254 3/4	249 1/4	251	247 1/2	251 1/2
1992	264 1/4	273 1/2	264 1/4	249 1/2	259 1/2	253 1/4	220 1/4	217 1/4	215 1/4	207 1/4	221 1/2	216 1/2
1993	214 1/2	219 1/4	230 1/4	232 1/2	224 1/2	229	235 3/4	237 1/2	244 3/4	257 3/4	285 1/2	306
1994	290 1/4	293 3/4	274 3/4	272	278 3/4	244 1/2	218 3/4	222 3/4	215 3/4	215 3/4	223	231
1995	229 1/2	242	250	255 1/4	266	278	281 3/4	293 3/4	311 3/4	332 1/2	337 3/4	369 1/4
1996	369	389 1/4	409	452	477 1/4	397 3/4	354 1/4	343 3/4	296 3/4	266	271	258 1/4
1997	270 1/4	295 1/4	310	293 1/4	270 3/4	238	265 1/2	269 1/4	257 3/4	279 3/4	280 3/4	265
1998	273	270 1/4	259	252 1/4	238 1/2	253 1/4	217 1/2	199 1/2	209	219	230	213 1/2
1999	214 1/2	210 1/4	225 1/2	218 3/4	219 1/2	216 1/4	203 1/4	219 1/4	208 1/4	199 1/2	200 1/2	204 1/2
2000	220	224	236	232	225	195 3/4	180 1/4	196 1/2	197 3/4	206	220 1/2	231 3/4
2001	209	222 1/2	203 1/4	207 1/2	192 3/4	197 1/4	218 3/4	232 1/4	214 1/2	205 1/2	220 1/2	209
2002	206	207 1/2	202 1/2	200 1/4	214	233	247 1/4	268	251 1/2	247 1/2	241 1/4	235 3/4
2003	238 1/4	233 1/4	236 1/2	231 1/4	244 1/4	223 3/4	206	241 3/4	220 1/4	247 1/4	248 3/4	246
2004	276 1/4	303	320	321 1/2	304	262 1/2	217 1/4	237 3/4	205 1/2	202 1/2	203 3/4	204 3/4
2005	197	222 3/4	213	213 1/2	222	222 1/4	236 1/2	216 1/2	205 1/2	196 1/4	201 3/4	215 3/4
2006	218 3/4	238 3/4	236	249	251 1/4	246	239	248	262 1/2	320 3/4	390 1/2	390 1/4
2007	404	435 1/2	374 1/2	367 1/2	390 1/4	340	325 3/4	340	373	375 1/2	401 1/2	455 1/2
2008	501 1/4	556 1/2	567 1/4	612 1/4	599 1/4							

CORN NEAR-TERM CONTRACT MONTHLY PERCENT CHANGES

	Jan	Feb	Mar	Apr	May	Jun	Jul	Aug	Sep	Oct	Nov	Dec	Year's Change
1970	−0.6	2.3	−0.2	5.2	0.1	6.4	−4.9	18.0	−3.2	−2.4	4.4	2.1	28.4
1971	−1.0	−0.9	−4.2	−1.1	3.7	0.2	−11.8	−10.5	−4.8	2.5	3.5	3.0	−20.7
1972	−2.1	0.4	2.5	2.1	−1.2	−1.0	2.8	5.2	4.4	−2.4	5.2	7.6	25.4
1973	4.4	−1.8	−2.0	6.0	32.4	−8.5	44.2	−13.0	0.7	−5.5	11.1	1.4	73.7
1974	12.3	7.0	−13.9	−0.1	−4.2	8.7	31.2	−9.8	13.2	−1.7	−1.4	−8.9	27.2
1975	−8.9	−15.7	13.9	−4.5	−5.2	−7.9	15.3	5.5	0.2	−8.4	0.5	−6.3	−23.5
1976	1.3	4.9	−4.5	3.1	6.2	−1.8	−1.8	−0.2	−4.6	−5.4	−1.4	3.1	−1.9
1977	−1.2	3.4	−3.9	0.3	−1.2	−9.5	−14.0	−1.3	5.9	5.4	6.9	−2.2	−12.8
1978	1.1	1.0	12.1	−3.7	9.2	−6.7	−9.3	−2.5	1.8	3.5	1.7	−2.7	3.6
1979	1.1	5.3	1.9	5.7	0.8	11.8	−6.0	1.9	−1.5	−6.4	10.1	−0.7	24.8
1980	−5.0	0.5	−6.5	7.8	−0.6	5.1	15.3	6.6	−2.4	7.1	9.5	−7.6	30.7
1981	−6.0	4.0	−1.4	0.8	−4.3	−4.9	1.2	−9.5	−6.0	−0.2	−2.5	−3.5	−28.4
1982	1.3	−1.5	1.6	4.4	−3.9	−3.5	−7.4	−6.6	−3.3	−3.0	12.0	1.6	−9.5
1983	9.4	5.1	11.1	1.8	−4.3	−2.4	7.7	12.3	−1.3	−2.8	−1.2	−1.0	37.8
1984	−2.4	0.9	6.3	−3.1	2.4	−6.3	−10.4	−3.7	−1.8	−1.4	1.4	−3.2	−20.2
1985	1.2	−0.5	3.7	−0.5	−1.9	−6.9	−9.6	−5.3	2.7	3.6	4.7	1.8	−7.8
1986	−1.7	−7.0	3.4	−0.9	1.8	−22.4	−10.2	N/C	7.0	−2.0	2.6	−10.0	−35.5
1987	−1.9	−2.1	5.7	13.4	2.4	−1.2	−12.3	1.8	8.0	−0.1	9.5	−6.0	15.5
1988	6.5	6.4	0.2	0.7	6.2	50.6	−18.6	7.8	−3.6	−1.2	−4.2	5.2	54.0
1989	−3.4	1.4	−3.6	0.7	−3.6	−2.0	−12.9	6.4	−1.6	1.9	1.8	−0.8	−15.7
1990	−0.6	6.3	3.2	8.3	−1.8	4.1	−10.1	−10.4	−2.3	0.5	3.7	−2.5	−3.3
1991	5.4	2.8	0.7	0.5	−3.2	−8.9	15.2	−1.3	−2.2	0.7	−1.4	1.6	8.5
1992	5.1	3.5	−3.4	−5.6	4.0	−2.4	−13.0	−1.4	−0.9	−3.7	6.9	−2.3	−13.9
1993	−0.9	2.2	5.0	1.0	−3.4	2.0	2.9	0.7	3.1	5.3	10.8	7.2	41.3
1994	−5.1	1.2	−6.5	−1.0	2.5	−12.3	−10.5	1.8	−3.1	N/C	3.4	3.6	−24.5
1995	−0.6	5.4	3.3	2.1	4.2	4.5	1.3	4.3	6.1	6.7	1.6	9.3	59.8
1996	−0.1	5.5	5.1	10.5	5.6	−16.7	−10.9	−3.0	−13.7	−10.4	1.9	−4.7	−30.1
1997	4.6	9.3	5.0	−5.4	−7.7	−12.1	11.6	1.4	−4.3	8.5	0.4	−5.6	2.6
1998	3.0	−1.0	−4.2	−2.6	−5.5	6.2	−14.1	−8.3	4.8	4.8	5.0	−7.2	−19.4
1999	0.5	−2.0	7.3	−3.0	0.3	−1.5	−6.0	7.9	−5.0	−4.2	0.5	2.0	−4.2
2000	7.6	1.8	5.4	−1.7	−3.0	−13.0	−7.9	9.0	0.6	4.2	7.0	5.1	13.3
2001	−9.8	6.5	−8.7	2.1	−7.1	2.3	10.9	6.2	−7.6	−4.2	7.3	−5.2	−9.8
2002	−1.4	0.7	−2.4	−1.0	6.7	8.9	6.1	8.4	−6.2	−1.6	−2.4	−2.4	12.8
2003	1.1	−2.1	1.4	−2.2	5.6	−8.4	−7.9	17.4	−8.9	12.3	0.6	−1.1	4.3
2004	12.3	9.7	5.6	0.5	−5.4	−13.7	−17.2	9.4	−13.6	−1.5	0.6	0.5	−16.8
2005	−3.8	13.1	−4.4	0.2	4.0	0.1	6.4	−8.5	−5.1	−4.5	2.8	6.9	5.4
2006	1.4	9.1	−1.2	5.5	0.9	−2.1	−2.8	3.8	5.8	22.2	21.7	−0.1	80.9
2007	3.5	7.8	−14.0	−1.9	6.2	−12.9	−4.2	4.4	9.7	0.7	6.9	13.4	16.7
2008	10.0	11.0	1.9	7.9	−2.1								
TOTALS	36.6	103.9	21.3	52.3	35.6	−78.1	−61.7	44.9	−33.0	16.9	151.5	−8.6	
AVG.	0.9	2.7	0.5	1.3	0.9	−2.1	−1.6	1.2	−0.9	0.4	4.0	−0.2	
# Up	20	29	22	23	20	13	14	21	15	16	31	17	
# Down	19	10	17	16	19	25	24	16	23	21	7	21	

SOYBEANS CYCLE, SEASONAL PATTERN & TRADING GUIDE

Soybeans are traded at the CME Group, which was formerly the Chicago Board of Trade. One futures contract is 5,000 bushels, and every penny move represents a $50 change in value per contract position. The contract symbol is S and it has several tradable contract months, beginning with the March then May, July, September, and November contracts.

This commodity is now traded both electronically and through the open outcry session; the pit-traded hours are from 9:30 AM until 1:15PM (CT). The daily trading limit is set at 70 cents per bushel above or below the previous day's settlement price. This represents a $3,500 move per contract. There are no trading limits in the spot month (limits are lifted beginning on first notice day).

The United States is the leading producer of soybeans, followed by Brazil and China. For the most part, this crop is grown in the Corn Belt which consists of Illinois, Iowa, Indiana, Ohio, Missouri, and Minnesota. Generally, it is planted in April through June, but it can be delayed if necessary. For this reason, soybeans can be used as an alternative crop for corn and cotton when weather affects the planting of other crops such as a wet, cold weather condition. Harvesting is generally complete by October.

There are three soybean-related futures contracts: soybeans, soybean meal, and bean oil. Soybeans are the cash crop and are grown to yield soybean meal and bean oil. Soybean meal is used to enrich the feed for hogs, cattle, and poultry. Bean oil is used in food-related products like shortening, salad dressings, and cooking oils. Of the two by-products, soybean meal is more valuable because there is little in the form of a competing product except for animal bone meal or fish meal, which are used as an animal feed.

Unfortunately, it cannot be stored for extended periods, making its price more volatile. The seasonal price patterns show a peak in May as the U.S. crop is now in the ground and developing and the Southern Hemisphere crop is being marketed. Under normal growing conditions, with the exception of droughts, the July-August period is usually a bearish time for soybeans. The seasonal lows occur, in general, into fall, due to the harvest and when there are fresh supplies. This also puts pressure on bean meal and bean oil.

SOYBEANS ONE-YEAR SEASONAL PATTERN

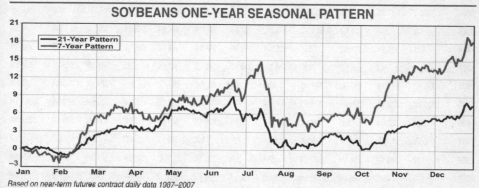

Based on near-term futures contract daily data 1987–2007

SOYBEANS NEAR-TERM CONTRACT ANNUAL HIGHS, LOWS & CLOSES SINCE 1969

YEAR	HIGH DATE	HIGH CLOSE	LOW DATE	LOW CLOSE	YEAR CLOSE	YEAR	HIGH DATE	HIGH CLOSE	LOW DATE	LOW CLOSE	YEAR CLOSE
1969	05/13	271 3/8	09/02	234 7/8	251 7/8	1989	01/06	829 1/2	10/13	544 1/4	582 1/4
1970	10/27	312	01/05	251 1/4	297 7/8	1990	07/03	663 3/4	01/25	558 1/4	574 3/4
1971	07/16	347 1/2	04/08	289 3/4	317	1991	08/02	642 3/4	07/08	515 3/4	557
1972	12/12	435 1/2	01/14	307	426 1/2	1992	06/02	630	10/02	527 1/4	574 1/4
1973	06/04	1211	01/08	422	586 1/4	1993	07/19	737	02/08	564 3/4	712 1/2
1974	10/04	949	05/06	523	715	1994	05/23	732 1/4	10/07	527 1/4	561 1/2
1975	01/02	723 1/2	12/15	445 1/4	459	1995	12/29	744 3/4	02/01	546 1/2	744 3/4
1976	07/09	750 1/4	01/26	456 3/4	711 1/4	1996	04/25	831	11/01	666 1/2	687 3/4
1977	04/21	1046 1/2	09/14	505 1/4	603 3/4	1997	05/06	892	07/02	607 1/2	676 1/4
1978	05/30	745 1/4	02/09	558 1/2	690 1/2	1998	02/10	693	08/31	511 1/2	541 1/4
1979	06/22	838 1/2	10/26	655 1/2	664 3/4	1999	01/08	555	07/08	410	469 3/4
1980	11/05	954 1/2	04/01	579 1/2	818 1/2	2000	05/04	572 1/4	08/07	446 3/4	509 3/4
1981	01/06	842 3/4	12/21	606 3/4	626 1/4	2001	07/17	528	12/31	422 1/4	422 1/4
1982	04/23	676	10/04	518 1/4	573 1/4	2002	09/11	588 3/4	01/02	418 1/4	565
1983	09/09	948	01/04	571 1/2	832 3/4	2003	10/29	803 1/2	07/31	509	794
1984	05/21	893 1/4	12/12	584 3/4	585 1/4	2004	03/22	1055 3/4	11/05	505 1/4	547 1/4
1985	03/19	609	11/25	484 3/4	542 3/4	2005	06/24	748 1/4	02/04	499 1/2	613 1/2
1986	01/08	554 1/2	08/25	468 1/4	494 3/4	2006	12/29	697 1/4	09/12	538 1/2	697 1/4
1987	12/23	618 1/2	02/26	480 1/2	614 3/4	2007	12/26	1239 1/2	01/09	664 1/2	1214 1/4
1988	06/21	1046 1/2	02/02	597	819 1/4	2008*	03/03	1559 1/2	01/23	1189 1/2	AT PRESS-TIME

*Through May 30, 2008

SOYBEANS NEAR-TERM CONTRACT MONTHLY CLOSING PRICES

	Jan	Feb	Mar	Apr	May	Jun	Jul	Aug	Sep	Oct	Nov	Dec
1969	264 1/2	266 3/8	262 1/2	270	267 1/8	263 1/4	246 1/2	236 1/2	236 3/8	249 5/8	243 7/8	251 7/8
1970	254 1/8	261	259 1/4	268 5/8	271	290	283 3/4	279 1/4	286	308	299	297 7/8
1971	307 3/8	307 3/4	300 1/2	295 7/8	311	323	330 1/8	315	309 3/4	323 1/4	310 1/2	317
1972	314 3/8	335 1/8	343 1/2	350 1/2	350	338 3/4	334 1/2	336 5/8	347 5/8	354 7/8	379 1/2	426 1/2
1973	490 3/8	609 1/4	538 3/4	678 1/4	1058	860	910	701	645	540 1/2	602 1/2	586 1/4
1974	644	627 1/4	616 1/4	548 1/4	547	570 1/2	895	732 1/2	878	823 3/4	782 1/2	715
1975	602 3/4	507 1/4	610	533	502 3/4	496 3/4	582 1/2	569 1/2	568 3/4	503 1/2	485 1/2	459
1976	467 1/2	486 1/2	469 3/4	487 1/4	579	677 1/2	608 1/2	673	632	684	674 1/2	711 1/4
1977	723 1/2	782 1/4	893 1/2	983	960	713 1/2	566 1/2	516	534 1/4	559	585 3/4	603 3/4
1978	564 3/4	590 1/2	689 1/2	702 1/2	737	652 1/4	621 3/4	640 1/2	651	718	678	690 1/2
1979	706	766	771 1/4	735	739	741 1/2	715 1/2	721 3/4	712 1/4	667 3/4	681 3/4	664 3/4
1980	673	657 1/2	583	615 1/2	623 3/4	688	783 3/4	817	811	923	933	818 1/2
1981	725 1/2	761	783 1/2	801 1/4	764 3/4	710	739 1/4	671 1/2	648	671 1/2	646 1/2	626 1/4
1982	656 3/4	632 3/4	640	665 3/4	635 3/4	618	600 3/4	559 1/2	534 1/4	547	573 1/2	573 1/4
1983	604 1/2	575 1/2	637	657 1/4	607 1/2	619	708 1/2	911 1/2	866	830 1/2	796 1/2	832 3/4
1984	730 3/4	765	789	782 1/2	847	738 1/4	612 1/2	636 1/2	591 3/4	631	609	585 1/4
1985	601 1/4	573	605 1/2	594 1/2	567 1/2	551 3/4	521 3/4	511 3/4	512 3/4	527 1/2	499	542 3/4
1986	533	529 3/4	541 1/2	551	525 1/4	488 3/4	500 1/4	479 1/2	486 1/2	500	503 1/2	494 3/4
1987	500 1/4	483	496 1/2	537	548 3/4	543 1/2	524 1/2	504 1/4	532	541 1/2	605 1/4	614 3/4
1988	609 1/2	642 1/2	653 1/2	698 1/2	798	986	778 1/2	867 1/2	813	789 1/4	763 3/4	819 1/4
1989	772 3/4	773 1/2	738 1/4	729 1/2	714	670	588	587 1/2	568	572 1/4	582 3/4	582 1/4
1990	561	580 3/4	595	648 1/2	607 1/4	638 3/4	599 1/4	613 3/4	617 1/2	609 1/4	589 1/2	574 3/4
1991	566 3/4	588	574 3/4	589 1/2	581 3/4	531	590	590 1/2	587	567	557	557
1992	572	589 1/4	588 1/4	580 1/4	614	611	555 1/2	541	540 3/4	552 3/4	563 3/4	574 1/4
1993	574	580	588 1/4	591 1/4	608 1/2	656 1/4	686 1/2	663 1/2	629 3/4	629 1/2	671 1/2	712 1/2
1994	686 3/4	683 3/4	681 3/4	676 1/2	701	640 1/2	575 1/4	573 3/4	536	554	563 1/2	561 1/2
1995	547 1/2	564 3/4	574	580	580 3/4	588 1/2	606	623	646	684 1/2	686 1/4	744 3/4
1996	738 3/4	745	751	795	788 1/4	757 1/2	747	794 1/2	758	669	712 3/4	687 3/4
1997	738 1/4	793 1/4	855 3/4	887	880 1/2	644	685	625 1/2	621 1/2	696 1/4	718 1/4	676 1/4
1998	672 3/4	658 1/4	645	638 1/2	618 1/2	632	560 3/4	511 1/2	520 1/4	568 1/4	593 1/2	541 1/4
1999	506 3/4	458	483 3/4	486 1/2	461 3/4	450 1/2	433 1/4	483	491 1/4	482 3/4	476 1/4	469 3/4
2000	508	511	545 1/2	539 1/4	517 1/2	482 3/4	454	505	490 1/2	470 1/4	506	509 3/4
2001	459 1/2	455 3/4	428 1/2	438	451	474 1/4	512 1/2	486	451 1/4	436 3/4	444 1/2	422 1/4
2002	430 1/4	440 1/4	476 1/4	466 3/4	508 3/4	528 3/4	536 1/2	544 3/4	545 3/4	566 1/2	578 3/4	565
2003	564	575	574 1/2	627 1/4	624 1/2	614 1/4	509	589	677 1/4	797 3/4	756 1/4	794
2004	819 1/2	937 1/2	995	1013	814	782 1/2	569	627 1/4	527	533 1/2	534 3/4	547 1/4
2005	514 3/4	622	627 1/2	626 1/4	680 1/4	656	686 3/4	598 3/4	573 1/4	576	558	613 1/2
2006	594 1/4	594	571 1/2	601	579 1/2	600 1/2	599 3/4	555 3/4	547 1/2	644 1/4	685 1/2	697 1/4
2007	719 1/2	787 1/2	761 1/4	743	806 1/4	855 3/4	857 1/2	882 1/2	991 1/4	1025 3/4	1080	1214 1/4
2008	1274 1/2	1536 1/2	1197 1/4	1314	1363 1/2							

SOYBEANS NEAR-TERM CONTRACT MONTHLY PERCENT CHANGES

	Jan	Feb	Mar	Apr	May	Jun	Jul	Aug	Sep	Oct	Nov	Dec	Year's Change
1969	0.2	0.7	-1.5	2.9	-1.1	-1.5	-6.4	-4.1	-0.1	5.6	-2.3	3.3	-4.5
1970	0.9	2.7	-0.7	3.6	0.9	7.0	-2.2	-1.6	2.4	7.7	-2.9	-0.4	18.3
1971	3.2	0.1	-2.4	-1.5	5.1	3.9	2.2	-4.6	-1.7	4.4	-3.9	2.1	6.4
1972	-0.8	6.6	2.5	2.0	-0.1	-3.2	-1.3	0.6	3.3	2.1	6.9	12.4	34.5
1973	15.0	24.2	-11.6	25.9	56.0	-18.7	5.8	-23.0	-8.0	-16.2	11.5	-2.7	37.5
1974	9.9	-2.6	-1.8	-11.0	-0.2	4.3	56.9	-18.2	19.9	-6.2	-5.0	-8.6	22.0
1975	-15.7	-15.8	20.3	-12.6	-5.7	-1.2	17.3	-2.2	-0.1	-11.5	-3.6	-5.5	-35.8
1976	1.9	4.1	-3.4	3.7	18.8	17.0	-10.2	10.6	-6.1	8.2	-1.4	5.4	55.0
1977	1.7	8.1	14.2	10.0	-2.3	-25.7	-20.6	-8.9	3.5	4.6	4.8	3.1	-15.1
1978	-6.5	4.6	16.8	1.9	4.9	-11.5	-4.7	3.0	1.6	10.3	-5.6	1.8	14.4
1979	2.2	8.5	0.7	-4.7	0.5	0.3	-3.5	0.9	-1.3	-6.2	2.1	-2.5	-3.7
1980	1.2	-2.3	-11.3	5.6	1.3	10.3	13.9	4.2	-0.7	13.8	1.1	-12.3	23.1
1981	-11.4	4.9	3.0	2.3	4.6	7.2	4.1	-9.2	-3.5	3.8	-3.7	-3.1	-23.5
1982	4.9	-3.7	1.1	4.0	-4.5	-2.8	-2.8	-6.9	-4.5	2.4	4.8	-0.04	-8.5
1983	5.5	-4.8	10.7	3.2	-7.6	1.9	14.5	28.7	-5.0	-4.1	-4.1	4.6	45.3
1984	-12.2	4.7	3.1	-0.8	8.2	-12.8	-17.0	3.9	-7.0	6.6	-3.5	-3.9	-29.7
1985	2.7	-4.7	5.7	-1.8	-4.5	-2.8	-5.4	-1.9	0.2	2.9	-5.4	8.8	-7.3
1986	-1.8	-0.6	2.2	1.8	-4.7	-6.9	2.4	-4.1	1.5	2.8	0.7	-1.7	-8.8
1987	1.1	-3.4	2.8	8.2	2.2	-1.0	-3.5	-3.9	5.5	1.8	11.8	1.6	24.3
1988	-0.9	5.4	1.7	6.9	14.2	23.6	-21.0	11.4	-6.3	-2.9	-3.2	7.3	33.3
1989	-5.7	0.1	-4.6	-1.2	-2.1	-6.2	-12.2	-0.1	-3.3	0.7	1.8	-0.1	-28.9
1990	-3.6	3.5	2.5	9.0	-6.4	5.2	-6.2	2.4	0.6	-1.3	-3.2	-2.5	-1.3
1991	-1.4	3.7	-2.3	2.6	-1.3	-8.7	11.1	0.1	-0.6	-3.4	-1.8	N/C	-3.1
1992	2.7	3.0	-0.2	-1.4	5.8	-0.5	-9.1	-2.6	-0.1	2.2	2.0	1.9	3.1
1993	-0.04	1.0	1.4	0.5	2.9	7.8	4.6	-3.4	-5.1	-0.04	6.7	6.1	24.1
1994	-3.6	-0.4	-0.3	-0.8	3.6	-8.6	-10.2	-0.3	-6.6	3.4	1.7	-0.4	-21.2
1995	-2.5	3.2	1.6	1.0	0.1	1.3	3.0	2.8	3.7	6.0	0.3	8.5	32.6
1996	-0.8	0.8	0.8	5.0	-0.8	-0.9	-1.4	6.4	-4.6	-11.7	6.5	-3.5	-7.7
1997	7.3	7.5	7.9	3.7	-0.7	-26.9	6.4	-8.7	-0.6	12.0	3.2	-5.8	-1.7
1998	-0.5	-2.2	-2.0	-1.0	-3.1	2.2	-11.3	-8.8	1.8	9.1	4.4	-8.8	-20.0
1999	-6.4	-9.6	5.6	0.6	-5.1	-2.4	-3.8	11.5	1.7	-1.7	-1.3	-1.4	-13.2
2000	8.1	0.6	6.8	-1.1	-4.0	-6.7	-6.0	11.2	-2.9	-4.1	7.6	0.7	8.5
2001	-9.9	-0.8	-6.0	2.2	3.0	5.2	8.1	-5.2	-7.2	-3.2	1.8	-5.0	-17.2
2002	1.9	2.3	8.2	-2.0	9.0	3.9	1.5	1.5	0.2	3.8	2.2	-2.4	33.8
2003	-0.2	2.0	-0.1	9.2	-0.4	-1.6	-17.1	15.7	15.0	17.8	-5.2	5.0	40.5
2004	3.2	14.4	6.1	1.8	-19.6	-3.9	-27.3	10.2	-16.0	1.2	0.2	2.3	-31.1
2005	-5.9	20.8	0.9	-0.2	8.6	-3.6	4.7	-12.8	-4.3	0.5	-3.1	9.9	12.1
2006	-3.1	-0.04	-3.8	5.2	-3.6	3.6	-0.1	-7.3	-1.5	17.7	6.4	1.7	13.7
2007	3.2	9.5	-3.3	-2.4	8.5	6.1	0.2	2.9	12.3	3.5	5.3	12.4	74.1
2008	5.0	20.6	-22.1	9.8	3.8								
TOTALS	-11.1	116.7	49.2	91.0	75.0	-64.7	-46.6	-9.8	-23.9	82.2	34.6	28.3	
AVG.	-0.3	2.9	1.2	2.3	1.9	-1.7	-1.2	-0.3	-0.6	2.1	0.9	0.7	
# Up	20	27	23	26	19	16	16	18	15	26	22	19	
# Down	20	13	17	14	21	23	23	21	24	13	17	19	

WHEAT CYCLE, SEASONAL PATTERN & TRADING GUIDE

CBOT wheat is traded at the CME Group, which was formerly the Chicago Board of Trade. One futures contract is 5,000 bushels, and every penny move represents a $50 change in value per contract position. The contract symbol is W and it has several tradable contract months, beginning with the March then May, July, September, and December contracts.

This commodity is now traded both electronically and through the open outcry session; the pit-traded hours are from 9:30 AM until 1:15PM (CT).The daily price limit move is 30 cents from the previous day's settlement price, which represents at $1,500 mover per contract. However, there are no price limits in the expiring contract during the delivery month or on the two business days prior to the first day of the delivery month.

This grade of wheat is called winter wheat since it is planted in the fall and harvested in midsummer. CBOT wheat is a lower-end soft red wheat that is primarily used in pastries, cakes and cookies, and other related products. Early 2008 saw a record price high traded at 1334.5 in the front contract month after ongoing concerns about declining world wheat supplies and a deterioration in the crop condition led by a severe drought in Australia. Because of limited alternatives, foreign buyers have flocked to the United States for wheat supplies. Due to the decline in the U.S. dollar, this gave added incentive to foreigners because a weaker dollar gave them added purchasing power. This pushed the first four-month export sales in 2008 to 880 million bushels, which was up 500 million over the same period in 2007 and 245 million bushels larger than wheat's previous highest pace for this period set in 1995/96.

Due to ongoing weather problems across the globe in wheat-producing countries, on top of increased global demand plus with the weaker U.S. dollar, the door remains wide open for prices to continue to remain firm in 2009, and these considerations may magnify the price moves during the seasonally strong period next year. Since harvest is typically around the June-July time period, this is when supplies are most abundant even when we are in years when crops yields are less than average. This is what we call the harvest lows as we now begin to sell and export our inventories. After the new year, prices tend to continue to decline as Southern Hemisphere supplies enter the world market, and this may explain a well-known phenomenon called the "February Break," whereby wheat prices usually show some degree of decline during the month of February.

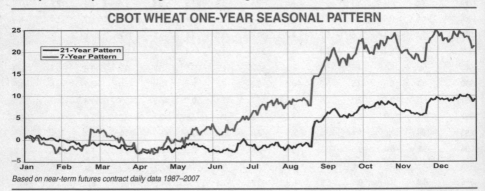

CBOT WHEAT ONE-YEAR SEASONAL PATTERN

21-Year Pattern
7-Year Pattern

Based on near-term futures contract daily data 1987–2007

CBOT WHEAT NEAR-TERM CONTRACT ANNUAL HIGHS, LOWS & CLOSES SINCE 1969

YEAR	HIGH DATE	HIGH CLOSE	LOW DATE	LOW CLOSE	YEAR CLOSE	YEAR	HIGH DATE	HIGH CLOSE	LOW DATE	LOW CLOSE	YEAR CLOSE
1969	12/24	148	07/28	121 1/4	147 3/8	1989	01/06	448 3/4	06/08	381 1/4	409 1/4
1970	11/05	179	05/28	134 1/2	168 1/2	1990	01/03	410	11/20	245 1/4	260 1/2
1971	01/15	172 1/2	08/11	141 1/2	163 1/8	1991	12/26	405 3/4	01/15	246 1/4	404 3/4
1972	12/14	269 1/2	06/23	141 1/8	264	1992	02/10	459 1/2	08/13	305 3/4	353 3/4
1973	12/31	545	03/21	214 3/4	545	1993	01/19	392 1/2	06/17	277 1/2	378 1/4
1974	02/15	631 1/2	05/09	336	458 1/2	1994	10/11	416 1/4	07/06	313 1/2	401 1/2
1975	08/22	463	06/02	295 3/4	335 3/4	1995	12/29	512 1/4	03/10	341 1/2	512 1/4
1976	02/27	401 3/4	11/11	255 3/4	277 1/2	1996	04/25	628 1/2	11/05	368 3/4	381 1/4
1977	02/24	293 3/4	08/19	217 1/4	279 1/4	1997	04/22	447	07/07	321 3/4	325 3/4
1978	11/30	369	02/28	260 3/4	343 1/4	1998	03/11	348	08/05	246 3/4	276 1/4
1979	06/22	489 1/2	04/23	326 1/2	454 1/4	1999	03/29	294 1/4	12/13	237 3/4	248 1/2
1980	10/28	541 1/2	04/18	380 1/2	501	2000	06/22	289 3/4	08/07	233 1/2	279 1/2
1981	01/02	508 1/2	12/23	376 1/4	391 1/2	2001	11/23	296 1/4	06/28	254 1/2	289
1982	01/08	402	10/21	301 3/4	330 3/4	2002	09/09	422	04/29	265	325
1983	08/22	423 1/4	02/28	321 1/2	363 1/2	2003	12/03	414 3/4	03/28	279 1/4	377
1984	04/04	377 1/4	02/13	321 3/4	347 3/4	2004	03/22	422 3/4	12/02	296 1/4	307 1/2
1985	04/08	370 3/4	08/20	280 1/4	343 1/4	2005	03/15	368	02/04	287 3/4	339 1/4
1986	01/02	339 1/2	07/01	240 1/2	274 1/2	2006	10/16	542 1/2	01/18	322 1/2	501
1987	12/18	321	07/21	256 3/4	310 3/4	2007	12/14	979 1/2	04/03	419	885
1988	12/23	440 1/2	03/10	297 3/4	440	2008*	03/12	1282 1/2	05/29	743 1/2	AT PRESS-TIME

*Through May 30, 2008

WHEAT NEAR-TERM CONTRACT MONTHLY CLOSING PRICES

	Jan	Feb	Mar	Apr	May	Jun	Jul	Aug	Sep	Oct	Nov	Dec
1969	134 3/8	131 5/8	125 7/8	130 1/8	128 1/8	127 3/4	123 3/4	133 5/8	134 7/8	135 1/4	143 5/8	147 3/8
1970	143 3/4	147 1/4	144 1/4	142 1/4	134 1/2	142	147 1/8	164 1/4	168 3/8	174 1/2	172 1/4	168 1/2
1971	166 1/2	162	158 1/8	151 3/4	157 1/2	156 1/2	147 5/8	149 3/4	146 7/8	161 3/8	155 1/2	163 1/8
1972	164 5/8	155	157 3/4	147 1/8	145 1/2	146	157 3/8	193 1/4	215 3/4	220 1/2	245 1/2	264
1973	247	235 3/4	222 3/4	233 3/8	281 1/4	268	364	497 1/2	491 1/2	430 1/2	472	545
1974	564 1/2	572	431 1/2	377	352 1/2	414	472	443 1/2	493	520 3/4	508 1/2	458 1/2
1975	379 1/2	349	387 1/4	328 3/4	305 1/2	307 1/2	366 3/4	425 1/2	429 1/2	386 1/4	355 1/2	335 3/4
1976	349 3/4	401 3/4	343 1/2	337 1/2	356 1/2	373 1/4	341	323 1/2	288 1/2	275	265 3/4	277 1/2
1977	274 1/4	275	272 3/4	265 1/2	246 1/4	251 1/2	225 1/2	230	252 1/4	259	275	279 1/4
1978	266 3/4	260 3/4	313 1/2	312	332	317 1/4	315 3/4	330 1/2	342 1/2	361 1/2	369	343 1/4
1979	351 1/2	353 1/4	339 3/4	347 1/2	366 3/4	433 1/2	410 1/2	456 1/4	450 3/4	421 1/4	456	454 1/4
1980	467 3/4	447 1/4	383 1/2	399 1/4	402 3/4	433 1/2	465	477	503 1/2	528 3/4	540 3/4	501
1981	465 3/4	457 1/2	433 3/4	443	412 1/4	389 3/4	407 1/2	417	424 3/4	439 1/4	439 1/2	391 1/2
1982	377	366 3/4	370 1/4	374 3/4	351 1/2	355 3/4	342 3/4	356 1/4	319 3/4	317 1/2	346	330 3/4
1983	343 1/2	321 1/2	360 1/4	361 1/2	343 1/4	356 3/4	372 3/4	410 1/4	370 3/4	354 1/2	355 3/4	363 1/2
1984	328 3/4	331 1/4	374	341 3/4	356	359 1/4	349 1/4	352	347	362 1/4	353 3/4	347 3/4
1985	350 3/4	336 1/4	356 1/2	327	315	321 1/4	295 1/4	287 3/4	297	323 3/4	334 3/4	343 1/4
1986	327 1/4	286 1/4	304 1/4	293 1/2	248 1/2	246	257 1/2	261 1/4	265 1/4	287	286 1/4	274 1/2
1987	288 1/4	280	284 1/2	274	274 1/4	263 1/4	261 1/4	286 3/4	289 1/4	296 1/2	318 1/4	310 3/4
1988	326	323 1/2	299 1/4	315 1/2	351 1/2	395 1/2	368 1/4	415 3/4	414 3/4	415 3/4	427 1/2	440
1989	440 1/2	434 3/4	403 3/4	405	387 1/2	404 3/4	384 1/2	399 1/4	407 1/4	394 1/2	407 3/4	409 1/4
1990	375 3/4	362 1/4	351 3/4	345 3/4	333 3/4	331	288 1/4	277 1/2	277 3/4	262	261 3/4	260 1/2
1991	263	269 1/2	286 3/4	283 1/4	287	275	294	321	332 1/2	363 1/2	366	404 3/4
1992	440 1/4	400	379	353 1/2	349 1/2	352 1/2	317 1/4	333	350 1/4	354 1/2	371	353 3/4
1993	380	333 1/4	347 1/4	301 1/4	288 1/4	287 1/4	304	315 1/2	318 3/4	335 1/2	350 1/2	378 1/4
1994	371 3/4	345 1/4	329 3/4	330 3/4	327 1/2	322 1/4	330 1/2	379 1/4	403 1/2	384 1/2	384 1/2	401 1/2
1995	373 1/2	347 1/4	343 1/4	351	373 1/4	446	464 1/4	462 3/4	492 1/4	497 3/4	495	512 1/4
1996	519 1/2	501 1/2	499 1/4	567	528 3/4	482 1/2	440	453 1/4	436	371 1/4	377 1/2	381 1/4
1997	359 3/4	375 1/4	397 1/2	433 1/2	360 1/2	332 1/4	362	394	354 1/4	360 1/2	357 3/4	325 3/4
1998	337 1/4	338 1/4	320 1/4	301 1/4	284 1/4	287 1/2	252 1/2	254	269 1/4	294 1/4	294 1/4	276 1/4
1999	275 1/2	248 1/2	280 1/4	268	252 1/4	264 1/4	263 3/4	282 1/4	275 3/4	255 3/4	249 1/2	248 1/2
2000	256 1/4	259	262 1/4	254 3/4	274 3/4	271 1/4	246 1/4	268 1/4	265	254 3/4	273 3/4	279 1/2
2001	273	276 3/4	255	283 1/4	267	258	278 1/2	289	270 3/4	293 1/4	289 1/2	289
2002	286	276	285	268 3/4	282 1/4	313	334	370	396 1/2	402 1/4	379 3/4	325
2003	320 1/2	310 1/4	286 3/4	282 3/4	324 1/4	310 1/2	348 1/2	381	360 1/4	369 1/2	406 3/4	377
2004	389	390 3/4	408	390	362	345 1/2	312 1/4	322 3/4	306 3/4	316 1/2	301 1/4	307 1/2
2005	291	345 1/4	331	326	331 3/4	331 1/4	327 3/4	317 1/2	346 1/4	317	320 3/4	339 1/4
2006	343 1/4	381	347 3/4	358 1/2	393 1/2	396	397 1/2	422 1/4	443	483	521 1/2	501
2007	467 1/2	488	438	495 1/2	517	597	630	775 1/2	939	808	885 1/2	885
2008	929 1/2	1086	929	801	761 1/2							

165

WHEAT NEAR-TERM CONTRACT MONTHLY PERCENT CHANGES

	Jan	Feb	Mar	Apr	May	Jun	Jul	Aug	Sep	Oct	Nov	Dec	Year's Change
1969	−0.8	−2.0	−4.4	3.4	−1.5	−0.3	−3.1	8.0	0.9	0.3	6.2	2.6	8.8
1970	−2.5	2.4	−2.0	−1.4	−5.4	5.6	3.6	11.6	2.5	3.6	−1.3	−2.2	14.3
1971	−1.2	−2.7	−2.4	−4.0	3.8	−0.6	−5.7	1.4	−1.9	9.9	−3.6	4.9	−3.2
1972	0.9	−5.8	1.8	−6.7	−1.1	0.3	7.8	22.8	11.6	2.2	11.3	7.5	61.8
1973	−6.4	−4.6	−5.5	4.8	20.5	−4.7	35.8	36.7	−1.2	−12.4	9.6	15.5	106.4
1974	3.6	1.3	−24.6	−12.6	−6.5	17.4	14.0	−6.0	11.2	5.6	−2.4	−9.8	−15.9
1975	−17.2	−8.0	11.0	−15.1	−7.1	0.7	19.3	16.0	0.9	−10.1	−8.0	−5.6	−26.8
1976	4.2	14.9	−14.5	−1.7	5.6	4.7	−8.6	−5.1	−10.8	−4.7	−3.4	4.4	−17.3
1977	−1.2	0.3	−0.8	−2.7	−7.3	2.1	−10.3	2.0	9.7	2.7	6.2	1.5	0.6
1978	−4.5	−2.2	20.2	−0.5	6.4	−4.4	−0.5	4.7	3.6	5.5	2.1	−7.0	22.9
1979	2.4	0.5	−3.8	2.3	5.5	18.2	−5.3	11.1	−1.2	−6.5	8.2	−0.4	32.3
1980	3.0	−4.4	−14.3	4.1	0.9	7.6	7.3	2.6	5.6	5.0	2.3	−7.4	10.3
1981	−7.0	−1.8	−5.2	2.1	−6.9	−5.5	4.6	2.3	1.9	3.4	0.1	−10.9	−21.9
1982	−3.7	−2.7	1.0	1.2	−6.2	1.2	−3.7	3.9	−10.2	−0.7	9.0	−4.4	−15.5
1983	3.9	−6.4	12.1	0.3	−5.0	3.9	4.5	10.1	−9.6	−4.4	0.4	2.2	9.9
1984	−9.6	0.8	12.9	−8.6	4.2	0.9	−2.8	0.8	−1.4	4.5	−2.4	−1.7	−4.3
1985	0.9	−4.1	6.0	−8.3	−3.7	2.0	−8.1	−2.5	3.2	9.0	3.4	2.5	−1.3
1986	−4.7	−12.5	6.3	−3.5	−15.3	−1.0	4.7	1.5	1.5	8.2	−0.3	−4.1	−20.0
1987	5.0	−2.9	1.6	−3.7	0.1	−4.0	−0.8	9.8	0.9	2.5	7.3	−2.4	13.2
1988	4.9	−0.8	−7.5	5.4	11.4	12.5	−6.9	12.9	−0.2	0.2	2.8	2.9	41.6
1989	0.1	−1.3	−7.1	0.3	−4.3	4.5	−5.0	3.8	2.0	−3.1	3.4	0.4	−7.0
1990	−8.2	−3.6	−2.9	−1.7	−3.5	−0.8	−12.9	−3.7	0.1	−5.7	−0.1	−0.5	−36.3
1991	1.0	2.5	6.4	−1.2	1.3	−4.2	6.9	9.2	3.6	9.3	0.7	10.6	55.4
1992	8.8	−9.1	−5.2	−6.7	−1.1	0.9	−10.0	5.0	5.2	1.2	4.7	−4.6	−12.6
1993	7.4	−12.3	4.2	−13.2	−4.3	−0.3	5.8	3.8	1.0	5.3	4.5	7.9	6.9
1994	−1.7	−7.1	−4.5	0.3	−1.0	−1.6	2.6	14.8	6.4	−4.7	N/C	4.4	6.1
1995	−7.0	−7.0	−1.2	2.3	6.3	19.5	4.1	−0.3	6.4	1.1	−0.6	3.5	27.6
1996	1.4	−3.5	−0.4	13.6	−6.7	−8.7	−8.8	3.0	−3.8	−14.9	1.7	1.0	−25.6
1997	−5.6	4.3	5.9	9.1	−16.8	−7.8	9.0	8.8	−10.1	1.8	−0.8	−8.9	−14.6
1998	3.5	0.3	−5.3	−5.9	−5.6	1.1	−12.2	0.6	6.0	9.3	N/C	−6.1	−15.2
1999	−0.3	−9.8	12.8	−4.4	−5.9	4.8	−0.2	7.0	−2.3	−7.3	−2.4	−0.4	−10.0
2000	3.1	1.1	1.3	−2.9	7.9	−1.3	−9.2	8.9	−1.2	−3.9	7.5	2.1	12.5
2001	−2.3	1.4	−7.9	11.1	−5.7	−3.4	7.9	3.8	−6.3	8.3	−1.3	−0.2	3.4
2002	−1.0	−3.5	3.3	−5.7	5.0	10.9	6.7	10.8	7.2	1.5	−5.6	−14.4	12.5
2003	−1.4	−3.2	−7.6	−1.4	14.7	−4.2	12.2	9.3	−5.4	2.6	10.1	−7.3	16.0
2004	3.2	0.4	4.4	−4.4	−7.2	−4.6	−9.6	3.4	−5.0	3.2	−4.8	2.1	−18.4
2005	−5.4	18.6	−4.1	−1.5	1.8	−0.1	−1.1	−3.1	9.1	−8.4	1.2	5.8	10.3
2006	1.2	11.0	−8.7	3.1	9.8	0.6	0.4	6.2	4.9	9.0	8.0	−3.9	47.7
2007	−6.7	4.4	−10.2	13.1	4.3	15.5	5.5	23.1	21.1	−14.0	9.6	−0.1	76.6
2008	5.0	16.8	−14.5	−13.8	−4.9								
TOTALS	−34.9	−40.3	−53.4	−55.1	−23.5	77.4	37.9	259.0	55.9	14.4	83.3	−20.5	
AVG.	−0.9	−1.0	−1.3	−1.4	−0.6	2.0	1.0	6.6	1.4	0.4	2.3	−0.5	
# Up	19	16	16	16	17	21	19	33	24	25	23	18	
# Down	21	24	24	24	23	18	20	6	15	14	14	21	

COCOA CYCLE, SEASONAL PATTERN & TRADING GUIDE

Cocoa is now traded through the Atlanta, Georgia-based, Intercontinental Commodity Exchange (ICE). One futures contract is 10 metric tons, and every penny move represents a $1,000 change in value per contract position. The contract symbol is CC, it has a tradable contract starting with March, May, July, September, and December. The trading hours for this commodity are from 8:00 AM until 11:50 AM (CT). There are no daily price limits.

The cocoa bean grows on a tropical plant, thriving only in hot, rainy climates with cultivation generally confined to areas not more than 20 degrees north or south of the equator. The tree takes four or five years after planting to yield cocoa beans, and then it takes anywhere from 8 to 10 years to achieve maximum production. That is why it is susceptible to frost scares. The fruit of the cocoa tree appears as pods primarily on the trees trunk and lower main branches. When ripe, these pods are cut down and opened, and the beans are removed, fermented, and dried. The cocoa butter extracted from the bean is used in a number of products, ranging from cosmetic to pharmaceuticals, but its main use is in the manufacture of chocolate candy.

Currently, the Ivory Coast is the world's leading cocoa producing nation. Ghana and Indonesia rank next among major world producers, followed by Brazil, Nigeria, and Malaysia. The leading cocoa bean importing nations are the Netherlands, United States, and Germany. These countries accounted for about 54% of world imports. The United States is the leading importer of cocoa products such as cocoa butter, liquor, and pow- der— accounting for 12% of world imports. This market has two crop seasons due to the production areas of Ghana and South America. The market has a strong seasonal tendency to bottom in June due to the new crop harvest and peaks in March as supplies have declined and as confectioners and processors have accrued inven- tories ahead of both Valentine's Day and Easter, when consumption is high.

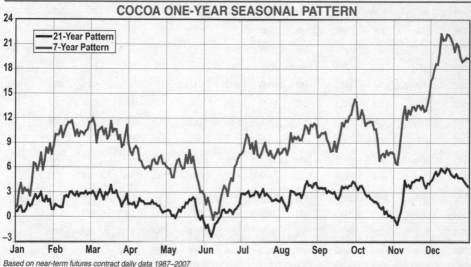

COCOA ONE-YEAR SEASONAL PATTERN

21-Year Pattern
7-Year Pattern

Based on near-term futures contract daily data 1987–2007

COCOA NEAR-TERM CONTRACT ANNUAL HIGHS, LOWS & CLOSES SINCE 1981

YEAR	HIGH DATE	HIGH CLOSE	LOW DATE	LOW CLOSE	YEAR CLOSE	YEAR	HIGH DATE	HIGH CLOSE	LOW DATE	LOW CLOSE	YEAR CLOSE
1981	09/02	2272	06/05	1403	2054	1995	02/24	1461	07/10	1216	1258
1982	01/05	2159	07/19	1344	1603	1996	06/12	1458	03/13	1211	1374
1983	12/30	2755	01/04	1590	2755	1997	12/15	1762	01/23	1260	1630
1984	05/22	2730	08/01	1963	2052	1998	05/14	1748	12/30	1376	1379
1985	03/29	2469	06/24	1968	2298	1999	01/12	1392	11/08	806	836
1986	01/02	2307	06/02	1722	1935	2000	03/16	935	11/27	714	758
1987	07/15	2125	12/08	1743	1814	2001	11/29	1349	01/03	753	1310
1988	01/21	1942	09/29	1116	1500	2002	10/10	2374	01/18	1286	2021
1989	02/15	1566	12/14	898	925	2003	01/31	2409	10/17	1367	1515
1990	05/24	1493	01/03	912	1150	2004	11/08	1792	05/17	1314	1547
1991	12/16	1333	07/09	904	1245	2005	03/18	1844	11/07	1322	1504
1992	01/02	1253	06/24	831	936	2006	07/10	1734	10/16	1406	1635
1993	12/03	1316	06/07	849	1144	2007	12/19	2132	01/26	1578	2035
1994	07/15	1522	02/02	1051	1280	2008*	03/13	2921	01/02	2097	AT PRESS-TIME

*Through May 30, 2008

COCOA NEAR-TERM CONTRACT MONTHLY CLOSING PRICES

	Jan	Feb	Mar	Apr	May	Jun	Jul	Aug	Sep	Oct	Nov	Dec
1981	1944	1992	2027	1944	1681	1554	2047	2178	2215	1931	1911	2054
1982	1942	1940	1638	1660	1488	1477	1395	1475	1529	1372	1465	1603
1983	1826	1740	1704	1935	2072	2143	2337	2093	2072	1963	2224	2755
1984	2521	2377	2562	2545	2616	2347	1981	2326	2174	2277	2117	2052
1985	2271	2163	2469	2093	2075	2031	2087	2222	2273	2103	2214	2298
1986	2146	2040	1862	1798	1759	1800	1942	2129	2011	1876	1886	1935
1987	1820	1888	1928	1977	1881	1997	1962	1988	1823	1807	1866	1814
1988	1760	1621	1570	1622	1619	1580	1468	1256	1132	1309	1476	1500
1989	1446	1485	1431	1211	1128	1229	1267	1149	1040	977	939	925
1990	962	1055	1183	1297	1415	1246	1248	1319	1281	1153	1283	1150
1991	1128	1138	1105	1035	1030	908	1036	1091	1220	1208	1231	1245
1992	1177	1116	986	933	864	954	1013	1092	1009	932	1008	936
1993	912	936	919	936	894	903	939	1079	1151	1120	1263	1144
1994	1088	1139	1148	1128	1388	1305	1490	1357	1320	1327	1228	1280
1995	1363	1427	1308	1408	1362	1289	1236	1336	1293	1311	1308	1258
1996	1242	1268	1306	1368	1376	1384	1333	1352	1377	1353	1416	1374
1997	1314	1286	1453	1400	1469	1713	1513	1717	1679	1603	1582	1630
1998	1556	1614	1652	1686	1673	1575	1552	1614	1512	1506	1441	1379
1999	1331	1278	1192	1019	874	1039	1001	951	1029	874	899	836
2000	795	778	800	774	842	835	825	795	797	755	729	758
2001	1020	1137	1073	987	936	964	957	949	1077	1017	1339	1310
2002	1344	1450	1494	1510	1598	1647	1787	2002	2191	1927	1703	2021
2003	2409	2034	1960	1991	1493	1651	1465	1761	1626	1440	1438	1515
2004	1520	1570	1549	1413	1465	1341	1645	1686	1453	1469	1651	1547
2005	1525	1730	1613	1492	1422	1452	1479	1404	1413	1351	1415	1504
2006	1484	1461	1489	1521	1473	1639	1486	1485	1472	1484	1557	1635
2007	1617	1732	1953	1798	1883	2062	1942	1824	2036	1945	1983	2035
2008	2326	2777	2321	2776	2723							

COCOA NEAR-TERM CONTRACT MONTHLY PERCENT CHANGES

	Jan	Feb	Mar	Apr	May	Jun	Jul	Aug	Sep	Oct	Nov	Dec	Year's Change
1981	−5.2	2.5	1.8	−4.1	−13.5	−7.6	31.7	6.4	1.7	−12.8	−1.0	7.5	0.2
1982	−5.5	−0.1	−15.6	1.3	−10.4	−0.7	−5.6	5.7	3.7	−10.3	6.8	9.4	−22.0
1983	13.9	−4.7	−2.1	13.6	7.1	3.4	9.1	−10.4	−1.0	−5.3	13.3	23.9	71.9
1984	−8.5	−5.7	7.8	−0.7	2.8	−10.3	−15.6	17.4	−6.5	4.7	−7.0	−3.1	−25.5
1985	10.7	−4.8	14.1	−15.2	−0.9	−2.1	2.8	6.5	2.3	−7.5	5.3	3.8	12.0
1986	−6.6	−4.9	−8.7	−3.4	−2.2	2.3	7.9	9.6	−5.5	−6.7	0.5	2.6	−15.8
1987	−5.9	3.7	2.1	2.5	−4.9	6.2	−1.8	1.3	−8.3	−0.9	3.3	−2.8	−6.3
1988	−3.0	−7.9	−3.1	3.3	−0.2	−2.4	−7.1	−14.4	−9.9	15.6	12.8	1.6	−17.3
1989	−3.6	2.7	−3.6	−15.4	−6.9	9.0	3.1	−9.3	−9.5	−6.1	−3.9	−1.5	−38.3
1990	4.0	9.7	12.1	9.6	9.1	−11.9	0.2	5.7	−2.9	−10.0	11.3	−10.4	24.3
1991	−1.9	0.9	−2.9	−6.3	−0.5	−11.8	14.1	5.3	11.8	−1.0	1.9	1.1	8.3
1992	−5.5	−5.2	−11.6	−5.4	−7.4	10.4	6.2	7.8	−7.6	−7.6	8.2	−7.1	−24.8
1993	−2.6	2.6	−1.8	1.8	−4.5	1.0	4.0	14.9	6.7	−2.7	12.8	−9.4	22.2
1994	−4.9	4.7	0.8	−1.7	23.0	−6.0	14.2	−8.9	−2.7	0.5	−7.5	4.2	11.9
1995	6.5	4.7	−8.3	7.6	−3.3	−5.4	−4.1	8.1	−3.2	1.4	−0.2	−3.8	−1.7
1996	−1.3	2.1	3.0	4.7	0.6	0.6	−3.7	1.4	1.8	−1.7	4.7	−3.0	9.2
1997	−4.4	−2.1	13.0	−3.6	4.9	16.6	−11.7	13.5	−2.2	−4.5	−1.3	3.0	18.6
1998	−4.5	3.7	2.4	2.1	−0.8	−5.9	−1.5	4.0	−6.3	−0.4	−4.3	−4.3	−15.4
1999	−3.5	−4.0	−6.7	−14.5	−14.2	18.9	−3.7	5.0	8.2	−15.1	2.9	−7.0	−39.4
2000	−4.9	−2.1	2.8	−3.2	8.8	−0.8	−1.2	−3.6	0.3	−5.3	−3.4	4.0	−9.3
2001	34.6	11.5	−5.6	−8.0	−5.2	3.0	−0.7	−0.8	13.5	−5.6	31.7	−2.2	72.8
2002	2.6	7.9	3.0	1.1	5.8	3.1	8.5	12.0	9.4	−12.0	−11.6	18.7	54.3
2003	19.2	−15.6	−3.6	1.6	−25.0	10.6	−11.3	20.2	−7.7	−11.4	−0.1	5.4	−25.0
2004	0.3	3.3	−1.3	−8.8	3.7	−8.5	22.7	2.5	−13.8	1.1	12.4	−6.3	2.1
2005	−1.4	13.4	−6.8	−7.5	−4.7	2.1	1.9	−5.1	0.6	−4.4	4.7	6.3	−2.8
2006	−1.3	−1.5	1.9	2.1	−3.2	11.3	−9.3	−0.1	−0.9	0.8	4.9	5.0	8.7
2007	−1.1	7.1	12.8	−7.9	4.7	9.5	−5.8	−6.1	11.6	−4.5	2.0	2.6	24.5
2008	14.3	19.4	−16.4	19.6	−1.9								
TOTALS	30.5	41.3	−20.5	−34.8	−39.2	34.6	43.3	78.6	−16.4	−111.7	99.2	38.2	
AVG.	1.1	1.5	−0.7	−1.2	−1.4	1.3	1.6	2.9	−0.6	−4.1	3.7	1.4	
# Up	9	16	13	13	10	15	13	17	12	6	17	15	
# Down	19	12	15	15	18	12	14	10	15	21	10	12	

COFFEE CYCLE, SEASONAL PATTERN & TRADING GUIDE

Coffee is now traded through the Atlanta, Georgia-based, Intercontinental Commodity Exchange (ICE). One futures contract is 37,000 pounds (250 bags) and every penny move represents a $375 change in value per contract position. The contract symbol is KC. It has a tradable contract starting with March, May, July, September and December. The trading hours for this commodity are from 8:15 AM until 12:35 PM (CT). The daily price fluctuations are 6.00 cents with variable limits effective under certain conditions. However, there are no price limits on the two nearby months.

Coffee is produced from trees, or bushes, that grow primarily in subtropical climates. Coffee beans are the seeds of cherry-sized berries, the fruit of the coffee tree. Coffee is primarily classified in two types — Arabica and Robusta. Arabian coffees, which make up the bulk of world production, are grown mainly in the tropical highlands of the Western Hemisphere. Robusta coffees are produced largely in the low, hot areas of Africa and Asia. Their flavors are less mild than the Arabica coffees. South and Central America produce the majority of coffee trade in world commerce. Brazil and Colombia, the largest growers of Arabica coffees, accounted for about 41% of world green coffee production on average.

The demand for coffee is price inelastic. This means that when coffee prices rise, people do not reduce their coffee consumption proportionally, and when coffee prices fall, consumer demand for coffee does not proportionally increase to any great extent, unless it is met by a substantial price increase due to crop devastation due to frost damage as did occur in the late 1970s. Coffee also has a strong seasonal tendency to peak in May right before the Brazil harvest, as the market builds a price premium as a hedge against a potential frost scare. Then prices tend to decline through the summer months and bottom in August as roasters build inventories ahead of the highest consumptions months of fall into winter.

COFFEE ONE-YEAR SEASONAL PATTERN

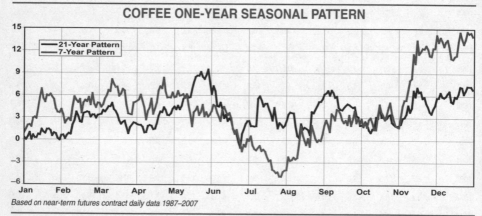

Based on near-term futures contract daily data 1987–2007

COFFEE NEAR-TERM CONTRACT ANNUAL HIGHS, LOWS & CLOSES SINCE 1974

YEAR	HIGH DATE	HIGH CLOSE	LOW DATE	LOW CLOSE	YEAR CLOSE	YEAR	HIGH DATE	HIGH CLOSE	LOW DATE	LOW CLOSE	YEAR CLOSE
1974	02/11	81.95	09/16	50.17	59.62	1992	12/21	81.90	09/09	50.90	77.55
1975	08/04	87.90	04/10	47.00	87.25	1993	09/10	83.15	04/08	53.50	71.55
1976	12/30	224.45	01/06	86.90	224.45	1994	07/12	246.80	01/05	71.55	168.85
1977	04/14	339.86	10/21	149.06	192.03	1995	03/10	187.75	12/28	93.90	94.90
1978	01/16	201.25	07/25	109.00	132.88	1996	04/22	130.95	01/02	91.25	116.90
1979	06/29	221.53	02/16	122.91	181.56	1997	05/29	314.80	01/06	114.05	162.45
1980	05/15	203.07	11/10	108.03	126.80	1998	02/05	181.95	09/18	101.10	117.75
1981	11/04	149.71	06/26	85.44	139.71	1999	12/03	144.05	10/01	81.35	125.90
1982	02/10	157.75	04/19	118.07	129.83	2000	07/18	119.05	12/19	65.05	65.55
1983	12/13	149.58	02/16	119.44	138.79	2001	01/22	71.25	10/22	42.50	46.20
1984	05/21	156.45	10/01	133.57	142.25	2002	12/02	72.85	02/08	44.55	60.20
1985	12/23	246.66	07/23	131.32	241.29	2003	09/11	72.05	03/27	57.15	64.95
1986	01/07	273.45	12/30	132.59	136.83	2004	12/29	107.95	08/05	65.90	103.75
1987	01/08	134.02	04/01	99.28	125.96	2005	03/10	138.10	09/19	86.45	107.10
1988	12/30	159.34	08/02	108.83	159.34	2006	12/14	128.90	07/24	94.05	126.20
1989	01/03	165.90	10/09	68.72	79.57	2007	10/12	139.30	05/03	104.35	136.20
1990	03/05	104.24	01/16	77.55	88.65	2008*	02/28	167.50	03/31	127.40	AT PRESS-TIME
1991	03/06	95.85	11/06	76.50	77.70						

*Through May 30, 2008

COFFEE NEAR-TERM CONTRACT MONTHLY CLOSING PRICES

	Jan	Feb	Mar	Apr	May	Jun	Jul	Aug	Sep	Oct	Nov	Dec
1974	72.65	74.50	74.90	73.15	73.13	70.90	69.25	59.35	54.20	57.60	61.63	59.62
1975	54.75	51.75	51.90	48.95	54.11	55.25	84.05	83.70	80.93	80.10	79.90	87.25
1976	95.00	96.52	108.70	125.50	141.05	152.85	141.75	147.90	166.25	178.50	186.98	224.45
1977	222.93	267.49	308.75	301.99	273.12	235.92	222.00	180.50	165.50	184.50	170.33	192.03
1978	190.00	159.46	168.65	154.13	171.00	146.18	128.46	151.30	149.65	153.06	133.98	132.88
1979	127.76	127.47	137.49	156.04	155.82	221.53	198.00	207.46	213.81	212.30	205.85	181.56
1980	166.39	183.26	182.25	184.65	194.05	177.92	143.06	134.92	126.66	125.14	121.38	126.80
1981	122.36	123.09	128.66	126.84	113.78	92.02	123.13	98.08	129.15	141.12	129.68	139.71
1982	149.14	141.26	128.56	129.31	138.23	133.46	126.81	126.83	144.87	139.41	136.08	129.83
1983	122.81	120.12	123.23	124.35	131.75	125.19	126.07	129.90	136.48	141.54	144.01	138.79
1984	142.44	144.84	151.37	147.17	144.35	142.65	139.01	146.85	135.95	138.66	136.76	142.25
1985	150.05	139.96	144.43	145.67	144.10	143.56	133.49	138.63	138.00	161.55	168.56	241.29
1986	214.43	246.96	246.41	233.27	187.98	169.28	169.47	204.36	201.36	173.71	150.85	136.83
1987	123.98	129.31	100.04	120.56	119.46	105.75	101.54	118.52	112.77	122.52	129.70	125.96
1988	131.55	135.31	134.51	132.60	133.77	131.43	124.72	123.83	131.93	123.61	123.77	159.34
1989	132.64	127.32	128.13	127.45	130.68	108.06	78.99	85.76	80.60	74.85	77.70	79.57
1990	79.99	93.79	92.14	93.73	94.05	85.60	93.80	102.85	93.00	90.50	86.90	88.65
1991	83.00	92.75	94.70	89.35	86.70	85.90	81.40	89.00	82.90	80.55	83.80	77.70
1992	72.15	70.90	68.50	62.90	63.30	58.10	56.25	54.20	55.70	68.45	73.00	77.55
1993	58.30	64.85	58.60	64.20	63.55	61.35	76.55	77.90	74.50	79.30	77.60	71.55
1994	72.35	76.40	82.20	89.50	126.00	191.60	202.75	210.90	208.85	187.40	160.80	168.85
1995	155.50	181.25	166.30	174.15	153.85	130.30	145.70	147.50	117.25	121.55	104.85	94.90
1996	128.60	115.90	115.45	124.45	116.10	121.45	106.40	118.25	102.95	117.20	107.75	116.90
1997	139.40	176.85	191.15	210.40	276.40	172.40	184.50	179.90	162.50	148.65	155.05	162.45
1998	174.70	162.15	146.25	131.45	132.50	110.20	129.20	116.35	105.15	110.00	110.10	117.75
1999	103.90	102.90	109.70	104.00	121.60	101.40	91.10	89.85	82.45	100.20	134.60	125.90
2000	111.10	100.40	103.70	98.00	93.00	87.45	86.45	79.70	83.00	74.40	71.70	65.55
2001	63.75	65.90	60.30	64.45	57.15	58.50	51.95	54.35	48.30	43.90	46.20	46.20
2002	45.10	46.30	57.20	52.85	51.90	48.85	46.80	53.20	54.50	65.95	70.60	60.20
2003	65.30	59.15	58.65	69.25	58.35	61.10	63.45	63.40	62.90	58.65	60.65	64.95
2004	75.50	76.75	73.75	69.10	85.55	75.30	66.45	72.60	82.35	74.40	97.45	103.75
2005	105.35	121.55	126.40	127.95	118.35	108.05	103.15	101.05	93.45	96.65	97.00	107.10
2006	118.20	113.70	107.00	109.70	98.95	101.10	99.35	108.00	107.65	108.25	124.30	126.20
2007	117.65	118.50	109.25	106.15	111.90	112.80	114.30	115.85	128.65	121.35	129.20	136.20
2008	138.15	166.80	127.40	135.45	133.90							

COFFEE NEAR-TERM CONTRACT MONTHLY PERCENT CHANGES

	Jan	Feb	Mar	Apr	May	Jun	Jul	Aug	Sep	Oct	Nov	Dec	Year's Change
1974	7.8	2.5	0.5	-2.3	-0.0	-3.0	-2.3	-14.3	-8.7	6.3	7.0	-3.3	-11.5
1975	-8.2	-5.5	0.3	-5.7	10.5	2.1	52.1	-0.4	-3.3	-1.0	-0.2	9.2	46.3
1976	8.9	1.6	12.6	15.5	12.4	8.4	-7.3	4.3	12.4	7.4	4.8	20.0	157.2
1977	-0.7	20.0	15.4	-2.2	-9.6	-13.6	-5.9	-18.7	-8.3	11.5	-7.7	12.7	-14.4
1978	-1.1	-16.1	5.8	-8.6	10.9	-14.5	-12.1	17.8	-1.1	2.3	-12.5	-0.8	-30.8
1979	-3.9	-0.2	7.9	13.5	-0.1	42.2	-10.6	4.8	3.1	-0.7	-3.0	-11.8	36.6
1980	-8.4	10.1	-0.6	1.3	5.1	-8.3	-19.6	-5.7	-6.1	-1.2	-3.0	4.5	-30.2
1981	-3.5	0.6	4.5	-1.4	-10.3	-19.1	33.8	-20.3	31.7	9.3	-8.1	7.7	10.2
1982	6.7	-5.3	-9.0	0.6	6.9	-3.5	-5.0	0.0	14.2	-3.8	-2.4	-4.6	-7.1
1983	-5.4	-2.2	2.6	0.9	6.0	-5.0	0.7	3.0	5.1	3.7	1.7	-3.6	6.9
1984	2.6	1.7	4.5	-2.8	-1.9	-1.2	-2.6	5.6	-7.4	2.0	-1.4	4.0	2.5
1985	5.5	-6.7	3.2	0.9	-1.1	-0.4	-7.0	3.9	-0.5	17.1	4.3	43.1	69.6
1986	-11.1	15.2	-0.2	-5.3	-19.4	-9.9	0.1	20.6	-1.5	-13.7	-13.2	-9.3	-43.3
1987	-9.4	4.3	-22.6	20.5	-0.9	-11.5	-4.0	16.7	-4.9	8.6	5.9	-2.9	-7.9
1988	4.4	2.9	-0.6	-1.4	0.9	-1.7	-5.1	-0.7	6.5	-6.3	0.1	28.7	26.5
1989	-16.8	-4.0	0.6	-0.5	2.5	-17.3	-26.9	8.6	-6.0	-7.1	3.8	2.4	-50.1
1990	0.5	17.3	-1.8	1.7	0.3	-9.0	9.6	9.6	-9.6	-2.7	-4.0	2.0	11.4
1991	-6.4	11.7	2.1	-5.6	-3.0	-0.9	-5.2	9.3	-6.9	-2.8	4.0	-7.3	-12.4
1992	-7.1	-1.7	-3.4	-8.2	0.6	-8.2	-3.2	-3.6	2.8	22.9	6.6	6.2	-0.2
1993	-24.8	11.2	-9.6	9.6	-1.0	-3.5	24.8	1.8	-4.4	6.4	-2.1	-7.8	-7.7
1994	1.1	5.6	7.6	8.9	40.8	52.1	5.8	4.0	-1.0	-10.3	-14.2	5.0	136.0
1995	-7.9	16.6	-8.2	4.7	-11.7	-15.3	11.8	1.2	-20.5	3.7	-13.7	-9.5	-43.8
1996	35.5	-9.9	-0.4	7.8	-6.7	4.6	-12.4	11.1	-12.9	13.8	-8.1	8.5	23.2
1997	19.2	26.9	8.1	10.1	31.4	-37.6	7.0	-2.5	-9.7	-8.5	4.3	4.8	39.0
1998	7.5	-7.2	-9.8	-10.1	0.8	-16.8	17.2	-9.9	-9.6	4.6	0.1	6.9	-27.5
1999	-11.8	-1.0	6.6	-5.2	16.9	-16.6	-10.2	-1.4	-8.2	21.5	34.3	-6.5	6.9
2000	-11.8	-9.6	3.3	-5.5	-5.1	-6.0	-1.1	-7.8	4.1	-10.4	-3.6	-8.6	-47.9
2001	-2.7	3.4	-8.5	6.9	-11.3	2.4	-11.2	4.6	-11.1	-9.1	5.2	N/C	-29.5
2002	-2.4	2.7	23.5	-7.6	-1.8	-5.9	-4.2	13.7	2.4	21.0	7.1	-14.7	30.3
2003	8.5	-9.4	-0.8	18.1	-15.7	4.7	3.8	-0.1	-0.8	-6.8	3.4	7.1	7.9
2004	16.2	1.7	-3.9	-6.3	23.8	-12.0	-11.8	9.3	13.4	-9.7	31.0	6.5	59.7
2005	1.5	15.4	4.0	1.2	-7.5	-8.7	-4.5	-2.0	-7.5	3.4	0.4	10.4	3.2
2006	10.4	-3.8	-5.9	2.5	-9.8	2.2	-1.7	8.7	-0.3	0.6	14.8	1.5	17.8
2007	-6.8	0.7	-7.8	-2.8	5.4	0.8	1.3	1.4	11.0	-5.7	6.5	5.4	7.9
2008	1.4	20.7	-23.6	6.3	-1.1								
TOTALS	-12.5	110.2	-3.6	49.5	57.2	-130.0	-5.9	72.6	-43.6	66.3	48.1	105.9	
AVG.	-0.4	3.1	-0.1	1.4	1.6	-3.8	-0.2	2.1	-1.3	2.0	1.4	3.1	
# Up	16	21	18	18	16	9	12	21	11	18	19	20	
# Down	19	14	17	17	19	25	22	13	23	16	15	13	

SUGAR CYCLE, SEASONAL PATTERN & TRADING GUIDE

Sugar is now traded through the Atlanta, Georgia-based, Intercontinental Commodity Exchange (ICE). One futures contract is 112,000 pounds, (50 long tons), and every penny move represents a $1,120 change in value per contract position. The contract symbol is SB, it has a tradable contract starting with March, May, July, and October. However, beginning in 2009 they will be listing a January contract. The electronic trading hours for this commodity are from 01:30 until 14:15 (CT). There are no daily price limits.

Sugar prices are not only affected by beet and cane supply but also by domestic and international demand for its by-products like molasses, methanol, and ethanol. It is a highly regulated industry; thus, many countries such as the United States that impose trade barriers, including production quotas, guaranteed prices and import tariffs, impart a significant degree of distortion to international prices. The relatively longer plantation cycle, combined with restrictive trade practices, has in the past been the catalyst for the volatility in sugar prices.

In India, sugar production follows a three to five-year cycle. Higher production leads to increased availability of sugar, thereby declining the sugar prices. This leads to lower profitability for the companies and delayed payment to the farmers. As a result of higher sugarcane arrears, the farmers switch to other crops, thereby leading to a fall in the area under cultivation for sugar. This then leads to lower production and lower sugar availability, followed by higher sugar prices, higher profitability, and lower arrears, and thus the cycle continues. Because of the many areas around the globe that produce sugar, it does have many seasonal price swings, but overall it tends to bottom in late August through early September and peaks in November prior to the Northern Hemisphere harvest of both cane and sugar beet production.

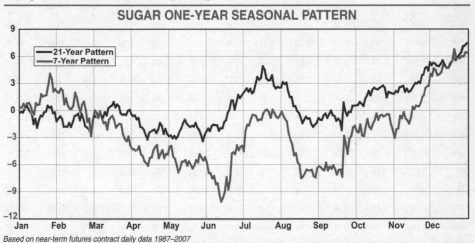

SUGAR ONE-YEAR SEASONAL PATTERN

- 21-Year Pattern
- 7-Year Pattern

Based on near-term futures contract daily data 1987–2007

SUGAR NEAR-TERM CONTRACT ANNUAL HIGHS, LOWS & CLOSES SINCE 1975

YEAR	HIGH DATE	HIGH CLOSE	LOW DATE	LOW CLOSE	YEAR CLOSE	YEAR	HIGH DATE	HIGH CLOSE	LOW DATE	LOW CLOSE	YEAR CLOSE
1975	01/03	45.60	06/25	11.54	14.40	1992	06/17	11.05	02/11	7.88	8.41
1976	05/07	15.74	12/27	7.65	8.04	1993	05/14	13.19	02/02	8.04	10.77
1977	04/22	10.95	07/12	7.12	9.40	1994	12/30	15.17	01/19	10.28	15.17
1978	10/30	9.75	07/25	6.01	8.43	1995	01/06	15.74	07/14	9.69	11.60
1979	12/26	16.98	04/20	7.64	16.31	1996	02/16	12.66	12/03	10.27	11.00
1980	11/05	45.64	01/03	15.37	30.58	1997	12/01	12.49	01/23	10.15	12.22
1981	01/06	33.78	09/17	10.76	13.18	1998	01/05	12.02	09/18	6.67	7.86
1982	01/27	13.99	09/15	5.99	6.85	1999	01/07	8.80	04/28	4.08	6.12
1983	05/31	13.36	01/12	6.10	8.18	2000	10/16	11.39	02/28	4.88	10.20
1984	01/12	8.15	09/17	3.80	4.16	2001	01/08	10.47	10/09	6.15	7.39
1985	12/05	6.51	06/20	2.70	5.62	2002	01/09	8.03	06/28	4.96	7.61
1986	04/07	9.39	09/19	4.81	6.16	2003	02/20	9.07	12/31	5.67	5.67
1987	12/31	9.49	08/28	5.60	9.49	2004	10/12	9.32	02/09	5.36	9.04
1988	07/19	15.30	02/26	7.74	11.15	2005	12/29	14.79	04/15	8.08	14.68
1989	11/17	15.36	01/24	9.40	13.16	2006	02/03	19.30	09/25	10.87	11.75
1990	03/16	16.13	10/15	9.13	9.37	2007	01/03	11.51	06/13	8.45	10.82
1991	06/19	9.97	05/10	7.63	9.00	2008*	03/03	14.91	05/29	9.97	AT PRESS-TIME

*Through May 30, 2008

173

SUGAR NEAR-TERM CONTRACT MONTHLY CLOSING PRICES

	Jan	Feb	Mar	Apr	May	Jun	Jul	Aug	Sep	Oct	Nov	Dec
1975	35.65	28.40	25.40	18.90	15.20	13.65	17.09	17.05	13.75	14.22	13.13	14.40
1976	13.35	13.73	14.06	14.26	13.74	13.81	12.07	9.85	8.81	8.21	8.51	8.04
1977	8.89	8.75	9.37	10.23	8.63	8.30	7.98	7.72	8.33	8.63	9.27	9.40
1978	9.41	8.79	7.98	7.91	7.51	6.95	6.35	7.39	9.23	9.42	8.48	8.43
1979	8.22	8.88	8.51	8.20	7.88	8.75	8.47	9.69	11.56	14.08	16.86	16.31
1980	22.01	24.88	19.70	24.81	35.17	34.93	30.05	33.18	41.16	43.34	35.11	30.58
1981	26.79	24.03	21.12	16.78	17.99	15.40	16.70	12.42	13.11	12.52	13.01	13.18
1982	13.58	12.58	10.97	9.12	7.80	7.91	7.49	6.63	7.11	7.84	8.32	6.85
1983	6.20	6.32	7.09	7.98	13.36	11.55	11.68	10.39	10.94	9.36	9.57	8.18
1984	7.50	6.71	6.86	6.48	5.88	5.58	4.55	4.62	5.44	5.83	5.28	4.16
1985	4.32	4.12	3.85	3.55	3.14	2.95	4.50	4.75	5.65	6.14	6.13	5.62
1986	5.92	6.30	9.18	9.24	7.32	6.85	6.57	5.22	6.28	6.90	6.60	6.16
1987	7.74	8.24	6.72	7.31	6.72	6.97	5.94	5.63	6.96	7.59	8.01	9.49
1988	9.64	7.91	8.88	8.51	9.47	12.63	11.54	10.25	9.64	10.59	11.07	11.15
1989	10.49	11.63	12.62	11.54	10.86	14.43	14.65	13.39	14.16	13.97	14.15	13.16
1990	14.73	14.46	15.69	16.02	13.68	12.77	11.09	10.33	10.11	9.42	9.82	9.37
1991	8.79	8.78	8.90	7.73	8.05	8.52	9.68	8.83	9.01	8.98	8.92	9.00
1992	8.18	8.02	8.68	9.36	10.03	9.76	9.51	9.23	8.71	8.77	8.41	8.41
1993	8.30	9.96	11.89	12.82	10.76	10.45	9.36	9.07	10.45	10.62	10.36	10.77
1994	10.59	11.80	11.96	11.67	12.04	11.68	11.68	12.14	12.40	12.80	14.71	15.17
1995	14.12	14.42	14.28	11.56	11.72	10.79	10.50	10.86	10.18	10.56	10.97	11.60
1996	12.15	11.60	11.79	10.39	11.21	11.15	11.70	11.78	10.89	10.30	10.66	11.00
1997	10.45	10.97	10.79	10.96	11.17	11.19	11.68	11.60	11.56	12.39	12.24	12.22
1998	11.23	9.85	10.19	8.46	8.28	8.58	8.76	7.55	7.65	7.71	8.23	7.86
1999	7.11	6.26	5.91	4.33	5.00	6.22	5.98	6.82	6.93	6.88	5.78	6.12
2000	5.42	4.99	5.90	6.64	7.55	8.48	10.40	10.56	9.45	9.90	9.75	10.20
2001	9.95	8.99	7.75	8.50	8.55	9.36	7.93	7.91	6.63	6.74	7.68	7.39
2002	6.38	5.69	5.93	5.36	5.90	4.96	5.80	5.98	6.44	7.36	7.41	7.61
2003	8.64	8.45	7.68	7.20	7.08	6.22	7.21	6.29	6.44	5.93	6.25	5.67
2004	5.86	6.12	6.40	6.95	7.06	7.69	8.28	7.99	9.06	8.60	8.84	9.04
2005	9.22	9.17	8.70	8.66	8.76	9.33	9.83	10.07	11.23	11.33	12.43	14.68
2006	18.02	17.12	17.90	17.43	15.46	16.34	14.91	11.80	11.75	11.55	12.37	11.75
2007	10.60	10.56	9.88	9.10	9.34	9.52	10.33	9.48	10.15	9.98	9.75	10.82
2008	12.36	14.62	11.69	11.81	10.02							

SUGAR NEAR-TERM CONTRACT MONTHLY PERCENT CHANGES

	Jan	Feb	Mar	Apr	May	Jun	Jul	Aug	Sep	Oct	Nov	Dec	Year's Change
1975	−24.5	−20.3	−10.6	−25.6	−19.6	−10.2	25.2	−0.2	−19.4	3.4	−7.7	9.7	−69.5
1976	−7.3	2.8	2.4	1.4	−3.6	0.5	−12.6	−18.4	−10.6	−6.8	3.7	−5.5	−44.2
1977	10.6	−1.6	7.1	9.2	−15.6	−3.8	−3.9	−3.3	7.9	3.6	7.4	1.4	16.9
1978	0.1	−6.6	−9.2	−0.9	−5.1	−7.5	−8.6	16.4	24.9	2.1	−10.0	−0.6	−10.3
1979	−2.5	8.0	−4.2	−3.6	−3.9	11.0	−3.2	14.4	19.3	21.8	19.7	−3.3	93.5
1980	34.9	13.0	−20.8	25.9	41.8	−0.7	−14.0	10.4	24.1	5.3	−19.0	−12.9	87.5
1981	−12.4	−10.3	−12.1	−20.5	7.2	−14.4	8.4	−25.6	5.6	−4.5	3.9	1.3	−56.9
1982	3.0	−7.4	−12.8	−16.9	−14.5	1.4	−5.3	−11.5	7.2	10.3	6.1	−17.7	−48.0
1983	−9.5	1.9	12.2	12.6	67.4	−13.5	1.1	−11.0	5.3	−14.4	2.2	−14.5	19.4
1984	−8.3	−10.5	2.2	−5.5	−9.3	−5.1	−18.5	1.5	17.7	7.2	−9.4	−21.2	−49.1
1985	3.8	−4.6	−6.6	−7.8	−11.5	−6.1	52.5	5.6	18.9	8.7	−0.2	−8.3	35.1
1986	5.3	6.4	45.7	0.7	−20.8	−6.4	−4.1	−20.5	20.3	9.9	−4.3	−6.7	9.6
1987	25.6	6.5	−18.4	8.8	−8.1	3.7	−14.8	−5.2	23.6	9.1	5.5	18.5	54.1
1988	1.6	−17.9	12.3	−4.2	11.3	33.4	−8.6	−11.2	−6.0	9.9	4.5	0.7	17.5
1989	−5.9	10.9	8.5	−8.6	−5.9	32.9	1.5	−8.6	5.8	−1.3	1.3	−7.0	18.0
1990	11.9	−1.8	8.5	2.1	−14.6	−6.7	−13.2	−6.9	−2.1	−6.8	4.2	−4.6	−28.8
1991	−6.2	−0.1	1.4	−13.1	4.1	5.8	13.6	−8.8	2.0	−0.3	−0.7	0.9	−3.9
1992	−9.1	−2.0	8.2	7.8	7.2	−2.7	−2.6	−2.9	−5.6	0.7	−4.1	N/C	−6.6
1993	−1.3	20.0	19.4	7.8	−16.1	−2.9	−10.4	−3.1	15.2	1.6	−2.4	4.0	28.1
1994	−1.7	11.4	1.4	−2.4	3.2	−3.0	N/C	3.9	2.1	3.2	14.9	3.1	40.9
1995	−6.9	2.1	−1.0	−19.0	1.4	−7.9	−2.7	3.4	−6.3	3.7	3.9	5.7	−23.5
1996	4.7	−4.5	1.6	−11.9	7.9	−0.5	4.9	0.7	−7.6	−5.4	3.5	3.2	−5.2
1997	−5.0	5.0	−1.6	1.6	1.9	0.2	4.4	−0.7	−0.3	7.2	−1.2	−0.2	11.1
1998	−8.1	−12.3	3.5	−17.0	−2.1	3.6	2.1	−13.8	1.3	0.8	6.7	−4.5	−35.7
1999	−9.5	−12.0	−5.6	−26.7	15.5	24.4	−3.9	14.0	1.6	−0.7	−16.0	5.9	−22.1
2000	−11.4	−7.9	18.2	12.5	13.7	12.3	22.6	1.5	−10.5	4.8	−1.5	4.6	66.7
2001	−2.5	−9.6	−13.8	9.7	0.6	9.5	−15.3	−0.3	−16.2	1.7	13.9	−3.8	−27.5
2002	−13.7	−10.8	4.2	−9.6	10.1	−15.9	16.9	3.1	7.7	14.3	0.7	2.7	3.0
2003	13.5	−2.2	−9.1	−6.2	−1.7	−12.1	15.9	−12.8	2.4	−7.9	5.4	−9.3	−25.5
2004	3.4	4.4	4.6	8.6	1.6	8.9	7.7	−3.5	13.4	−5.1	2.8	2.3	59.4
2005	2.0	−0.5	−5.1	−0.5	1.2	6.5	5.4	2.4	11.5	0.9	9.7	18.1	62.4
2006	22.8	−5.0	4.6	−2.6	−11.3	5.7	−8.8	−20.9	−0.4	−1.7	7.1	−5.0	−20.0
2007	−9.8	−0.4	−6.4	−7.9	2.6	1.9	8.5	−8.2	7.1	−1.7	−2.3	11.0	−7.9
2008	14.2	18.3	−20.0	1.0	−15.2								
TOTALS	1.8	−37.6	8.7	−100.8	19.8	42.3	40.2	−120.1	159.9	73.6	48.3	−32.0	
AVG.	0.1	−1.1	0.3	−3.0	0.6	1.3	1.2	−3.6	4.8	2.2	1.5	−1.0	
# Up	15	13	18	14	17	16	15	12	22	21	20	16	
# Down	19	21	16	20	17	17	17	21	11	12	13	16	

LIVE CATTLE CYCLE, SEASONAL PATTERN & TRADING GUIDE

Live cattle is traded at the Chicago Mercantile Exchange. One futures contract is 40,000 pounds, every penny move represents a $400 change in value per contract position. There is a daily trading limit of 3.00 cents, which means the market cannot trade higher or lower than the previous close by more than 3.00 cents. That would represent a $1200 dollar-value change. The contract symbol is LC and it has several tradable months starting with February, April, June, August, October, and then December. This commodity is now traded both electronically and through the open outcry session; the pit traded hours are from 9:05 AM until 1:00 PM (CT).

Beef inventories here in the United States have declined in the last decade as production costs have increased as a result of higher feed and transportation costs. Breeding is both costly and requires a lengthy start-up time. For example, females can first be bred between 14 to 18 months of age, but gestation is approximately nine months. Once the herd population is reduced, it may take up to three years to begin building up calf inventories.

Global demand has also increased as a result of a weaker U.S. dollar. This scenario is lending to a decrease in inventory that may lead to sharply higher prices in 2009. Cattle prices are prone not only to seasonal tendencies, but also to cyclical forces as the country's herd population expands and contracts in response to production costs and farm operation profit margins. Typically, the seasonal low is in June, with a minor peak in November, and then typically beef prices form a seasonal high in March, as packers have purchased inventory ahead of the summer grilling season.

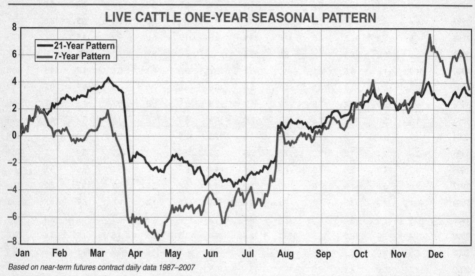

LIVE CATTLE ONE-YEAR SEASONAL PATTERN

— 21-Year Pattern
— 7-Year Pattern

Based on near-term futures contract daily data 1987–2007

LIVE CATTLE NEAR-TERM CONTRACT ANNUAL HIGHS, LOWS & CLOSES SINCE 1972

	HIGH		LOW		YEAR		HIGH		LOW		YEAR
YEAR	DATE	CLOSE	DATE	CLOSE	CLOSE	YEAR	DATE	CLOSE	DATE	CLOSE	CLOSE
1972	12/29	40.825	08/22	32.800	40.825	1991	03/08	81.900	08/08	68.650	72.400
1973	08/13	60.775	09/25	38.550	48.650	1992	03/09	79.525	05/28	69.225	77.125
1974	01/28	53.825	06/11	33.825	39.575	1993	03/22	83.725	12/02	72.225	73.450
1975	06/18	52.075	03/03	34.300	42.925	1994	03/04	77.200	06/27	62.275	72.675
1976	04/20	49.550	01/26	36.275	40.400	1995	01/20	75.000	05/10	59.100	66.425
1977	05/02	46.250	01/14	36.375	42.375	1996	09/13	73.275	04/25	54.800	64.975
1978	05/26	61.975	01/10	41.175	58.925	1997	07/28	71.275	07/08	62.925	66.450
1979	04/26	78.825	08/07	56.525	70.675	1998	04/30	69.500	12/15	57.625	60.525
1980	07/25	73.950	04/02	60.600	68.075	1999	11/16	70.775	01/04	59.625	69.600
1981	04/27	72.150	12/31	54.650	54.650	2000	12/18	78.225	09/06	66.300	77.925
1982	05/17	73.125	12/06	55.150	58.325	2001	03/06	81.650	11/12	61.750	70.700
1983	04/13	70.750	09/02	55.550	67.850	2002	12/31	79.625	05/21	59.400	79.625
1984	03/23	72.125	09/26	60.725	66.675	2003	11/26	98.475	06/16	67.050	73.525
1985	02/04	68.800	07/26	51.675	61.150	2004	12/27	91.775	02/04	71.375	87.825
1986	01/27	63.300	06/03	50.125	55.525	2005	12/20	97.275	07/11	78.075	96.375
1987	05/11	70.125	01/02	55.975	63.125	2006	01/10	96.550	04/04	73.125	92.500
1988	10/12	75.250	06/23	62.225	73.950	2007	03/12	102.025	06/26	88.625	96.175
1989	03/21	78.675	05/30	66.650	77.375	2008*	05/30	101.850	04/02	87.550	AT PRESS-TIME
1990	11/26	79.750	04/26	72.600	77.200						

*Through May 30, 2008

176

LIVE CATTLE NEAR-TERM CONTRACT MONTHLY CLOSING PRICES

	Jan	Feb	Mar	Apr	May	Jun	Jul	Aug	Sep	Oct	Nov	Dec
1972	34.725	34.675	33.775	35.375	36.225	38.075	33.800	33.850	37.150	35.750	38.000	40.825
1973	43.450	45.075	44.200	44.425	47.050	47.525	56.775	49.250	44.225	43.250	45.325	48.650
1974	53.175	44.600	45.400	43.700	37.275	42.575	50.725	40.650	43.400	41.075	41.300	39.575
1975	36.575	35.800	42.325	46.600	46.700	48.700	39.700	44.925	47.325	43.050	44.450	42.925
1976	37.600	37.800	44.150	47.075	47.225	42.000	41.125	40.750	37.250	39.550	40.800	40.400
1977	39.150	37.475	41.425	45.600	42.850	41.475	38.225	38.900	40.775	40.975	39.975	42.375
1978	43.700	46.100	50.475	53.675	58.925	51.525	52.650	53.175	56.175	53.550	57.725	58.925
1979	66.700	71.100	71.350	78.350	69.650	66.725	59.400	68.450	73.000	67.325	72.600	70.675
1980	69.300	68.575	63.600	64.825	65.375	68.700	70.575	68.725	68.925	69.225	71.175	68.075
1981	66.025	65.050	68.550	70.175	67.100	66.325	64.975	66.925	65.825	63.800	62.350	54.650
1982	61.700	64.225	66.425	69.575	68.075	63.250	62.425	61.650	59.025	59.525	58.250	58.325
1983	60.400	64.575	69.625	66.125	62.525	61.425	60.475	55.975	60.750	59.425	62.750	67.850
1984	66.125	70.400	68.700	66.175	62.600	64.725	61.600	63.600	63.550	63.975	66.525	66.675
1985	68.050	65.025	67.200	62.650	62.875	58.350	55.925	56.100	61.825	66.250	65.075	61.150
1986	61.900	61.375	58.250	57.200	51.400	56.700	59.050	61.775	56.200	59.575	59.175	55.525
1987	62.875	64.975	63.425	67.200	62.400	63.300	62.775	66.050	66.600	62.400	61.725	63.125
1988	67.800	71.500	70.875	70.900	67.825	64.600	69.100	71.775	73.775	74.175	72.625	73.950
1989	76.425	78.050	73.025	71.450	66.950	70.150	75.525	73.750	74.325	74.450	74.100	77.375
1990	76.025	75.450	72.925	72.975	73.100	73.075	78.975	76.325	76.450	77.450	75.150	77.200
1991	77.525	80.225	77.125	76.100	73.725	72.225	73.200	70.050	76.775	73.500	74.725	72.400
1992	77.150	77.400	74.775	73.100	69.475	72.425	73.625	73.750	73.650	73.775	74.150	77.125
1993	76.850	80.225	76.250	76.775	73.375	75.050	75.200	75.150	74.125	74.050	72.500	73.450
1994	76.450	77.100	74.275	71.300	65.750	64.150	71.725	70.850	68.500	70.000	67.250	72.675
1995	74.150	74.275	61.700	62.950	59.700	62.800	65.875	63.325	66.650	68.350	67.625	66.425
1996	63.850	63.925	62.475	57.350	64.525	65.825	68.550	72.225	68.150	66.675	63.675	64.975
1997	66.825	69.625	65.075	64.750	64.925	64.450	70.625	67.200	67.100	67.525	68.625	66.450
1998	67.475	64.375	65.775	69.500	66.300	65.025	59.925	59.000	61.750	65.000	62.775	60.525
1999	65.075	68.025	63.600	62.825	62.800	62.625	64.375	66.550	69.300	68.650	70.050	69.600
2000	72.050	71.175	68.975	69.275	67.250	66.725	68.800	66.975	70.675	72.675	74.050	77.925
2001	76.825	81.375	72.675	71.650	74.475	74.000	73.900	73.150	67.325	68.075	70.175	70.700
2002	75.525	74.200	65.800	63.625	60.950	63.550	67.750	67.200	70.625	73.200	78.475	79.625
2003	79.975	75.825	70.375	71.925	69.750	69.875	77.700	82.850	84.950	90.900	93.175	73.525
2004	73.425	76.850	76.225	80.400	88.625	85.750	88.750	84.650	87.275	84.475	89.550	87.825
2005	88.325	86.050	85.250	85.625	84.700	79.300	83.400	82.250	90.000	90.925	95.725	96.375
2006	91.575	87.225	74.350	73.500	80.075	85.675	88.700	93.125	89.850	87.825	89.100	92.500
2007	93.175	97.050	94.875	94.125	91.475	90.275	99.950	96.900	99.800	94.925	95.775	96.175
2008	94.275	94.325	87.750	93.475	101.850							

LIVE CATTLE NEAR-TERM CONTRACT MONTHLY PERCENT CHANGES

	Jan	Feb	Mar	Apr	May	Jun	Jul	Aug	Sep	Oct	Nov	Dec	Year's Change
1972	1.5	−0.1	−2.6	4.7	2.4	5.1	−11.2	0.1	9.7	−3.8	6.3	7.4	19.4
1973	6.4	3.7	−1.9	0.5	5.9	1.0	19.5	−13.3	−10.2	−2.2	4.8	7.3	19.2
1974	9.3	−16.1	1.8	−3.7	−14.7	14.2	19.1	−19.9	6.8	−5.4	0.5	−4.2	−18.7
1975	−7.6	−2.1	18.2	10.1	0.2	4.3	−18.5	13.2	5.3	−9.0	3.3	−3.4	8.5
1976	−12.4	0.5	16.8	6.6	0.3	−11.1	−2.1	−0.9	−8.6	6.2	3.2	−1.0	−5.9
1977	−3.1	−4.3	10.5	10.1	−6.0	−3.2	−7.8	1.8	4.8	0.5	−2.4	6.0	4.9
1978	3.1	5.5	9.5	6.3	9.8	−12.6	2.2	1.0	5.6	−4.7	7.8	2.1	39.1
1979	13.2	6.6	0.4	9.8	−11.1	−4.2	−11.0	15.2	6.6	−7.8	7.8	−2.7	19.9
1980	−1.9	−1.0	−7.3	1.9	0.8	5.1	2.7	−2.6	0.3	0.4	2.8	−4.4	−3.7
1981	−3.0	−1.5	5.4	2.4	−4.4	−1.2	−2.0	3.0	−1.6	−3.1	−2.3	−12.3	−19.7
1982	12.9	4.1	3.4	4.7	−2.2	−7.1	−1.3	−1.2	−4.3	0.8	−2.1	0.1	6.7
1983	3.6	6.9	7.8	−5.0	−5.4	−1.8	−1.5	−7.4	8.5	−2.2	5.6	8.1	16.3
1984	−2.5	6.5	−2.4	−3.7	−5.4	3.4	−4.8	3.2	−0.1	0.7	4.0	0.2	−1.7
1985	2.1	−4.4	3.3	−6.8	0.4	−7.2	−4.2	0.3	10.2	7.2	−1.8	−6.0	−8.3
1986	1.2	−0.8	−5.1	−1.8	−10.1	10.3	4.1	4.6	−9.0	6.0	−0.7	−6.2	−9.2
1987	13.2	3.3	−2.4	6.0	−7.1	1.4	−0.8	5.2	0.8	−6.3	−1.1	2.3	13.7
1988	7.4	5.5	−0.9	0.04	−4.3	−4.8	7.0	3.9	2.8	0.5	−2.1	1.8	17.1
1989	3.3	2.1	−6.4	−2.2	−6.3	4.8	7.7	−2.4	0.8	0.2	−0.5	4.4	4.6
1990	−1.7	−0.8	−3.3	0.1	0.2	−0.03	8.1	−3.4	0.2	1.3	−3.0	2.7	−0.2
1991	0.4	3.5	−3.9	−1.3	−3.1	−2.0	1.3	−4.3	9.6	−4.3	1.7	−3.1	−6.2
1992	6.6	0.3	−3.4	−2.2	−5.0	4.2	1.7	0.2	−0.1	0.2	0.5	4.0	6.5
1993	−0.4	4.4	−5.0	0.7	−4.4	2.3	0.2	−0.1	−1.4	−0.1	−2.1	1.3	−4.8
1994	4.1	0.9	−3.7	−4.0	−7.8	−2.4	11.8	−1.2	−3.3	2.2	−3.9	8.1	−1.1
1995	2.0	0.2	−16.9	2.0	−5.2	5.2	4.9	−3.9	5.3	2.6	−1.1	−1.8	−8.6
1996	−3.9	0.1	−2.3	−8.2	12.5	2.0	4.1	5.4	−5.6	−2.2	−4.5	2.0	−2.2
1997	2.8	4.2	−6.5	−0.5	0.3	−0.7	9.6	−4.8	−0.1	0.6	1.6	−3.2	2.3
1998	1.5	−4.6	2.2	5.7	−4.6	−1.9	−7.8	−1.5	4.7	5.3	−3.4	−3.6	−8.9
1999	7.5	4.5	−6.5	−1.2	−0.04	−0.3	2.8	3.4	4.1	−0.9	2.0	−0.6	15.0
2000	3.5	−1.2	−3.1	0.4	−2.9	−0.8	3.1	−2.7	5.5	2.8	1.9	5.2	12.0
2001	−1.4	5.9	−10.7	−1.4	3.9	−0.6	−0.1	−1.0	−8.0	1.1	3.1	0.7	−9.3
2002	6.8	−1.8	−11.3	−3.3	−4.2	4.3	6.6	−0.8	5.1	3.6	7.2	1.5	12.6
2003	0.4	−5.2	−7.2	2.2	−3.0	0.2	11.2	6.6	2.5	7.0	2.5	−21.1	−7.7
2004	−0.1	4.7	−0.8	5.5	10.2	−3.2	3.5	−4.6	3.1	−3.2	6.0	−1.9	19.4
2005	0.6	−2.6	−0.9	0.4	−1.1	−6.4	5.2	−1.4	9.4	1.0	5.3	0.7	9.7
2006	−5.0	−4.8	−14.8	−1.1	8.9	7.0	3.5	5.0	−3.5	−2.3	1.5	3.8	−4.0
2007	0.7	4.2	−2.2	−0.8	−2.8	−1.3	10.7	−3.1	3.0	−4.9	0.9	0.4	4.0
2008	−2.0	0.1	−7.0	6.5	9.0								
TOTALS	69.1	26.4	−59.2	39.4	−56.3	2.0	77.5	−8.4	58.9	−12.2	49.3	−5.4	
AVG.	1.9	0.7	−1.6	1.1	−1.5	0.1	2.2	−0.2	1.6	−0.3	1.4	−0.2	
# Up	24	22	11	21	14	16	23	16	23	20	22	21	
# Down	13	15	26	16	23	20	13	20	13	16	14	15	

LEAN HOGS CYCLE, SEASONAL PATTERN & TRADING GUIDE

Lean hogs is traded at the Chicago Mercantile Exchange. One futures contract is 40,000 pounds, every penny move represents a $400 change in value per contract position. There is a daily trading limit of 3.00 cents, which means the market cannot trade higher or lower than the previous close by more than 3.00 cents. That would represent a $1200 value change. The contract symbol is LH, and it has several tradable months starting with February, April, May, June, July, August, October, and then December. This commodity is now traded both electronically and through the open outcry session; the pit traded hours are from 9:05 AM until 1:00 PM (CT).

Unlike beef, pork production actually increased in early 2007, causing prices to decline. Several factors came into play. One was due to an increase in imports from Canada and in addition U.S. producers had enjoyed years of profitability, which created an incentive for increased production. The breeding cycle is significantly shorter for raising pork than it is for cattle. Female pigs can start breeding at an average of 7 months of age and gestation period is less than four months.

Demand for pork has increased in recent years, building a solid base as consumers are switching to a lower cholesterol and leaner protein meat source in dietary needs. This in turn has helped to increase the overall demand for pork, which has been named "the other white meat." The price action of the hog market also has a reasonably defined seasonal price pattern. Pork supply is heaviest both in supply and in weight at the end of October into November, when feed grain is more abundant and less expensive due to harvest pressure. From March through May we typically see packers buy in, preparing for summer grill season demand, and then as hog inventories start to decline we see a typical peak in May. During summer months, demand tends to decline as consumption declines, as fewer people cook indoors.

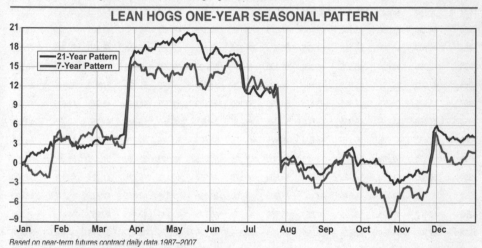

LEAN HOGS ONE-YEAR SEASONAL PATTERN

21-Year Pattern
7-Year Pattern

Based on near-term futures contract daily data 1987–2007

LEAN HOGS NEAR-TERM CONTRACT ANNUAL HIGHS, LOWS & CLOSES SINCE 1970

	HIGH		LOW		YEAR		HIGH		LOW		YEAR
YEAR	DATE	CLOSE	DATE	CLOSE	CLOSE	YEAR	DATE	CLOSE	DATE	CLOSE	CLOSE
1970	01/06	28.450	10/28	16.150	16.350	1990	05/21	67.000	02/02	46.550	48.875
1971	12/30	25.050	01/08	16.050	25.050	1991	04/30	58.925	12/30	39.125	39.300
1972	12/27	32.975	02/28	23.350	32.550	1992	05/08	48.950	07/28	37.725	43.625
1973	08/13	57.050	02/07	30.075	44.300	1993	03/31	56.225	01/06	42.450	45.350
1974	01/07	48.100	06/11	24.025	41.900	1994	03/28	53.425	11/23	31.650	39.350
1975	10/02	65.050	01/17	36.975	48.475	1995	12/13	50.725	01/06	37.100	48.575
1976	06/14	53.275	11/03	29.825	37.625	1996	12/30	79.500	01/31	44.350	79.225
1977	06/03	47.700	08/01	33.850	43.325	1997	04/17	85.450	12/31	57.700	57.700
1978	05/16	56.050	01/30	41.325	49.100	1998	06/16	62.800	12/16	27.950	32.650
1979	01/19	54.125	08/01	31.425	41.675	1999	05/10	60.700	01/04	30.725	54.500
1980	11/28	57.450	04/02	32.050	47.750	2000	04/24	77.475	10/30	50.750	56.825
1981	06/08	56.850	03/20	38.825	43.350	2001	04/16	73.175	10/25	47.575	57.050
1982	09/08	64.750	01/04	43.825	56.750	2002	02/05	62.725	09/03	30.050	51.600
1983	01/14	59.700	10/10	40.200	51.250	2003	06/09	68.450	11/26	48.450	53.425
1984	04/03	57.750	02/23	44.250	53.325	2004	06/23	78.125	01/12	51.775	76.400
1985	01/02	53.750	09/09	34.800	46.625	2005	04/01	80.800	07/27	56.625	65.275
1986	07/25	59.600	02/28	38.075	47.250	2006	06/19	76.925	01/26	57.175	61.700
1987	06/15	59.275	12/22	40.650	41.075	2007	04/16	77.850	11/06	51.125	57.875
1988	05/31	54.725	09/06	37.550	46.525	2008*	05/14	78.175	01/11	54.000	AT PRESS-TIME
1989	11/24	51.125	09/11	38.750	48.700						

*Through May 30, 2008

LEAN HOGS NEAR-TERM CONTRACT MONTHLY CLOSING PRICES

	Jan	Feb	Mar	Apr	May	Jun	Jul	Aug	Sep	Oct	Nov	Dec
1970	27.500	27.900	27.250	27.100	25.875	24.550	20.675	19.675	19.400	16.150	16.950	16.350
1971	17.675	17.600	19.875	20.575	22.900	21.275	19.125	18.125	20.800	21.250	23.575	25.050
1972	25.975	23.875	27.200	27.825	28.750	29.150	26.300	27.900	29.325	29.100	29.600	32.550
1973	31.125	35.875	36.275	37.175	40.450	43.050	55.575	46.775	43.450	43.850	44.975	44.300
1974	45.050	38.250	36.750	33.300	28.500	35.325	41.325	34.275	43.500	41.575	44.300	41.900
1975	40.175	38.600	45.250	46.800	49.875	52.725	48.700	55.525	63.675	51.100	50.200	48.475
1976	40.550	43.825	47.700	51.050	50.475	47.375	38.075	38.425	32.950	30.100	31.700	37.625
1977	34.925	34.700	38.425	43.650	46.550	45.250	34.500	37.825	36.950	39.125	39.350	43.325
1978	42.750	44.075	50.850	51.850	54.525	44.500	45.850	46.475	52.250	50.400	52.200	49.100
1979	51.125	52.300	48.000	50.250	43.850	35.550	32.400	36.875	37.200	37.725	42.325	41.675
1980	38.950	36.850	34.300	34.475	34.775	40.250	43.700	42.250	50.750	49.925	57.450	47.750
1981	47.350	43.600	49.825	49.000	56.075	51.275	49.350	49.450	50.250	48.700	45.525	43.350
1982	49.450	45.825	55.475	59.925	62.650	57.800	59.525	61.750	59.550	54.475	58.125	56.750
1983	54.200	51.350	52.100	49.300	47.075	45.125	40.325	43.050	40.950	43.325	47.525	51.250
1984	46.800	45.650	56.125	54.425	56.075	55.775	47.425	47.550	45.950	48.450	53.925	53.325
1985	48.750	46.625	49.575	46.300	51.100	48.350	40.000	36.300	43.200	46.725	47.650	46.625
1986	42.000	38.075	43.825	46.600	48.125	56.075	54.700	57.725	51.600	51.600	52.450	47.250
1987	45.975	43.275	47.825	53.475	54.800	53.100	48.800	50.375	45.275	42.975	42.625	41.075
1988	44.150	43.250	49.300	48.800	54.725	45.275	39.325	38.550	43.025	41.150	43.775	46.525
1989	43.475	43.725	46.475	46.625	46.975	47.425	39.825	40.475	44.375	46.575	49.800	48.700
1990	46.875	50.350	57.025	63.125	62.400	58.300	54.825	48.300	52.700	51.775	48.200	48.875
1991	50.500	51.875	58.425	58.925	54.800	50.575	45.250	44.175	44.725	41.725	42.475	39.300
1992	40.025	39.725	45.675	48.100	45.000	44.700	37.850	40.050	42.875	42.425	43.375	43.625
1993	43.800	45.525	56.225	51.350	49.650	44.900	45.725	47.175	47.400	49.050	46.475	45.350
1994	51.700	49.500	52.850	51.225	47.225	45.350	42.325	38.575	36.400	35.275	34.400	39.350
1995	39.650	39.750	42.950	42.350	44.325	46.625	44.225	44.650	46.600	43.700	48.275	48.575
1996	44.350	48.550	54.850	59.750	58.225	51.525	53.625	52.425	57.300	54.400	78.350	79.225
1997	74.750	74.475	81.875	83.550	80.650	81.950	75.150	70.450	63.425	62.225	60.475	57.700
1998	57.625	49.025	59.975	59.925	59.800	54.925	42.450	37.275	40.400	37.400	36.575	32.650
1999	43.025	43.000	52.350	59.075	55.500	44.575	43.350	45.800	46.625	46.525	56.175	54.500
2000	60.250	58.075	73.150	76.650	68.600	69.025	57.450	52.925	54.200	51.175	56.675	56.825
2001	57.150	62.800	69.000	67.575	66.600	69.050	60.175	58.250	54.825	51.650	55.250	57.050
2002	60.900	60.350	60.500	52.050	47.775	46.725	41.700	30.875	40.550	43.125	54.200	51.600
2003	56.850	54.550	58.350	62.775	67.525	63.975	51.300	54.775	53.600	53.325	55.200	53.425
2004	59.200	62.025	74.650	74.075	75.275	76.700	69.225	65.975	69.125	67.450	77.150	76.400
2005	75.550	74.225	79.275	77.450	71.400	65.025	57.525	63.700	63.350	61.675	67.350	65.275
2006	61.825	61.475	65.275	67.000	66.425	70.375	61.750	66.900	60.850	64.950	65.175	61.700
2007	68.225	67.750	75.400	75.100	74.525	70.675	75.200	66.825	62.250	53.875	62.300	57.875
2008	66.450	59.950	67.950	73.475	78.100							

LEAN HOGS NEAR-TERM CONTRACT MONTHLY PERCENT CHANGES

	Jan	Feb	Mar	Apr	May	Jun	Jul	Aug	Sep	Oct	Nov	Dec	Year's Change
1970	0.9	1.5	-2.3	-0.6	-4.5	-5.1	-15.8	-4.8	-1.4	-16.8	5.0	-3.5	-40.0
1971	8.1	-0.4	12.9	3.5	11.3	-7.1	-10.1	-5.2	14.8	2.2	10.9	6.3	53.2
1973	3.7	-8.1	13.9	2.3	3.3	1.4	-9.8	6.1	5.1	-0.8	1.7	10.0	29.9
1973	-4.4	15.3	1.1	2.5	8.8	6.4	29.1	-15.8	-7.1	0.9	2.6	-1.5	36.1
1974	1.7	-15.1	-3.9	-9.4	-14.4	23.9	17.0	-17.1	26.9	-4.4	6.6	-5.4	-5.4
1975	-4.1	-3.9	17.2	3.4	6.6	5.7	-7.6	14.0	14.7	-19.7	-1.8	-3.4	15.7
1976	-16.3	8.1	8.8	7.0	-1.1	-6.1	-19.6	0.9	-14.2	-8.6	5.3	18.7	-22.4
1977	-7.2	-0.6	10.7	13.6	6.6	-2.8	-23.8	9.6	-2.3	5.9	0.6	10.1	15.1
1978	-1.3	3.1	15.4	2.0	5.2	-18.4	3.0	1.4	12.4	-3.5	3.6	-5.9	13.3
1979	4.1	2.3	-8.2	4.7	-12.7	-18.9	-8.9	13.8	0.9	1.4	12.2	-1.5	-15.1
1980	-6.5	-5.4	-6.9	0.5	0.9	15.7	8.6	-3.3	20.1	-1.6	15.1	-16.9	14.6
1981	-0.8	-7.9	14.3	-1.7	14.4	-8.6	-3.8	0.2	1.6	-3.1	-6.5	-4.8	-9.2
1982	14.1	-7.3	21.1	8.0	4.5	-7.7	3.0	3.7	-3.6	-8.5	6.7	-2.4	30.9
1983	-4.5	-5.3	1.5	-5.4	-4.5	-4.1	-10.6	6.8	-4.9	5.8	9.7	7.8	-9.7
1984	-8.7	-2.5	22.9	-3.0	3.0	-0.5	-15.0	0.3	-3.4	5.4	11.3	-1.1	4.0
1985	-8.6	-4.4	6.3	-6.6	10.4	-5.4	-17.3	-9.3	19.0	8.2	2.0	-2.2	-12.6
1986	-9.9	-9.3	15.1	6.3	3.3	16.5	-2.5	5.5	-10.6	N/C	1.6	-9.9	1.3
1987	-2.7	-5.9	10.5	11.8	2.5	-3.1	-8.1	3.2	-10.1	-5.1	-0.8	-3.6	-13.1
1988	7.5	-2.0	14.0	-1.0	12.1	-17.3	-13.1	-2.0	11.6	-4.4	6.4	6.3	13.3
1989	-6.6	0.6	6.3	0.3	0.8	1.0	-16.0	1.6	9.6	5.0	6.9	-2.2	4.7
1990	-3.7	7.4	13.3	10.7	-1.1	-6.6	-6.0	-11.9	9.1	-1.8	-6.9	1.4	0.4
1991	3.3	2.7	12.6	0.9	-7.0	-7.7	-10.5	-2.4	1.2	-6.7	1.8	-7.5	-19.6
1992	1.8	-0.7	15.0	5.3	-6.4	-0.7	-15.3	5.8	7.1	-1.0	2.2	0.6	11.0
1993	0.4	3.9	23.5	-8.7	-3.3	-9.6	1.8	3.2	0.5	3.5	-5.2	-2.4	4.0
1994	14.0	-4.3	6.8	-3.1	-7.8	-4.0	-6.7	-8.9	-5.6	-3.1	-2.5	14.4	-13.2
1995	0.8	0.3	8.1	-1.4	4.7	5.2	-5.1	1.0	4.4	-6.2	10.5	0.6	23.4
1996	-8.7	9.5	13.0	8.9	-2.6	-11.5	4.1	-2.2	9.3	-5.1	44.0	1.1	63.1
1997	-5.6	-0.4	9.9	2.0	-3.5	1.6	-8.3	-6.3	-10.0	-1.9	-2.8	-4.6	-27.2
1998	-0.1	-14.9	22.3	-0.1	-0.2	-8.2	-22.7	-12.2	8.4	-7.4	-2.2	-10.7	-43.4
1999	31.8	-0.1	21.7	12.8	-6.1	-19.7	-2.7	5.7	1.8	-0.2	20.7	-3.0	66.9
2000	10.6	-3.6	26.0	4.8	-10.5	0.6	-16.8	-7.9	2.4	-5.6	10.7	0.3	4.3
2001	0.6	9.9	9.9	-2.1	-1.4	3.7	-12.9	-3.2	-5.9	-5.8	7.0	3.3	0.4
2002	6.7	-0.9	0.2	-14.0	-8.2	-2.2	-10.8	-26.0	31.3	6.4	25.7	-4.8	-9.6
2003	10.2	-4.0	7.0	7.6	7.6	-5.3	-19.8	6.8	-2.1	-0.5	3.5	-3.2	3.5
2004	10.8	4.8	20.4	-0.8	1.6	1.9	-9.7	-4.7	4.8	-2.4	14.4	-1.0	43.0
2005	-1.1	-1.8	6.8	-2.3	-7.8	-8.9	-11.5	10.7	-0.5	-2.6	9.2	-3.1	-14.6
2006	-5.3	-0.6	6.2	2.6	-0.9	5.9	-12.3	8.3	-9.0	6.7	0.3	-5.3	-5.5
2007	10.6	-0.7	11.3	-0.4	-0.8	-5.2	6.4	-11.1	-6.8	-13.5	15.6	-7.1	-6.2
2008	14.8	-9.8	13.3	8.1	6.3								
TOTALS	50.4	-50.5	418.0	69.0	9.1	-105.2	-280.1	-45.7	119.5	-88.9	245.1	-36.1	
AVG.	1.3	-1.3	10.7	1.8	0.2	-2.8	-7.4	-1.2	3.1	-2.3	6.5	-1.0	
# Up	20	13	35	23	19	13	8	20	22	11	30	13	
# Down	19	26	4	16	20	25	30	18	16	26	8	25	

BRITISH POUND CYCLE, SEASONAL PATTERN & TRADING GUIDE

The British pound currency futures contract is traded at the Chicago Mercantile Exchange. Unlike the spot Forex markets, we have more data to study the pound's seasonality's due to the fact there is a warehouse of historic data since this market was traded in a centralized and regulated environment. One futures contract size is 62,000 worth of sterling or pounds, and a penny move represents a $625 change in value per contract position. The contract symbol is BP; it has a tradable contract starting with March, June, September, and December. This is considered an electronic traded market with nearly 24 hour access but the outcry trading hours are from 7:20 AM until 2:00 PM (CT) there are no daily price limits.

The British economy is driven by manufacturing, agricultural production, and energy production from oil, coal and natural gas, which is considered to account for as much as 10% of Britain's gross domestic production. In addition, London is considered the world's leading international financial service center. Their economy runs on a fiscal year which begins in April. Since the pound is valued against the U.S. dollar, we have a tendency to see bottoms in March as multiconglomerate international companies adjust their books for fiscal yearend adjustments, and we see a major peak in December against the U.S. dollar, as money flows go back into the U.S. for yearend tax adjustment purposes also referred to as repatriation of funds.

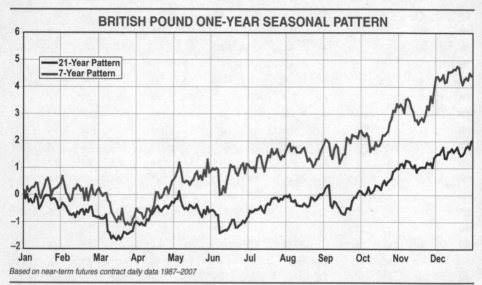

BRITISH POUND ONE-YEAR SEASONAL PATTERN

- 21-Year Pattern
- 7-Year Pattern

Based on near-term futures contract daily data 1987–2007

BRITISH POUND NEAR-TERM CONTRACT ANNUAL HIGHS, LOWS & CLOSES SINCE 1976

YEAR	HIGH DATE	HIGH CLOSE	LOW DATE	LOW CLOSE	YEAR CLOSE	YEAR	HIGH DATE	HIGH CLOSE	LOW DATE	LOW CLOSE	YEAR CLOSE
1976	02/26	202.40	10/28	154.05	166.40	1993	04/26	158.02	02/12	141.18	146.84
1977	12/30	191.95	01/03	166.95	191.95	1994	10/25	163.74	02/09	145.78	156.70
1978	10/30	209.75	05/19	180.05	204.10	1995	03/07	164.42	12/12	152.88	155.14
1979	07/24	231.75	02/02	197.20	220.15	1996	12/31	171.24	05/01	149.02	171.24
1980	10/23	244.55	04/03	213.55	241.85	1997	11/12	170.32	08/12	157.54	164.66
1981	01/20	244.40	09/25	177.35	190.40	1998	10/08	170.52	01/09	160.68	165.68
1982	01/04	193.20	11/24	158.65	162.95	1999	10/21	167.70	07/09	154.86	161.90
1983	01/03	162.80	12/13	141.95	146.25	2000	01/20	165.38	11/24	140.06	149.48
1984	02/28	148.85	12/31	115.40	115.40	2001	01/05	150.30	06/12	136.84	144.86
1985	11/29	148.85	02/25	105.00	143.90	2002	12/31	160.22	01/28	140.38	160.22
1986	04/28	154.90	02/04	136.65	147.20	2003	12/31	177.39	04/07	154.48	177.39
1987	12/31	188.25	01/07	145.75	188.25	2004	12/07	194.53	05/11	175.12	190.71
1988	04/18	189.65	09/22	165.38	179.92	2005	03/04	192.30	11/25	171.28	171.87
1989	01/03	180.98	06/14	149.26	158.88	2006	12/01	198.06	03/10	172.82	195.72
1990	11/27	197.30	03/21	156.88	190.94	2007	11/08	210.64	03/05	192.23	197.85
1991	02/06	198.90	07/02	158.58	184.48	2008*	03/07	201.37	02/07	193.63	AT PRESS-TIME
1992	09/02	199.96	12/28	147.96	149.86						

*Through May 30, 2008

BRITISH POUND NEAR-TERM CONTRACT MONTHLY CLOSING PRICES

	Jan	Feb	Mar	Apr	May	Jun	Jul	Aug	Sep	Oct	Nov	Dec
1976	201.80	202.30	189.90	182.80	175.60	175.70	176.70	177.25	162.55	156.15	164.90	166.40
1977	169.70	171.10	170.70	171.45	171.30	171.05	173.40	174.20	175.25	183.50	181.70	191.95
1978	195.30	193.95	186.00	181.45	183.85	184.00	192.70	193.80	195.75	206.45	194.05	204.10
1979	197.75	202.40	206.45	206.65	206.85	216.10	223.50	226.00	219.20	207.70	219.20	220.15
1980	225.65	225.45	216.15	225.45	234.30	232.25	230.40	240.10	237.25	242.30	236.00	241.85
1981	236.60	220.00	224.80	214.90	207.75	194.55	184.45	183.95	180.90	187.75	195.85	190.40
1982	187.90	181.60	179.20	182.50	178.10	174.60	174.10	172.15	169.80	167.70	163.15	162.95
1983	151.80	150.65	148.25	156.15	160.20	152.80	151.45	149.65	149.45	149.30	146.40	146.25
1984	140.40	148.85	144.65	140.40	138.75	136.55	130.25	130.85	123.80	122.50	119.30	115.40
1985	111.95	107.30	123.20	122.45	129.00	129.60	140.75	138.75	138.50	143.65	148.85	143.90
1986	140.55	143.80	145.75	153.50	147.20	153.15	148.65	149.05	142.95	139.80	143.15	147.20
1987	150.50	154.35	159.55	166.15	162.85	161.00	158.65	162.95	161.75	171.90	182.95	188.25
1988	176.10	177.15	188.10	187.20	183.55	170.44	170.24	168.22	168.14	175.64	184.80	179.92
1989	174.52	174.14	167.84	167.96	156.90	154.22	165.40	156.54	160.12	156.86	156.72	158.88
1990	166.60	167.52	162.62	162.80	167.24	172.56	184.82	188.58	184.86	193.20	193.76	190.94
1991	195.16	190.52	171.90	171.82	169.30	160.42	167.62	167.70	173.38	172.86	176.38	184.48
1992	177.08	175.18	171.38	176.24	182.38	188.02	191.24	198.32	175.56	154.86	151.34	149.86
1993	148.00	142.54	150.44	156.74	155.98	148.30	147.76	148.88	148.82	147.66	148.54	146.84
1994	150.26	148.56	148.26	151.80	150.98	154.24	153.88	153.46	157.46	163.46	156.56	156.70
1995	157.96	158.42	162.00	161.04	158.96	159.04	159.66	155.12	157.82	157.94	153.08	155.14
1996	151.12	153.18	152.56	150.68	155.02	155.16	155.46	156.18	156.46	162.60	168.12	171.24
1997	159.78	162.92	163.86	162.26	164.04	166.06	163.72	161.94	161.14	167.18	168.68	164.66
1998	162.88	164.38	166.56	166.88	163.02	166.08	162.80	167.78	169.24	167.02	164.68	165.68
1999	164.50	160.12	161.08	160.86	160.10	157.92	162.26	160.68	164.64	164.48	159.90	161.90
2000	161.56	157.94	159.40	155.28	149.82	151.86	150.08	145.10	147.70	145.04	142.54	149.48
2001	146.24	144.56	141.58	142.90	141.58	140.94	142.28	145.38	146.68	145.16	142.28	144.86
2002	140.66	141.58	141.90	145.34	145.48	152.44	155.82	154.68	156.26	156.00	155.40	160.22
2003	164.20	157.26	157.24	159.44	163.76	164.68	160.46	157.40	165.36	168.94	172.03	177.39
2004	181.79	186.46	183.16	177.24	183.04	180.57	181.24	179.83	180.23	183.12	190.90	190.71
2005	187.78	192.18	188.26	190.30	181.66	178.63	175.49	180.18	176.03	176.93	172.89	171.87
2006	178.02	175.45	173.80	182.28	186.97	185.08	187.00	190.52	187.30	190.82	196.62	195.72
2007	196.38	196.37	196.69	199.86	197.94	200.55	203.33	201.61	204.19	207.85	205.58	197.85
2008	198.48	198.63	197.12	198.29	197.88							

BRITISH POUND NEAR-TERM CONTRACT MONTHLY PERCENT CHANGES

	Jan	Feb	Mar	Apr	May	Jun	Jul	Aug	Sep	Oct	Nov	Dec	Year's Change
1976	0.7	0.2	-6.1	-3.7	-3.9	0.1	0.6	0.3	-8.3	-3.9	5.6	0.9	-17.0
1977	2.0	0.8	-0.2	0.4	-0.1	-0.1	1.4	0.5	0.6	4.7	-1.0	5.6	15.4
1978	1.7	-0.7	-4.1	-2.4	1.3	0.1	4.7	0.6	1.0	5.5	-6.0	5.2	6.3
1979	-3.1	2.4	2.0	0.1	0.1	4.5	3.4	1.1	-3.0	-5.2	5.5	0.4	7.9
1980	2.5	-0.1	-4.1	4.3	3.9	-0.9	-0.8	4.2	-1.2	2.1	-2.6	2.5	9.9
1981	-2.2	-7.0	2.2	-4.4	-3.3	-6.4	-5.2	-0.3	-1.7	3.8	4.3	-2.8	-21.3
1982	-1.3	-3.4	-1.3	1.8	-2.4	-2.0	-0.3	-1.1	-1.4	-1.2	-2.7	-0.1	-14.4
1983	-6.8	-0.8	-1.6	5.3	2.6	-4.6	-0.9	-1.2	-0.1	-0.1	-1.9	-0.1	-10.2
1984	-4.0	6.0	-2.8	-2.9	-1.2	-1.6	-4.6	0.5	-5.4	-1.1	-2.6	-3.3	-21.1
1985	-3.0	-4.2	14.8	-0.6	5.3	0.5	8.6	-1.4	-0.2	3.7	3.6	-3.3	24.7
1986	-2.3	2.3	1.4	5.3	-4.1	4.0	-2.9	0.3	-4.1	-2.2	2.4	2.8	2.3
1987	2.2	2.6	3.4	4.1	-2.0	-1.1	-1.5	2.7	-0.7	6.3	6.4	2.9	27.9
1988	-6.5	0.6	6.2	-0.5	-1.9	-7.1	-0.1	-1.2	-0.1	4.5	5.2	-2.6	-4.4
1989	-3.0	-0.2	-3.6	0.1	-6.6	-1.7	7.2	-5.4	2.3	-2.0	-0.1	1.4	-11.7
1990	4.9	0.6	-2.9	0.1	2.7	3.2	7.1	2.0	-2.0	4.5	0.3	-1.5	20.2
1991	2.2	-2.4	-9.8	-0.1	-1.5	-5.2	4.5	0.1	3.4	-0.3	2.0	4.6	-3.4
1992	-4.0	-1.1	-2.2	2.8	3.5	3.1	1.7	3.7	-11.5	-11.8	-2.3	-1.0	-18.8
1993	-1.2	-3.7	5.5	4.2	-0.5	-4.9	-0.4	0.8	-0.04	-0.8	0.6	-1.1	-2.0
1994	2.3	-1.1	-0.2	2.4	-0.5	2.2	-0.2	-0.3	2.6	3.8	-4.2	0.1	6.7
1995	0.8	0.3	2.3	-0.6	-1.3	0.1	0.4	-2.8	1.7	0.1	-3.1	1.3	-1.0
1996	-2.6	1.4	-0.4	-1.2	2.9	0.1	0.2	0.5	0.2	3.9	3.4	1.9	10.4
1997	-6.7	2.0	0.6	-1.0	1.1	1.2	-1.4	-1.1	-0.5	3.7	0.9	-2.4	-3.8
1998	-1.1	0.9	1.3	0.2	-2.3	1.9	-2.0	3.1	0.9	-1.3	-1.4	0.6	0.6
1999	-0.7	-2.7	0.6	-0.1	-0.5	-1.4	2.7	-1.0	2.5	-0.1	-2.8	1.3	-2.3
2000	-0.2	-2.2	0.9	-2.6	-3.5	1.4	-1.2	-3.3	1.8	-1.8	-1.7	4.9	-7.7
2001	-2.2	-1.1	-2.1	0.9	-0.9	-0.5	1.0	2.2	0.9	-1.0	-2.0	1.8	-3.1
2002	-2.9	0.7	0.2	2.4	0.1	4.8	2.2	-0.7	1.0	-0.2	-0.4	3.1	10.6
2003	2.5	-4.2	-0.01	1.4	2.7	0.6	-2.6	-1.9	5.1	2.2	1.8	3.1	10.7
2004	2.5	2.6	-1.8	-3.2	3.3	-1.3	0.4	-0.8	0.2	1.6	4.2	-0.1	7.5
2005	-1.5	2.3	-2.0	1.1	-4.5	-1.7	-1.8	2.7	-2.3	0.5	-2.3	-0.6	-9.9
2006	3.6	-1.4	-0.9	4.9	2.6	-1.0	1.0	1.9	-1.7	1.9	3.0	-0.5	13.9
2007	0.3	-0.01	0.2	1.6	-1.0	1.3	1.4	-0.8	1.3	1.8	-1.1	-3.8	1.1
2008	0.3	0.1	-0.8	0.6	-0.2								
TOTALS	-26.8	-10.5	-5.3	20.7	-10.1	-12.4	22.6	3.9	-18.7	21.6	11.0	21.2	
AVG.	-0.8	-0.3	-0.2	0.6	-0.3	-0.4	0.7	0.1	-0.6	0.7	0.3	0.7	
# Up	14	16	14	20	13	16	17	17	15	17	15	18	
# Down	19	17	19	13	20	16	15	15	17	15	17	14	

EURO CYCLE, SEASONAL PATTERN & TRADING GUIDE

The euro currency futures contract is traded at the Chicago Mercantile Exchange. Unlike the spot Forex markets we have more data to study the euro's seasonality's due to the fact there is a warehouse of historic data since this market was traded in a centralized and regulated environment. One futures contract size is 125,000 worth of euros and every penny move represents a $1,250 change in value per contract position. The contract symbol is EU; it has a tradable contract starting with March, June, September, and December. This is considered an electronic traded market with nearly 24 hour access, but the outcry trading hours are from 7:20 AM until 2:00 PM (CT) there are no daily price limits.

The euro is quoted in terms of the U.S. dollar, which is or has been considered the world's reserve currency in which most internationally traded goods are priced. Two markets we discussed already are gold and crude oil. This contract from a historic perspective is relatively new; however, one can adjust the value to reflect the more historic theoretical value by combing the prices of the German Deutsche Mark, the French franc, and the Italian lira. The market has seen a tendency of bottoms in September as multiconglomerate international companies adjust their books for fiscal year-end adjustments and we see peaks in December against the U.S. dollar as money flows go back into the U.S. for year end tax adjustment purposes.

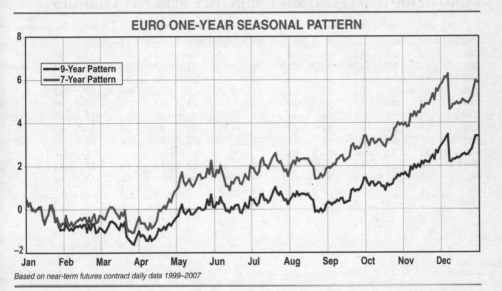

EURO ONE-YEAR SEASONAL PATTERN

Based on near-term futures contract daily data 1999–2007

EURO NEAR-TERM CONTRACT ANNUAL HIGHS, LOWS & CLOSES SINCE 1999

YEAR	HIGH DATE	HIGH CLOSE	LOW DATE	LOW CLOSE	YEAR CLOSE	YEAR	HIGH DATE	HIGH CLOSE	LOW DATE	LOW CLOSE	YEAR CLOSE
1999	01/04	116.09	12/03	106.68	107.35	2004	12/30	136.59	05/13	118.11	135.58
2000	01/11	108.44	10/25	97.82	103.60	2005	01/03	134.90	11/16	117.06	118.80
2001	01/05	104.45	12/24	87.35	88.78	2006	12/01	133.43	02/27	118.64	132.36
2002	12/31	104.71	01/31	85.68	104.71	2007	11/26	148.72	01/11	129.28	145.90
2003	12/31	125.34	01/02	103.30	125.34	2008*	04/22	159.64	02/07	144.45	AT PRESS-TIME

*Through May 30, 2008

EURO NEAR-TERM CONTRACT MONTHLY CLOSING PRICES

	Jan	Feb	Mar	Apr	May	Jun	Jul	Aug	Sep	Oct	Nov	Dec
1999	113.64	111.78	110.63	109.66	108.63	108.58	110.31	109.54	110.26	109.46	107.01	107.35
2000	105.12	104.85	104.52	102.04	103.31	104.39	102.93	100.83	100.67	98.90	100.02	103.60
2001	103.17	102.61	100.37	100.79	98.65	98.77	100.10	101.91	101.85	101.33	101.18	88.78
2002	85.68	86.82	86.82	89.90	93.17	98.85	97.49	98.02	98.34	98.71	99.35	104.71
2003	107.36	107.95	108.68	111.59	117.83	114.69	112.26	109.66	116.20	115.59	119.84	125.34
2004	124.48	124.89	122.80	119.69	122.10	121.78	120.07	121.69	124.32	127.87	132.92	135.58
2005	130.35	132.43	129.82	128.79	123.06	121.37	121.51	123.44	120.59	120.23	118.04	118.80
2006	121.78	119.29	121.79	126.52	128.24	128.50	128.13	128.23	127.39	127.96	132.60	132.36
2007	130.57	132.42	133.94	136.76	134.63	135.68	137.11	136.47	142.93	145.10	146.43	145.90
2008	148.59	151.85	157.29	156.09	155.46							

EURO NEAR-TERM CONTRACT MONTHLY PERCENT CHANGES

	Jan	Feb	Mar	Apr	May	Jun	Jul	Aug	Sep	Oct	Nov	Dec	Year's Change
1999	-1.7	-1.6	-1.0	-0.9	-0.9	-0.1	1.6	-0.7	0.7	-0.7	-2.2	0.3	-7.1
2000	-2.1	-0.3	-0.3	-2.4	1.2	1.0	-1.4	-2.0	-0.2	-1.8	1.1	3.6	-3.5
2001	-0.4	-0.5	-2.2	0.4	-2.1	0.1	1.3	1.8	-0.1	-0.5	-0.1	-12.3	-14.3
2002	-3.5	1.3	N/C	3.5	3.6	6.1	-1.4	0.5	0.3	0.4	0.6	5.4	17.9
2003	2.5	0.5	0.7	2.7	5.6	-2.7	-2.1	-2.3	6.0	-0.5	3.7	4.6	19.7
2004	-0.7	0.3	-1.7	-2.5	2.0	-0.3	-1.4	1.3	2.2	2.9	3.9	2.0	8.2
2005	-3.9	1.6	-2.0	-0.8	-4.4	-1.4	0.1	1.6	-2.3	-0.3	-1.8	0.6	-12.4
2006	2.5	-2.0	2.1	3.9	1.4	0.2	-0.3	0.1	-0.7	0.4	3.6	-0.2	11.4
2007	-1.4	1.4	1.1	2.1	-1.6	0.8	1.1	-0.5	4.7	1.5	0.9	-0.4	10.2
2008	1.8	2.2	3.6	-0.8	-0.4								
TOTALS	-6.9	2.9	0.3	5.2	4.4	3.7	-2.5	-0.2	10.6	1.4	9.7	3.6	
AVG.	-0.7	0.3	0.03	0.5	0.4	0.4	-0.3	-0.02	1.2	0.2	1.1	0.4	
# Up	3	6	4	5	5	5	4	5	5	4	6	6	
# Down	7	4	5	5	5	4	5	4	4	5	3	3	

SWISS FRANC CYCLE, SEASONAL PATTERN & TRADING GUIDE

The Swiss franc currency futures contract is traded at the Chicago Mercantile Exchange. Unlike the spot Forex markets, we have more data to study the franc's seasonality's due to the fact there is a warehouse of historic data since this market was traded in a centralized and regulated environment. One futures contract size is 125,000 worth of Swiss francs, and every penny move represents a $1,250 change in value per contract position. The contract symbol is SF; it has a tradable contract starting with March, June, September, and December. This is considered an electronic traded market with nearly 24 hour access but the outcry trading hours are from 7:20 AM until 2:00 PM (CT) there are no daily price limits.

The Swiss economy is driven by exporting technologically advanced machinery, agricultural products, and some chemical production. However, it is a major player in the banking community as a safe haven for international investors and a store house for gold bullion. Many times we see the value of the price in the Franc rise as gold prices move up as well as a decline in the U.S. dollar. In time of political and economic uncertainties, we also see the value rise in the franc against the U.S. dollar.

The economy runs on a fiscal year which begins in January and ends in December. Since the franc is valued against the U.S. dollar, we have a tendency to see bottoms in June–August, coincidently when gold prices have a tendency to bottom. And as multiconglomerate international companies adjust their books for fiscal year end adjustments, we see a major peak in December against the U.S. dollar, as money flows go back into the United States for yearend tax adjustment purposes, also referred to as repatriation of funds.

SWISS FRANC ONE-YEAR SEASONAL PATTERN

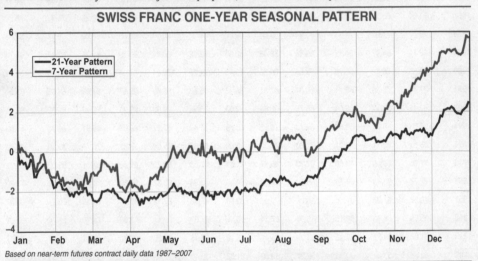

Based on near-term futures contract daily data 1987–2007

SWISS FRANC NEAR-TERM CONTRACT ANNUAL HIGHS, LOWS & CLOSES SINCE 1976

YEAR	HIGH DATE	HIGH CLOSE	LOW DATE	LOW CLOSE	YEAR CLOSE	YEAR	HIGH DATE	HIGH CLOSE	LOW DATE	LOW CLOSE	YEAR CLOSE
1976	06/02	41.70	01/02	38.44	41.24	1993	09/10	71.64	03/09	64.55	67.02
1977	12/30	50.79	03/09	39.15	50.79	1994	10/20	80.91	01/03	66.86	76.73
1978	10/30	69.22	01/18	50.14	63.47	1995	04/18	90.03	01/03	76.44	87.31
1979	10/01	66.26	05/29	57.72	63.94	1996	01/02	87.02	12/27	74.65	75.20
1980	01/07	64.91	04/07	54.42	56.97	1997	01/02	74.88	08/05	65.52	68.97
1981	01/06	58.34	08/10	45.86	56.68	1998	10/07	77.28	07/09	65.28	73.31
1982	01/04	56.48	11/11	44.90	50.70	1999	01/14	74.11	12/02	62.75	63.47
1983	01/10	52.65	09/01	45.68	46.58	2000	01/05	64.82	10/26	55.19	62.17
1984	03/08	48.04	12/31	38.79	38.79	2001	09/21	63.29	07/05	55.04	60.20
1985	12/31	49.08	03/05	34.27	49.08	2002	12/31	72.49	01/31	58.11	72.49
1986	09/19	62.52	01/14	48.02	62.47	2003	12/31	80.66	09/02	70.57	80.66
1987	12/31	79.50	01/05	61.71	79.50	2004	12/30	88.76	04/23	76.08	87.96
1988	01/04	78.44	08/23	62.41	67.28	2005	01/03	87.52	11/16	75.77	76.56
1989	01/03	67.16	05/22	55.87	64.74	2006	12/12	84.06	02/27	75.74	82.54
1990	11/20	80.29	01/02	62.98	78.75	2007	11/26	91.11	02/12	80.05	88.38
1991	02/06	81.06	07/11	62.66	73.00	2008*	03/17	101.23	01/02	89.81	AT PRESS-TIME
1992	09/01	80.77	04/21	64.21	67.81						

*Through May 30, 2008

SWISS FRANC NEAR-TERM CONTRACT MONTHLY CLOSING PRICES

	Jan	Feb	Mar	Apr	May	Jun	Jul	Aug	Sep	Oct	Nov	Dec
1976	38.61	39.04	39.74	40.03	40.83	40.92	40.71	40.40	41.26	41.29	40.94	41.24
1977	40.10	39.21	39.48	39.80	40.00	40.75	41.79	41.83	43.00	45.17	46.40	50.79
1978	50.87	55.17	54.66	51.81	52.89	54.81	57.90	61.02	66.45	68.22	58.01	63.47
1979	59.44	60.22	60.26	58.87	58.05	61.58	60.72	60.74	65.85	61.62	63.07	63.94
1980	61.69	58.60	55.33	60.62	60.51	61.89	60.59	60.91	61.47	58.88	57.61	56.97
1981	52.41	51.17	52.70	49.87	48.38	49.50	47.00	46.61	51.29	55.55	56.57	56.68
1982	54.66	52.66	52.83	51.79	50.24	48.60	48.05	47.24	46.68	45.55	47.40	50.70
1983	49.95	48.38	48.56	48.71	47.59	48.03	46.87	46.04	47.74	46.70	46.55	46.58
1984	44.94	46.20	47.37	44.95	44.46	43.52	40.88	41.63	40.02	40.58	39.15	38.79
1985	37.43	34.93	38.87	38.38	39.12	39.67	44.01	43.29	45.80	46.80	48.19	49.08
1986	49.64	53.16	51.75	54.93	51.74	56.45	59.98	61.19	61.12	58.63	60.99	62.47
1987	64.94	65.19	66.77	68.54	66.40	66.58	65.21	66.92	65.58	70.26	74.73	79.50
1988	73.46	71.93	74.01	71.94	69.26	67.08	64.32	63.26	63.83	66.69	69.14	67.28
1989	62.74	64.42	60.72	59.89	58.48	60.07	62.42	58.94	61.79	61.95	62.84	64.74
1990	66.55	66.69	66.76	68.86	69.85	70.45	74.23	76.24	77.04	77.75	78.29	78.75
1991	79.44	75.34	68.41	69.07	67.31	64.23	65.52	65.43	68.57	67.86	69.65	73.00
1992	69.42	67.17	66.04	65.76	68.53	72.02	75.32	79.90	80.23	72.47	69.62	67.81
1993	67.03	65.38	66.83	69.70	70.52	65.79	65.49	67.62	69.97	66.91	66.71	67.02
1994	68.61	70.12	70.91	71.38	71.23	75.06	74.60	75.08	77.83	79.71	75.39	76.73
1995	77.98	80.96	88.88	87.73	85.87	87.51	87.35	83.25	87.16	88.51	85.02	87.31
1996	82.77	83.44	84.64	80.72	80.12	80.30	83.88	83.37	80.39	79.14	76.83	75.20
1997	70.56	67.83	69.56	68.29	70.93	69.08	66.38	67.12	69.56	71.85	70.24	68.97
1998	68.09	68.43	66.18	66.94	67.54	66.28	67.39	69.41	73.08	74.36	71.74	73.31
1999	71.03	69.22	67.92	65.99	65.46	65.10	67.46	66.20	67.33	66.04	63.04	63.47
2000	60.56	60.27	60.55	58.27	59.50	61.62	60.17	57.48	58.28	55.87	57.89	62.17
2001	61.11	59.94	57.62	57.82	55.70	55.80	57.90	60.01	61.78	61.22	60.90	60.20
2002	58.11	58.91	59.43	61.98	63.73	67.56	67.31	66.70	67.91	67.68	67.39	72.49
2003	73.34	73.97	74.04	73.90	77.10	74.06	73.02	71.25	75.89	74.59	77.40	80.66
2004	79.55	79.28	79.08	77.29	79.92	80.17	78.10	78.91	80.54	83.86	87.82	87.96
2005	84.23	86.15	83.95	83.85	80.14	78.50	77.93	79.84	77.72	77.96	76.20	76.56
2006	78.54	76.32	77.35	80.97	82.21	82.41	81.73	81.40	80.60	80.81	83.60	82.54
2007	80.73	82.25	82.83	83.14	81.73	82.32	83.46	82.97	86.45	86.71	88.52	88.38
2008	92.56	95.90	100.66	96.76	95.93							

SWISS FRANC NEAR-TERM CONTRACT MONTHLY PERCENT CHANGES

	Jan	Feb	Mar	Apr	May	Jun	Jul	Aug	Sep	Oct	Nov	Dec	Year's Change
1976	0.6	1.1	1.8	0.7	2.0	0.2	−0.5	−0.8	2.1	0.1	−0.8	0.7	7.5
1977	−2.8	−2.2	0.7	0.8	0.5	1.9	2.6	0.1	2.8	5.0	2.7	9.5	23.2
1978	0.2	8.5	−0.9	−5.2	2.1	3.6	5.6	5.4	8.9	2.7	−15.0	9.4	25.0
1979	−6.3	1.3	0.1	−2.3	−1.4	6.1	−1.4	0.03	8.4	−6.4	2.4	1.4	0.7
1980	−3.5	−5.0	−5.6	9.6	−0.2	2.3	−2.1	0.5	0.9	−4.2	−2.2	−1.1	−10.9
1981	−8.0	−2.4	3.0	−5.4	−3.0	2.3	−5.1	−0.8	10.0	8.3	1.8	0.2	−0.5
1982	−3.6	−3.7	0.3	−2.0	−3.0	−3.3	−1.1	−1.7	−1.2	−2.4	4.1	7.0	−10.6
1983	−1.5	−3.1	0.4	0.3	−2.3	0.9	−2.4	−1.8	3.7	−2.2	−0.3	0.1	−8.1
1984	−3.5	2.8	2.5	−5.1	−1.1	−2.1	−6.1	1.8	−3.9	1.4	−3.5	−0.9	−16.7
1985	−3.5	−6.7	11.3	−1.3	1.9	1.4	10.9	−1.6	5.8	2.2	3.0	1.8	26.5
1986	1.1	7.1	−2.7	6.1	−5.8	9.1	6.3	2.0	−0.1	−4.1	4.0	2.4	27.3
1987	4.0	0.4	2.4	2.7	−3.1	0.3	−2.1	2.6	−2.0	7.1	6.4	6.4	27.3
1988	−7.6	−2.1	2.9	−2.8	−3.7	−3.1	−4.1	−1.6	0.9	4.5	3.7	−2.7	−15.4
1989	−6.7	2.7	−5.7	−1.4	−2.4	2.7	3.9	−5.6	4.8	0.3	1.4	3.0	−3.8
1990	2.8	0.2	0.1	3.1	1.4	0.9	5.4	2.7	1.0	0.9	0.7	0.6	21.6
1991	0.9	−5.2	−9.2	1.0	−2.5	−4.6	2.0	−0.1	4.8	−1.0	2.6	4.8	−7.3
1992	−4.9	−3.2	−1.7	−0.4	4.2	5.1	4.6	6.1	0.4	−9.7	−3.9	−2.6	−7.1
1993	−1.2	−2.5	2.2	4.3	1.2	−6.7	−0.5	3.3	3.5	−4.4	−0.3	0.5	−1.2
1994	2.4	2.2	1.1	0.7	−0.2	5.4	−0.6	0.6	3.7	2.4	−5.4	1.8	14.5
1995	1.6	3.8	9.8	−1.3	−2.1	1.9	−0.2	−4.7	4.7	1.5	−3.9	2.7	13.8
1996	−5.2	0.8	1.4	−4.6	−0.7	0.2	4.5	−0.6	−3.6	−1.6	−2.9	−2.1	−13.9
1997	−6.2	−3.9	2.6	−1.8	3.9	−2.6	−3.9	1.1	3.6	3.3	−2.2	−1.8	−8.3
1998	−1.3	0.5	−3.3	1.1	0.9	−1.9	1.7	3.0	5.3	1.8	−3.5	2.2	6.3
1999	−3.1	−2.5	−1.9	−2.8	−0.8	−0.5	3.6	−1.9	1.7	−1.9	−4.5	0.7	−13.4
2000	−4.6	−0.5	0.5	−3.8	2.1	3.6	−2.4	−4.5	1.4	−4.1	3.6	7.4	−2.0
2001	−1.7	−1.9	−3.9	0.3	−3.7	0.2	3.8	3.6	2.9	−0.9	−0.5	−1.1	−3.2
2002	−3.5	1.4	0.9	4.3	2.8	6.0	−0.4	−0.9	1.8	−0.3	−0.4	7.6	20.4
2003	1.2	0.9	0.1	−0.2	4.3	−3.9	−1.4	−2.4	6.5	−1.7	3.8	4.2	11.3
2004	−1.4	−0.3	−0.3	−2.3	3.4	0.3	−2.6	1.0	2.1	4.1	4.7	0.2	9.1
2005	−4.2	2.3	−2.6	−0.1	−4.4	−2.0	−0.7	2.5	−2.7	0.3	−2.3	0.5	−13.0
2006	2.6	−2.8	1.3	4.7	1.5	0.2	−0.8	−0.4	−1.0	0.3	3.5	−1.3	7.8
2007	−2.2	1.9	0.7	0.4	−1.7	0.7	1.4	−0.6	4.2	0.3	2.1	−0.2	7.1
2008	4.7	3.6	5.0	−3.9	−0.9								
TOTALS	−64.4	−6.5	13.3	−6.6	−10.8	24.6	17.9	6.3	81.4	1.6	−1.1	61.3	
AVG.	−2.0	−0.2	0.4	−0.2	−0.3	0.8	0.6	0.2	2.5	0.1	−0.03	1.9	
# Up	11	17	22	15	14	22	13	16	25	18	16	23	
# Down	22	16	11	18	19	10	19	16	7	14	16	9	

JAPANESE YEN CYCLE, SEASONAL PATTERN & TRADING GUIDE

The Japanese yen currency futures contract is traded at the Chicago Mercantile Exchange. Unlike the spot Forex markets, we have more data to study the yen's seasonality's due to the fact there is a warehouse of historic data since this market was traded in a centralized and regulated environment. One futures contract size is 12,500,000 worth of yen, and every penny move represents a $1,250 change in value per contract position. The contract symbol is JY; it has a tradable contract starting with March, June, September, and December. This is considered an electronic traded market with nearly 24-hour access, but the outcry trading hours are from 7:20 AM until 2:00 PM (CT). There are no daily price limits.

The Japanese economy has been considered the second most technologically advanced economy in the world, but the gap is closing with China and the combined euro zone nations. This market and economy is driven by finished good production, as they are a net importer of raw materials and the Japanese economy is heavily dependant on crude oil imports. The economy runs on a fiscal year from April through March, but since the yen contract is valued against the U.S. dollar, we have a tendency to see bottoms in late August as multiconglomerate international companies adjust their books for fiscal yearend adjustments and we see peaks in October against the U.S. dollar, as money flows go back into the U.S. for yearend tax adjustment purposes, also referred to as repatriation of funds.

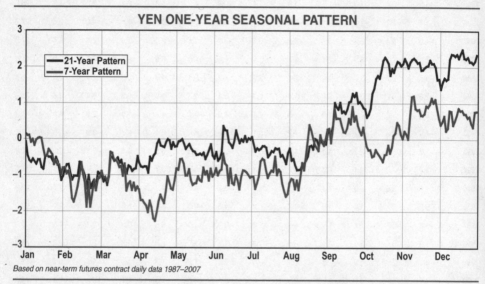

YEN ONE-YEAR SEASONAL PATTERN

- 21-Year Pattern
- 7-Year Pattern

Based on near-term futures contract daily data 1987–2007

YEN NEAR-TERM CONTRACT ANNUAL HIGHS, LOWS & CLOSES SINCE 1978

YEAR	HIGH DATE	HIGH CLOSE	LOW DATE	LOW CLOSE	YEAR CLOSE	YEAR	HIGH DATE	HIGH CLOSE	LOW DATE	LOW CLOSE	YEAR CLOSE
1978	10/30	57.23	02/03	41.45	52.70	1994	10/25	103.87	01/05	88.78	101.08
1979	01/02	52.72	11/26	39.99	41.97	1995	04/18	124.91	11/02	96.75	97.73
1980	12/30	50.33	04/07	38.48	50.25	1996	01/02	97.21	12/30	87.00	87.13
1981	01/05	51.13	08/04	41.21	46.24	1997	06/11	91.29	12/05	76.89	77.36
1982	01/04	46.43	11/03	36.10	43.15	1998	12/31	88.84	08/11	68.19	88.84
1983	01/10	44.26	09/01	40.51	43.71	1999	12/22	99.56	05/20	80.65	98.92
1984	03/08	45.48	12/31	39.87	39.87	2000	01/03	99.64	12/29	88.27	88.27
1985	12/31	50.04	02/22	38.07	50.04	2001	01/03	88.99	12/27	76.22	76.29
1986	09/19	65.97	01/03	49.30	63.54	2002	07/19	86.66	02/26	74.34	84.47
1987	12/31	83.16	01/05	62.99	83.16	2003	12/29	93.72	03/21	82.51	93.18
1988	12/08	82.87	09/01	73.41	80.69	2004	12/31	97.97	05/13	87.40	97.97
1989	01/03	81.49	06/14	67.65	69.68	2005	01/14	98.38	12/07	82.76	85.51
1990	10/18	80.30	04/17	62.73	73.84	2006	05/16	91.54	10/10	84.30	84.84
1991	12/31	79.91	06/10	70.30	79.91	2007	11/26	92.94	06/22	81.62	90.13
1992	09/29	83.68	04/23	74.13	80.04	2008*	03/17	103.05	01/10	91.85	AT PRESS-TIME
1993	08/17	98.93	01/15	79.25	89.59						

*Through May 30, 2008

JAPANESE YEN NEAR-TERM CONTRACT MONTHLY CLOSING PRICES

	Jan	Feb	Mar	Apr	May	Jun	Jul	Aug	Sep	Oct	Nov	Dec
1978	41.60	42.17	46.16	44.67	45.60	49.88	53.16	52.25	53.61	56.29	50.50	52.70
1979	49.95	49.69	48.13	45.40	45.39	46.27	46.34	45.70	44.99	42.77	40.17	41.97
1980	42.17	39.80	40.37	41.83	44.74	45.18	43.76	45.75	47.68	47.66	46.21	50.25
1981	48.98	47.83	47.94	46.76	44.95	44.83	42.16	43.24	43.75	43.44	46.86	46.24
1982	44.31	42.21	41.06	42.76	41.14	39.73	38.98	38.51	37.53	36.25	40.18	43.15
1983	41.77	41.78	42.06	42.17	41.77	42.06	41.23	40.73	42.71	42.75	43.12	43.71
1984	42.80	42.92	44.98	44.40	43.28	42.65	40.92	41.43	40.96	41.00	40.43	39.87
1985	39.28	38.53	40.14	39.72	39.94	40.39	42.46	41.84	46.40	47.38	49.42	50.04
1986	52.17	55.51	56.56	59.24	57.37	61.60	65.22	64.99	64.91	61.34	61.82	63.54
1987	65.16	65.31	68.93	71.56	69.62	68.63	66.93	70.33	68.74	72.54	75.82	83.16
1988	78.38	78.02	80.87	80.22	79.98	75.65	75.45	73.45	75.38	79.92	82.49	80.69
1989	77.14	78.97	76.32	75.75	70.06	70.07	73.48	68.98	72.43	70.24	70.12	69.68
1990	69.39	67.20	63.42	63.07	65.73	65.86	68.59	69.58	72.18	76.92	75.38	73.84
1991	76.14	75.10	70.55	73.22	72.27	72.47	72.66	73.05	75.10	76.38	76.95	79.91
1992	79.32	77.14	75.30	74.98	78.32	79.46	78.60	81.22	83.22	81.00	80.21	80.04
1993	80.11	84.56	87.04	90.10	93.17	93.49	95.51	95.47	94.30	92.27	91.66	89.59
1994	92.16	95.65	98.21	98.70	95.49	102.11	100.15	99.99	101.48	103.58	101.23	101.08
1995	100.75	103.55	116.57	119.54	118.74	119.21	114.00	102.94	101.26	98.60	98.15	97.73
1996	94.02	95.25	94.26	95.83	92.66	92.21	94.37	92.00	90.76	88.22	88.02	87.13
1997	82.81	83.43	81.78	79.25	86.22	88.26	84.81	82.81	83.92	83.59	78.42	77.36
1998	79.15	79.48	75.87	75.67	72.22	72.66	69.54	71.07	73.90	86.71	81.34	88.84
1999	86.37	84.16	84.86	84.20	82.50	83.48	87.87	91.47	95.00	96.59	98.33	98.92
2000	93.68	91.00	99.08	93.18	93.15	95.77	92.24	93.96	93.73	92.47	90.85	88.27
2001	86.47	85.36	80.08	81.32	84.07	80.79	80.32	84.32	84.15	81.98	81.03	76.29
2002	74.36	74.89	75.67	78.02	80.54	84.03	83.68	84.33	82.43	81.68	81.59	84.47
2003	83.52	84.74	84.82	84.24	83.87	83.69	83.04	85.80	89.96	90.99	91.34	93.18
2004	94.68	91.62	96.04	90.73	90.61	92.20	89.92	91.56	91.27	94.66	97.21	97.97
2005	96.75	95.77	93.83	95.69	92.27	90.92	89.40	90.54	88.77	86.42	83.65	85.51
2006	85.63	86.55	85.85	88.52	88.98	88.32	87.84	85.39	85.59	86.08	86.56	84.84
2007	83.36	84.73	85.75	84.17	82.34	82.01	84.69	86.45	87.97	87.16	90.12	90.13
2008	94.25	96.29	100.71	96.50	94.91							

191

JAPANESE YEN NEAR-TERM CONTRACT MONTHLY PERCENT CHANGES

	Jan	Feb	Mar	Apr	May	Jun	Jul	Aug	Sep	Oct	Nov	Dec	Year's Change
1978	−1.3	1.4	9.5	−3.2	2.1	9.4	6.6	−1.7	2.6	5.0	−10.3	4.4	25.0
1979	−5.2	−0.5	−3.1	−5.7	−0.02	1.9	0.2	−1.4	−1.6	−4.9	−6.1	4.5	−20.4
1980	0.5	−5.6	1.4	3.6	7.0	1.0	−3.1	4.5	4.2	−0.04	−3.0	8.7	19.7
1981	−2.5	−2.3	0.2	−2.5	−3.9	−0.3	−6.0	2.6	1.2	−0.7	7.9	−1.3	−8.0
1982	−4.2	−4.7	−2.7	4.1	−3.8	−3.4	−1.9	−1.2	−2.5	−3.4	10.8	7.4	−6.7
1983	−3.2	0.02	0.7	0.3	−0.9	0.7	−2.0	−1.2	4.9	0.1	0.9	1.4	1.3
1984	−2.1	0.3	4.8	−1.3	−2.5	−1.5	−4.1	1.2	−1.1	0.1	−1.4	−1.4	−8.8
1985	−1.5	−1.9	4.2	−1.0	0.6	1.1	5.1	−1.5	10.9	2.1	4.3	1.3	25.5
1986	4.3	6.4	1.9	4.7	−3.2	7.4	5.9	−0.4	−0.1	−5.5	0.8	2.8	27.0
1987	2.5	0.2	5.5	3.8	−2.7	−1.4	−2.5	5.1	−2.3	5.5	4.5	9.7	30.9
1988	−5.7	−0.5	3.7	−0.8	−0.3	−5.4	−0.3	−2.7	2.6	6.0	3.2	−2.2	−3.0
1989	−4.4	2.4	−3.4	−0.7	−7.5	0.01	4.9	−6.1	5.0	−3.0	−0.2	−0.6	−13.6
1990	−0.4	−3.2	−5.6	−0.6	4.2	0.2	4.1	1.4	3.7	6.6	−2.0	−2.0	6.0
1991	3.1	−1.4	−6.1	3.8	−1.3	0.3	0.3	0.5	2.8	1.7	0.7	3.8	8.2
1992	−0.7	−2.7	−2.4	−0.4	4.5	1.5	−1.1	3.3	2.5	−2.7	−1.0	−0.2	0.2
1993	0.1	5.6	2.9	3.5	3.4	0.3	2.2	−0.04	−1.2	−2.2	−0.7	−2.3	11.9
1994	2.9	3.8	2.7	0.5	−3.3	6.9	−1.9	−0.2	1.5	2.1	−2.3	−0.1	12.8
1995	−0.3	2.8	12.6	2.5	−0.7	0.4	−4.4	−9.7	−1.6	−2.6	−0.5	−0.4	−3.3
1996	−3.8	1.3	−1.0	1.7	−3.3	−0.5	2.3	−2.5	−1.3	−2.8	−0.2	−1.0	−10.8
1997	−5.0	0.7	−2.0	−3.1	8.8	2.4	−3.9	−2.4	1.3	−0.4	−6.2	−1.4	−11.2
1998	2.3	0.4	−4.5	−0.3	−4.6	0.6	−4.3	2.2	4.0	17.3	−6.2	9.2	14.8
1999	−2.8	−2.6	0.8	−0.8	−2.0	1.2	5.3	4.1	3.9	1.7	1.8	0.6	11.3
2000	−5.3	−2.9	8.9	−6.0	−0.03	2.8	−3.7	1.9	−0.2	−1.3	−1.8	−2.8	−10.8
2001	−2.0	−1.3	−6.2	1.5	3.4	−3.9	−0.6	5.0	−0.2	−2.6	−1.2	−5.8	−13.6
2002	−2.5	0.7	1.0	3.1	3.2	4.3	−0.4	0.8	−2.3	−0.9	−0.1	3.5	10.7
2003	−1.1	1.5	0.1	−0.7	−0.4	−0.2	−0.8	3.3	4.8	1.1	0.4	2.0	10.3
2004	1.6	−3.2	4.8	−5.5	−0.1	1.8	−2.5	1.8	−0.3	3.7	2.7	0.8	5.1
2005	−1.2	−1.0	−2.0	2.0	−3.6	−1.5	−1.7	1.3	−2.0	−2.6	−3.2	2.2	−12.7
2006	0.1	1.1	−0.8	3.1	0.5	−0.7	−0.5	−2.8	0.2	0.6	0.6	−2.0	−0.8
2007	−1.7	1.6	1.2	−1.8	−2.2	−0.4	3.3	2.1	1.8	−0.9	3.4	0.01	6.2
2008	4.6	2.2	4.6	−4.2	−1.6								
TOTALS	−34.9	−1.4	31.7	−0.4	−10.3	25.0	−5.5	7.3	41.2	17.1	−4.4	38.8	
AVG.	−1.1	−0.04	1.0	−0.01	−0.3	0.8	−0.2	0.2	1.4	0.6	−0.1	1.3	
# Up	10	17	19	14	10	19	11	16	17	14	13	16	
# Down	21	14	12	17	21	11	19	14	13	16	17	14